Managing Your
Emotions
for a
Healthier
Life

MARK W. BAKER, PHD

Published by Revell
a division of Baker Publishing Group
PO Box 6287, Grand Rapids, MI 49516-6287
www.revellbooks.com

Spire edition published 2020
ISBN 978-0-8007-3914-0

Previously published in 2017 under the title *Spiritual Wisdom for a Happier Life*

Printed in the United States of America

20   21   22   23   24   25   26   7   6   5   4   3   2   1

Contents

Part Four: Anxiety

Part Five: Sorrow

Part Eight: Love

Introduction

There are eight main emotions people feel every day all over the world. You know them because you have felt them. God has put down some pretty wise advice in the Bible for how to deal with these emotions, and that advice has been compiled for you in this book.

I spent the past twenty-five years as a psychologist studying what the Bible and modern psychology have to say about every human emotion. In the pages that follow, I will explain from a psychological perspective how healing is possible for our emotional pain today based upon God's wisdom taken from the Bible, and I will give you many examples of this from the real lives of people I have worked with and known. Some of the illustrations I use will be of everyday emotional experiences that are pretty common, and some will be of more severe psychological conditions, but all of them will be examples or composites of real people dealing with true-life emotional events. If you have ever felt you could use some help in the emotional side of your life, or perhaps have even considered talking to a psychologist, this book will give you a very good idea of how other people have been helped with their emotional struggles, some of which might be just like yours.

First, let me say just a word about emotions. Some scientists use the term *emotion* to refer to the physiological reaction stored in the right hemisphere of the brain that begins before the ability to think and express ourselves with the left hemisphere is even developed. Then, when we can put these right hemisphere emotions into words, we call them *feelings*. However, for our purposes in this book, this distinction is not necessary, so I will be using the terms interchangeably. So emotions, or feelings, are a physical reaction we have in our bodies that we give meaning to in our minds. They are an instantaneous way of evaluating what's happening to us. Scientists have tried to distill human emotions down to a finite list, and while they don't all agree on what that list is exactly, the eight sections listed in this book are a pretty good example of the eight basic emotions felt by human beings all over the world.

Emotions are not simply bodily sensations, such as hunger, thirst, sleepiness, or physical pain. They are physical reactions that we interpret to help us make meaning out of our lives. Emotions are a combination of something going on in our bodies and minds at the same time. This can be confusing, because we also have moods and general feelings that are vague, and some emotions are complex combinations of several feelings all at the same time. So understanding your emotions is not always easy to do. However, an awareness of the eight emotions I will describe for you will go a long way toward helping you identify and express what you are feeling and give you some handles on how to deal with your life in meaningful ways.

Many psychologists think humans are motivated to do what we do more by emotions than reasoning because the emotional part of the brain is many times faster than the thinking part, and having emotions responded to by caregivers is now known to be critical for the development of the human brain. Emotions are the filters through which we make meaning out of our day-to-day experiences, the markers that cause us to know whether something is significant or not, and the vehicle through which we intimately connect to others. In your most important experiences in life, you will not remember the facts with very much accuracy, but you are not likely to forget what you felt. When it comes to really meaningful things that happen to you, your emotions play a much greater part than your thinking in ways we are only beginning to understand.

This book is divided into eight parts; each part will address a different essential emotion. The first six parts address the painful emotions of hurt, guilt/shame, anger, anxiety, sorrow, and fear. The last two parts address happiness and love. While these last two emotions are about good feelings, the mishandling of them can lead to tremendous hurt for us all.

So how does God heal our hurt feelings? Well, certainly not by taking them away every time we ask him to. The fact that we struggle emotionally as a result of the way the world is made is inescapable. But God's role in the world did not stop with the act of creating it. He also provided us with tremendous wisdom on how to deal with the emotions that exist in our lives. If you have picked up this book to find some help for important feelings in your life, then I hope you will find God's soothing presence as a result of reading it.

My graduate degrees in psychology and theology, as well as my advanced training in psychodynamic psychotherapy, led me to the conclusion that good psychology and good theology point us toward health. Decades of psychological research support this conclusion, along with the many people who have shared with me how this has been true for them in very personal ways. We are emotional and spiritual creatures who hurt and love—you can't have one without the other. Learning how God can heal your emotional hurt will also teach you how God will bring more love and happiness into your life.

PART ONE

Hurt and Suffering

1

Why God Allows Pain

When Jesus was on the cross, he uttered the loneliest words ever spoken. Perhaps you were even confused as to why the Son of God himself would cry out in his suffering, "My God, my God, why have you forsaken me?" Theologians have wrestled with this statement over the years, but one thing is certain. This statement is not about a lack of faith. It is a statement about a psychological property of trauma. Extreme trauma makes you feel very alone. If you have ever felt isolated from others or even abandoned by God in your suffering, you are actually *not* alone. Jesus himself felt this type of pain.

One of the most helpful books written in the last century on the subject of suffering is *The Problem of Pain* by C. S. Lewis. He takes a realistic and sympathetic look at the intellectual problems raised by human suffering. Lewis says Christianity "creates rather than solves the problem of pain."[1] His argument is simple: "If God's goodness is inconsistent with hurting us, then either God is not good or there is no God."[2] Other religions that don't speak of a personal and loving God don't have this problem. Pain is simply a part of life, and there is no personally loving God to complain to about it. In this way, Christianity creates the problem of pain.

After Lewis wrote *The Problem of Pain* he met Joy Gresham, a divorced American poet studying in England. He went on to marry her and grew to love her more than any person he had ever known. But as life sometimes goes, she tragically died of cancer, leaving Lewis heartbroken, despondent, and profoundly alone. It was after his own intense suffering that Lewis wrote *A Grief Observed*,[3] his own story of surviving the intense pain of grief and loss. In it he wrote:

> Meanwhile, where is God? This is one of the most disquieting symptoms. When you are happy, so happy that you have no sense of needing Him . . . and turn to Him with gratitude and praise, you will be welcomed with open arms. But go to Him when your need is desperate, when all other help is vain and what do you find? A door slammed in your face, and a sound of bolting and double bolting on the inside. After that, silence. You may as well turn away.

Lewis's honesty helps us understand intense suffering. Trauma is alienating and makes us feel that no one understands. If suffering is too great, it can drive a wedge between us and others—even God. This is not a failing or a weakness. It is a property of trauma that you may experience someday. If this happens, you will probably feel afraid and alone. But do not stop there. Because the God of the Bible creates the problem of pain, you may not feel that the Bible offers a good answer as to *why* pain exists when you feel alone and traumatized, but it does offer some pretty good answers as to how to deal with it when you do. Let me share with you what some of those answers are.

2

Does Suffering Make You Bitter or Better?

The wisest people I know have suffered a great deal in life. But at the same time, the most bitter people I know have suffered a great deal in life. What's the difference? Pain is a powerful force. It is a physical vector that pushes you in a direction. It can push you in the direction of greater maturity and wisdom, or it can push you in the direction of discouragement and alienation. If you want to become a better person, and not a bitter one, then you need to know what it means to *persevere* toward something good in the midst of your pain.

The fact that you suffer in life does not make you either bitter or better—what you do with your suffering does. Pain is only a force that pushes you. It may push you hard and fast, or it may come slowly and over a long period of time. You can't choose the kind of suffering you are going to face in life, but you can choose the direction in which it pushes you.

Adam came to therapy because of the stress in his life. He worked long hours at a business consulting firm, and he was overwhelmed by his responsibilities both at work and at home. Adam had dedicated his life to Christ several years before and had hoped to be a pastor serving God in full-time ministry, but this never happened. Now he came to therapy to try to deal with the stress of a demanding job, a difficult home life, and thwarted dreams.

Adam was the youngest of three children and only seven when his parents divorced. His parents didn't believe in God, didn't like each other, and didn't have the time to be interested in him. He became self-sufficient at a young age and decided not to take the path of his older siblings, which led them into drugs and lives of self-destruction. Adam worked hard at school and always took part-time jobs to support himself. He decided early on that being responsible and trying to choose *the good* was going to serve him better in life. No one in his family seemed to be able to do that, and he didn't want to end up like any of them.

Adam became a Christian in high school and married a wonderful Christian girl shortly after graduation. Their dream was to become pastors and serve God by ministering to the needy of the world. Soon after they were married, they became pregnant with their first child. It seemed as though their dreams of happiness were finally being realized. But things are not always as they appear.

Sometime after their daughter was born, Adam and his wife learned that she would be seriously mentally handicapped for life. She would never reach mental maturity, never be self-sufficient, and always need constant supervision. They were devastated. Their only child would now be condemned to suffer daily, for life. How could God allow this to happen to two people who only wanted to serve him? Why did such suffering have to fall upon an innocent child?

Because of the special needs of their daughter, Adam had to take a job that could provide for the needs of his family and give up his vision of becoming a minister. He and his wife didn't like it, but because of their love for their daughter, they accepted this new plan for their lives. As always, Adam worked hard and tried to choose *the good*.

"I just can't seem to make ends meet," Adam said with frustration.

"It's overwhelming when the needs never end," I replied.

"People don't understand." He went on, "I have to fight with the very system that is designed to help us. Going to my brutally demanding job is the easy part of my day, and then I have to come home and deal with the real struggles of my life. I have always had dreams that God wanted me to be a preacher. But I don't have the luxury of dreams anymore. God's will for my life is to care for my family today."

"Having faith has never been easy. It's even more difficult when you don't know what to hope for," I said.

"Yeah," Adam said. "I guess my idea of God's will for my life has changed. I don't think I'll ever be a pastor. I'm just trying to find the strength to be the man my daughter needs me to be. I read that Saint Francis of Assisi once said, 'Preach the gospel everywhere, and when necessary, use words.' I think I understand that now. I'm just trying to be the gospel for my daughter."

Adam struggles with disappointment and frustration daily. Sometimes he doesn't feel like much of a witness to the good news of the gospel, and he often does not consider his life one that others would be attracted to. But Adam has not allowed the suffering in his life to push him in the same direction taken by everyone else in his family of origin. He could give up, become bitter, and end up like the rest of his family, giving over to a life of drugs and self-pity. Instead, even though he is disappointed and even angry with God at times, Adam still chooses the direction of his life. He gets up daily and points himself in the direction of *doing good* for his family with the faith that somehow God will give him the strength to persevere. The result? Adam is a better man. Even though he doesn't feel like it, he's one of the best men I know.

Suffering is a powerful force in life. You will not be able to avoid it. But you will be able to choose the *direction* in which it will push you. Will your pain drive you away from others into loneliness and bitterness, or will you choose to point yourself toward deeper relationships with others and the greater good in life to become a better person?

The Bible instructs us to "consider it pure joy, my brothers and sisters, whenever you face trials of many kinds, because you know that the testing of your faith develops perseverance." But perseverance is not patience. Patience is receptive and passive. It is good to be able to wait for things you do not have, and the capacity to be patient and hang on until something better comes along will serve you well in life. But for suffering to make you a better person, you must do more than simply patiently endure it; you must have perseverance in it. Like Adam, you must get up daily, suit up for life, and actively choose the good. This is not merely having a positive attitude during your trials; it is doing the hard work of making morally right choices in the midst of your suffering. Then the testing of your faith will produce perseverance. Perseverance is a kind of steadfastness for a greater good beyond your own self-interest that brings joy "whenever you face trials of many kinds."

The Bible tells you that God will help you with your suffering. But that does not mean God will necessarily remove suffering from your life. What it does mean is God has given you certain gifts to equip you to deal with the suffering you must face. The capacity for perseverance is one of those gifts from God to help you become a better person, and not a bitter one, in the face of your suffering.

3

Intense Suffering Creates Loneliness

Those who have been traumatized can be in a room full of people but still feel lonely anyway. They can have flashbacks that make them feel stuck back at some earlier point in time, making it difficult to be present in the moment. It is common for them to have the feeling that they no longer know who they are. Traumatic pain can disconnect you from your relationship with everyone, even yourself.[4] Don't feel ashamed if you have ever felt that no one could ever understand or care about the depth of your pain, not even God. Intense suffering creates loneliness.

Paul is a very gifted minister. He is a brilliant preacher, sensitive pastor, and strong leader of his church. He helped thousands of people over many years live better lives and grow closer to God. He was so committed to his ministry that he didn't marry until later in life. Fortunately, Paul met and fell in love with his soul mate, Alicia. She was beautiful, loved God, and was well liked by everyone. He considered himself to be the most fortunate man in the world. As much as Paul loved to help others, he loved Alicia even more.

Paul and Alicia had several wonderful years together and two beautiful children before tragedy struck. One day Alicia was taken from this world quite suddenly in an automobile accident. Paul was completely devastated. He now felt as much intense pain over the loss of her as he had felt intense love for her. He tried to make sense of this senseless tragedy, but he always came up short.

"How could a God I love so much allow such an unloving thing to happen?" he cried.

"I have no idea," I replied quietly. I was painfully aware that this was not a theological question. Paul had counseled hundreds of people in pain over the years, and what he needed from me was not help with his head. He needed help with his heart.

"And I have no idea how I will survive the pain," he mumbled.

"I can't begin to understand how much you must hurt," I replied.

I found out years later that this was actually comforting for Paul. In his moment of greatest suffering, the force of his pain had driven a wedge between him and everyone, even God. He had the profound sense that no one could understand how much he was hurting. Simple platitudes would have insulted him and made him feel even more alone. Paradoxically, the only thing that made him feel understood was my saying to him that I simply *couldn't* understand the depth of his pain. That was the closest anyone could come to grasping the severity of his suffering.

Because of his pain, Paul took a sabbatical from his pastorate. It took a while, but he eventually decided to stay in the ministry. Paul returned to the work he loved, but he carries a scar on his heart to this very day. I believe Paul survived this tragedy because even though he felt very alone in his suffering, he did not *stay* alone. He didn't want it at first, but he did allow a few others to be with him in his pain. There wasn't much we could say that was helpful; we were simply there. And our simply being there helped him make it through.

Traumatic suffering is disorienting and isolating. You may have the feeling that no one can understand the depth of your pain, but just because their *words* feel useless to you doesn't mean *they* are. Sometimes simply being there is not just the *only* thing your friends can do for you when you are in despair, it is actually the *best* thing.

Perseverance is not the only capacity God has given you to help you come out of intense suffering as a better person. He has also provided you with the capacity for relationships with others even when you feel painfully alone. As in the case of Paul, you may not feel you can do it or you may not even want it, but you can still choose to be with others to help you survive your pain.

The Bible offers you the wisdom that "for the despairing man there should be kindness from his friend; so that he does not forsake the fear of the Almighty" (NASB). Paul survived his suffering because of the relationships that sustained him through it. Even though he couldn't feel it at times, someone physically being there for him made a difference. You will be able to survive traumatic suffering better, just like Paul, if you allow others to be there with you, too. At those times when we feel abandoned by God, someone standing with us reminds us that we are not alone.

4

Are You a Survivor
or a Victim?

People are victimized by crimes of abuse daily. If you have been a victim of abuse or violence, it is important to realize that it was not your fault. It is a common tendency to blame the victim of a crime for somehow contributing to the suffering that was caused. This is a misguided attempt to make sense out of senseless suffering, and it is not helpful. Part of your healing is to stop blaming yourself for what happened to you. But while *being* a victim of abuse is not your fault, *staying* a victim might be.

Everyone goes through difficult circumstances in life. If the circumstances are *very* difficult, then you come through them as one of two things: a *survivor* or a *victim*.[5] Survivors are people who have suffered in life but still maintain a sense of what psychologists call *personal power*: a belief that they can make a difference when trials come their way again. Victims are people who have suffered in life but now believe they are powerless. Once you believe you are a victim because of what has happened to you in the past, you are destined to feel powerless about what is going to happen to you in the future.

It is important to understand what it means to have personal power, because many self-help books use the term in a self-centered way that is not helpful. Personal power is not power *over* others; it is power *with* them. It is *personal* because it is the power God has given you as one person to influence another person. It is not domination; it is inspiration. Survivors are people who have been victimized by suffering in life but still have the power to personally influence others. Victims believe they are powerless. When used as God intended, personal power inspires *others* to be the best they can be right alongside survivors—which makes it the opposite of self-centered.

Doris came to therapy because of the recommendation of her attorney. She was injured while working at a large accounting firm downtown. Her attorney was concerned that she might be depressed as a result of her injury, and he wanted me to look into this.

Doris was raised in a poor part of town, and she was the pride of her family for becoming educated and landing such a good job at a respectable company. She came from a very modest background, and now she was able to raise her standard of living. Doris was the success story of the family—at least until her injury.

Now Doris was afraid she was not going to be able to continue on her path of success. She experienced constant back pain, which made it very difficult for her to continue at her job. Her attorney told her that she should be compensated for her pain and suffering, and he thought that he could make it so that she would never have to work that hard again. Doris was confused, and in pain. The thought of getting a large sum of money sounded good to her, but the thought of never working hard again was depressing.

"I just don't know what to do," Doris said as she looked out the window of my office.

"What do you feel you can do?" I asked.

"Not much," she replied. "I mean, my attorney is telling me I need to see all these doctors, to build my case and all. He says we have a really good case and that the company should pay for what has happened to me. I don't know, things were going so well, and now this. It feels like my life is over and it was just getting started."

"That's sad," I said.

"I know. Sad is what I feel most of the time now. And I used to be so happy. What's happening to me?" Doris asked as she looked over at me.

The answer to Doris's question was not simple. Her physical pain was making her life more difficult. Constant pain is depressing, and she was suffering from that. But I didn't think her physical pain was the only cause of her depression. Doris also felt powerless.

Doris was encouraged to believe that she would never be able to work very hard at any job ever again, that she was powerless to change her future and should be compensated for this. A large financial payment was a great incentive for Doris to give up her belief that she would ever be hardworking and productive again. If Doris could convince others that she was truly powerless to work hard again, she would win her case. This made Doris feel like a victim.

Life is complicated. Sometimes the best thing to do legally or politically might not be the best thing to do psychologically—or the other way around, for that matter. Now, let me make it clear that I do not believe that all legal proceedings result in making people victims. I have some very good friends who are attorneys, and they do wonderful work to help empower people to do good things. But in Doris's case, the legal proceedings that were helping her financially were working against her psychologically. It was in her best interest legally to be a victim, but it was not in her best interest psychologically to stay that way.

Doris and I are working hard at helping her become a survivor of her suffering. She was powerless over what happened to her, and she is suffering today because of it. But Doris is rejecting the belief that she is a victim. Doris likes viewing herself as a hardworking person, and no amount of money is worth giving that up. Doris may have been hurt, but that doesn't make her weak. She refuses to believe she is powerless to be a productive person again, and this has made Doris a survivor of her suffering. Doris is starting to feel happy again, and she is becoming an inspiration to everyone who knows her—just like she was before.

God has not left you alone in your suffering. He has provided for you some things to make you a survivor and not a victim. He promises to give "strength to the weary and increases the power of the weak." But true strength and power are not shown by dominating others; they are demonstrated by the ability to empower them through the inspiring example of your life. God has given you the capacity to be a survivor of your suffering by inspiring others in it. Whether or not you are weary or injured may not be your fault. No matter what your circumstances, you can choose to be a survivor and ask God for the power to sustain you and show you how to inspire others in the midst of whatever you are going through. Then you will know the difference between being a survivor and a victim.

5

How to Trust Again

Being hurt by someone you depend upon damages your ability to trust. This is especially true when you have been wounded by someone as important as your parents. If you are abused or taken advantage of by the people who are supposed to make you feel safe, you learn that it just doesn't make sense to be vulnerable. Even if you need to be vulnerable to find the love you need, it just isn't safe to do so.

This is the reason we have laws to protect children from child abuse. Damaging a child's ability to be vulnerable leaves the child with the feeling that self-protection is more important than anything. The child then goes about the rest of life with the feeling that protecting yourself from getting hurt is more important than getting ahead. It's like trying to ride a bike up a hill with the brakes on: you won't fall backward, but it makes forward progress very difficult.

Charlene is an attractive and intelligent woman who is very good at her job but has difficulty sustaining an intimate relationship with a man. She came to me for help with her disappointing love life because she wanted to get married and have children someday.

"Where are all the good men?" she asked.

"You're having a hard time finding just one?" I replied.

"That's all I really need, but I don't think there are any men who can be trusted to show up, take responsibility for their part in the relationship, and hang in there when things get difficult. Are all men little boys just wanting to have a good time?"

"You seem frustrated with the opposite sex," I observed.

"Not really," she snapped back. "I mean, I don't hate men or anything. I just want a good relationship with a man. I'm willing to do *my* part; I just need someone to be willing to do *his*."

"I imagine you want my perspective as a man," I said. "But then, it might be difficult to trust me because I am a man, too."

"No, you're different. You're a doctor, so I have to trust you."

"It's good to have at least one man you can trust," I replied.

"Well," she said slowly, "I guess you *are* a man."

It didn't take long for me to realize that Charlene had a difficult time agreeing with anything I said. If I suggested a feeling she might be having, she would say that wasn't quite right. If I tried to repeat what she just said to me, she would disagree with that, too. Without realizing it, Charlene needed to oppose me. She didn't do it on purpose; she just didn't feel safe enough to let me in.

At some point in our work together, Charlene eventually revealed to me something that explained everything. She told me that she had been molested by her father. She had been in therapy before with a female therapist and discussed this extensively. She wouldn't say she was "over it," but she did feel she had dealt with it quite a bit. She confronted her father before he died, and she felt a good deal of satisfaction about making him face up to his selfish and damaging behavior.

But my work with Charlene didn't turn out to be with her abuse exactly; it was with its lingering effects on her. Because she had been molested by her own father, Charlene believed that being vulnerable with anyone, especially a man, would only lead to one thing: exploitation. If her own father would exploit her tender vulnerability as a child, then how could she trust that anyone else wouldn't? Charlene's automatic response to men was to protect herself from being too vulnerable. Opposing men felt like the safest thing to do, even if it conflicted with her goal of eventually getting married.

After months of many conversations about whether or not she should trust me, Charlene still struggles somewhat with her doubts about the trustworthiness of men, but she isn't as defensive as she used to be around them. She realizes that she plays a role in how safe she feels around men, and she is learning that vulnerability doesn't always lead to exploitation. As she is finding out in her relationship with me, sometimes it can lead to connection and safety. She just had to realize that she was too afraid of vulnerability to find out.

After people have suffered through the ending of painful relationships, they often ask me, "How will I ever trust again?" As in Charlene's case, they think they need to scrutinize other people carefully to determine whether or not they are safe. But what I eventually help them see is that gaining a better understanding of other people is not what helps you feel safe; it's knowing *yourself* better. Charlene didn't need to figure out all the men in the city; she needed to figure out herself, and then take the risk to be vulnerable again. As she is getting better at knowing clearly what she feels, she is getting better at spotting unsafe men. Her fear of vulnerability was keeping her from identifying subtle feelings within herself that were important indicators of whether or not a relationship was going to be safe. The more emotionally honest she could be with herself and me, the greater her ability was to spot a man who was willing to be safe for her, too. This turned out to be the thing that helped her most in developing the courage to trust again.

6

Are You Anticipating Disappointment?

Anticipating disappointment is a way some people try to protect themselves from future hurt. They are trying to be prepared, but this particular strategy has some pretty negative consequences. Their logic is: *If I see it coming, then it won't hurt as much.* As it turns out, anticipating disappointment is often worse than the disappointment itself.

Mia is a talented businesswoman who is happily married and the mother of two wonderful children. Her husband is a success-ful architect and a dedicated father. On the surface, they appear to have the perfect family: success at work and happiness at home. Who could ask for more?

But Mia came to therapy because things are not always the same on the inside as they appear to others on the surface. Mia worked in a corporate office where she was required to make business presentations often. She was good at her job and well respected by most of her colleagues, but this didn't always help her with how she felt prior to making her presentations. Although everyone was almost always pleased with the quality and effective-ness of her presentations, she was tortured for days every time she had to give one.

"I have another big presentation this Thursday," Mia told me anxiously.

"You sound nervous," I responded.

"Well, one of the partners from corporate will be there," she said, "and the last time he was at one of my presentations, he just sat there and didn't say a thing. Not a smile, or a nod, nothing. I mean, what was he thinking? Am I supposed to just drag out my dog-and-pony show to entertain this guy? I think he has a thing against women."

"It's stressful being a woman in a male-dominated career," I said.

"I know. I just never feel I'm giving them what they want. My dad was right. I should have never gone for my MBA," she said as she put her face in her hands.

Mia's anxiety about her presentations seemed odd since they usually went so well. You would think she would be confident about her ability to perform, but just one or two disappointing reactions and she would remember them for years.

As our therapy progressed, we discovered an important key to Mia's anxiety and fear about her work. She wasn't actually *experiencing* disappointment that often; she was *anticipating* it. Mia was the younger sister to Alan, her brilliant older brother whom her parents tended to favor. She grew up always hearing about his accomplishments and his importance as the eldest son in the family. Trying to live in his shadow made her feel like a constant disappointment to her parents. No matter how good she was in school, or successful she was at extracurricular activities, it was never as good as whatever Alan was doing. She would never be her brother, and there was nothing she could ever do about that. She would always only be "Alan's younger sister."

It is changing slowly, but Mia is realizing that trying to protect herself from the feeling of disappointment by anticipating
it is just not working for her. Just because she felt like a constant
disappointment to her parents as a child doesn't mean she has
to expect it as an adult. Sure, some people are going to be disappointed at times with her presentations, but that doesn't mean *she*
is a disappointment. Yes, it is disappointing to experience gender discrimination in the workplace, but that doesn't mean she is
disqualified from doing a good job. Mia isn't just Alan's younger
sister anymore. She is a successful woman in her job, but she was
anticipating that she was going to be a disappointment anyway.
Once she realized where this self-protective strategy came from,
she found it easier to surrender it as a source of suffering in her
life that she just didn't need.

The Bible tells us that there are people who "will look toward
the earth and see only distress and darkness and fearful gloom."
But negative anticipation only brings more suffering. Rather than
trying to anticipate it, you must develop the courage to tolerate it.
Feeling disappointment doesn't mean you *are* a disappointment.
It takes courage to live your life allowing disappointment to be
a part of it. Don't make it a goal to have a life without any disappointments; ask God for the strength to deal with them when
they come.

God says, "Whoever listens to me will live in safety and be at
ease, without fear of harm."[6] This obviously doesn't mean that no
harm will come your way; all you have to do is read the Bible to find
out that godly people have to deal with hurt and suffering in their
lives. What it does mean is that if you trust in God, you won't have
to *fear* harm—not because it won't happen to you, but because God
will give you the ability to be at ease with yourself when it does.
Working on *tolerating* disappointments more than *anticipating* them
helped Mia be at ease; it can help you, too.

7

Why You Hurt the One
You Love the Most

You say things to those you love that you would never say to your friends—because your friends would never stand for it. Sadly, if you talked to your friends in the same way that you talked to your spouse, you wouldn't have any friends. This is an unfortunate part of intimacy: *People take license with love.*

When you love someone, you want to go beyond the superficial. The Bible tells us that "an enemy multiplies kisses." It means they will "make nice" with people they don't like in order to give the appearance that everything is fine. Their kisses are insincere and overdone to cover over their real feelings about you. But "wounds from a friend can be trusted" because friends tell the truth to each other, and even though they may hurt each other at times, they can trust that they will deal with the genuine feelings between them. The problem comes with knowing how to be *real* when you are hurt by someone you love. Often in our attempt to be "real" with our hurt feelings, we think it gives us the license to hurt them back.

In order to love someone, you have to be vulnerable. You take off your superficial mask and let them see who you really are. This is necessary in love. However, being vulnerable is also when you get hurt. When this happens, it tempts you to do and say hurtful things in a stronger way to the people with whom you are most vulnerable. This is why you hurt the one you love the most.

Donna and Michael came for marital therapy because of their constant fighting, which is a common reason for seeking therapy. You start off marrying someone because of the exciting characteristics that are different from you that make you fall in love, but over the years those same differences become sources of irritation that can make you mad. Donna and Michael were no exception.

"Therapy isn't working. He hasn't changed one bit," Donna screamed at the beginning of our fifth session.

"What is it that you need?" I asked. I could see that I was going to have to fight to keep the session from spinning out of control. Coming to marital therapy to change your partner is a common mistake that people make. I needed each of them to stay focused on their own needs and feelings, and not fall into the trap of blaming each other, which gets us nowhere.

"I need him to stop being a liar!" she replied emphatically.

"Name calling isn't going to help," I said firmly. "So, try to say that in terms of your *feelings*, not what's wrong with him."

"Okay. I *feel* like he needs to stop being a liar," she said with a distinct edge in her voice.

"That's not a feeling," I replied. "What are *you* feeling right now?"

Donna's face changed. I could see that she was trying to understand what I was saying. She was used to talking in terms of his character defects and not expressing herself in terms of her own feelings. She wasn't getting anywhere by assassinating his character, and I was hoping to provide her with some tools that could help.

"I feel scared," she said as her lower lip began to quiver. "He told me I could quit work and he was going to take care of us financially, and now I find out that we are eighty thousand dollars in debt. How do you think I feel? I'm terrified that we'll end up broke." She burst into tears.

"Michael," I said calmly as I turned to him. "Did you know Donna felt this way?"

"Well, no," Michael said as he looked at his shoes. "All I knew was that she was mad, and I hate talking to her when she's that angry."

"And what do you feel hearing this now?"

"I feel terrible that she's scared," he said more confidently. "I don't want my wife to be afraid. We took out the second mortgage to have a cushion when we needed it, and I used it to pay for the construction on the house. I'm paying it back just fine. I didn't lie to her; I just thought it was my responsibility to take care of things, and that's exactly what I'm doing." Michael turned to face Donna. "I'm sorry that I didn't tell you I was drawing money from the second. I thought you wanted to leave those things up to me."

Donna and Michael actually loved each other very much. But when someone you love hurts you, anger will follow close behind. Donna was angry with Michael because she needed to feel safe with the man she loves. She was mad because she was fighting for the kind of marriage that would make her feel that way. But Michael wasn't getting that message. All he was hearing was that she didn't trust him and he was a failure as a husband.

Michael was trying to be a good husband to Donna, but he was afraid to talk to her about how he was going about it. He loved her and he wanted to take care of her. He worked hard to provide for his family, and everything he did was for their benefit. But Donna wasn't getting that message, either. The message she got was that he was tired of talking to her and just wanted her to leave him alone.

Over time, Donna and Michael stopped hurting each other as much. Donna does a better job these days refraining from attacking Michael's character, and Michael does a better job at opening up to her in ways that help her feel safe. Now they see that *how* you speak to someone is just as important as *what* it is you are trying to say. Making your point in marriage isn't going to do you much good if you have alienated your partner. Donna and Michael were fighting for connection—they just needed some help getting there.

What is it that you are supposed to trust in marriage? That your partner will never fail you? That you will never get hurt? You are going to be disappointed if you think so. What you are supposed to trust is that you are with someone who cares when they hurt you, and that they are willing to work it out with you when it happens. This is what friends do, which is why the Bible says "wounds from a friend can be trusted." Just don't forget that friends speak to each other with respect; and more importantly, trust that you will be loved, not that you won't get hurt. Then you can work out a real love relationship with someone who is both your lover and your friend.

8

Why Boundaries Are Hard but Helpful

Having the discipline to make use of boundaries is one of the ways you can protect yourself from becoming overwhelmed. Even though boundaries themselves hurt at times, they give you the protection you need for healthy growth.

Boundaries are a way of saying no and yes at the same time. As a child, you had to learn where you ended and others began. Understanding what no meant helped you to realize that the world didn't revolve around you, and learning your limits was an important part of learning how to be happy. Saying no to some things allows you to say yes to others. You may not always like it, but having boundaries is a good thing.

My wife, Barbara, and I thought a lot about where we were going to send our son Brendan to school. I'm not talking about college; I am referring to kindergarten. Because we live in a large city, we had lots of options. We wanted to find a place where he could thrive academically, but more importantly we wanted him to grow up to be a man of character. His spiritual and emotional development were just as important to us as his academic test scores. We found just the right place, a wonderful Christian school with caring teachers, active programs, and an emphasis on spiritual and emotional growth among its students. We couldn't have been more pleased to send him there.

To our delight, Brendan soon formed many friendships, and it didn't take long for him to become best friends with David. David was probably the brightest child in the class, and in kindergarten this automatically makes you one of the leaders. David was authoritative, always knew the rules to whatever games they were playing (or made them up if he didn't), and tended to see himself as in charge. Brendan loved David.

As happens among children, a pecking order was soon established. The less extroverted children sometimes got overlooked when it came time to take the lead in games, and the more authoritative children (like David and Brendan) got more than their fair share of the decision-making. And there was one boy in particular, Roberto, who sometimes was excluded from the games altogether.

Fortunately, Barbara has a keen insight into such things and instinctively knew what to do. She brought up her concerns with David's mother and suggested that they address what appeared to be unkind behavior toward the other children at times, especially Roberto. Unfortunately, David's mother didn't see a problem. To her, David was a natural leader and she wasn't going to do anything to squelch his innate abilities. She thought children should be allowed to work out their differences without parental interference, and if the other children couldn't stand up to David, then they needed to learn to be more assertive.

Barbara disagreed. Each day as she took Brendan to school, she would talk to him about taking turns, not excluding other children, and the consequences of hitting or pushing others to get his way. After some time-outs and lost privileges, Brendan began to be more respectful of the other children. He didn't like it, but through our discipline of setting boundaries on his behavior he learned how to get along better with the other children, including Roberto.

Then one day as Barbara dropped Brendan off at school, he ran up to David with all his enthusiasm to greet his best friend.

"Hey, David!" Brendan cried out with glee.

"Brendan!" David called back, wide-eyed. "Guess what?"

"What?" Brendan asked, eagerly awaiting the beginning of their next game together.

"I've decided that everyone is going to hate Roberto!" David shouted back.

"What?" asked Brendan with some amazement.

"That's right," David went on. "I don't like him, and everyone says that they are not going to be friends with him anymore."

After a moment, Brendan looked David in the eye and said as firmly as a six-year-old boy could, "No."

Somewhat shocked, David just stared back at Brendan.

"No," Brendan said. "That's not nice. If you're not going to be friends with Roberto, then I'm not going to be best friends with you anymore." At that, he simply ran off to join in a game some other children were playing nearby.

Within a short time, things got worse, but not for Roberto—for David. He began experiencing discipline problems in the classroom, the other children stopped following his lead in games, and several of the other mothers confronted David's mother about his hurtful behavior. Eventually, David's mother changed her mind about her parenting strategy. Refusing to set limits on David's hurtful behavior wasn't helping him develop properly. Setting boundaries for him not only helped him be less hurtful to others but also helped him to stop hurting himself since he was becoming ostracized as a bully.

I am not suggesting that Brendan was transformed by a few time-outs. Barbara and I spent a good deal of time and energy setting boundaries for him for years. And even though it was almost always difficult for him (and for us), it was worth it. He might have lost some fun by not always getting his way, but the trade-off was that he was developing his character. We believe whatever pain he was caused by our setting boundaries for him was much less than the hurt he would have received in life for not having them. God has told us, "No discipline seems pleasant at the time, but painful. Later on, however, it produces a harvest of righteousness and peace for those who have been trained by it."[7]

9

Hurt People Hurt People

Sometimes getting hurt makes you want to *even the scales*. You try to quantify your hurt, and then make someone else hurt in an equal amount. Of course, this isn't possible, which is why hurt people lash out in hurtful ways that don't make sense to anyone but the hurt person. Because of this, you should remember that when you are hurt you are in danger of hurting others, too.

A common mistake is to think someone is bad who makes you feel bad. This makes you feel justified in hurting that person. Your underlying reasoning is: Bad people make others feel bad, and bad people should be the ones getting hurt. Your pain might not be any less, but at least the world makes sense and *that* makes you feel a little better. Unfortunately, this rarely turns out well for anyone.

Ruth and Alex fell in love. They were both in their final year in college when they met, and they instantly felt they had so much in common. She wanted to become a nurse, then get married and have children and be a stay-at-home mom. Alex wanted to become a doctor and marry a woman with traditional values who would see her role as a homemaker as important. They agreed on political views and religion, and they were very attracted to each other. Everything felt just right. So, after six months of dating, they became engaged to be married.

But love does not always go as planned. After graduation, Alex went to medical school and Ruth took a job at a hospital in a town nearby as a nurse. They didn't spend much time together in the next year, but that was okay since they had a bigger life plan. They got together on weekends when Alex was able to get some time off, which was hard, but they both felt they were working for something that would make it all worthwhile.

Over time their relationship changed. Alex grew closer to his fellow medical students, and Ruth felt better understood by her girlfriends at the hospital than by Alex. Neither of them planned it, but one day when they were finally able to spend some time together face-to-face, they both knew they needed to talk.

"What are we doing?" Ruth asked after several minutes of silence.

"About what?" Alex asked.

"About us," Ruth said. "We're never affectionate anymore, we don't talk about anything other than your schedule, and I can't remember the last time you told me you loved me."

"I know," Alex said sadly. "I guess things have changed."

"What do you mean?" Ruth responded. "We agreed to be apart for now in order to build our dreams for the future. What are you trying to say, that you don't love me anymore?"

"I don't know," Alex said as he looked down. "We've just grown so far apart. I don't know if we should get married if we don't feel the same way anymore. I just don't know."

"Well, I do," Ruth said angrily. "I know that you promised to marry me when we got engaged, and I can't believe that you are going back on that promise now. After all this, after all I've done to make this work, and now you're telling me you *don't know* anymore? I hate that you can say that to me, and I hate you for doing this. I can't believe that you are telling me that our whole relationship has been nothing but a big lie. How could I have been so stupid!"

Sadly, Alex and Ruth broke up. Alex felt bad, and he regretted that their plans had not worked out, but Ruth was furious. She was hurt and humiliated. When people fall in love, they have an intense feeling of being connected that makes them feel that the other person is *there for them*. This brings with it an implied promise that they will *always* be there for them, and for Alex and Ruth this wasn't the case. Ruth now felt betrayed, and she was angry.

Over the next several weeks, Ruth couldn't stop thinking about Alex. Songs on the radio reminded her of him, doctors at the hospital made her think about what he was doing, and she hated her evenings because she felt so hurt and alone. She felt this wasn't right. What was once a promise now felt like a lie. Ruth just couldn't let it go.

Ruth was very vocal with their mutual friends about what she thought was Alex's lack of character, and she didn't hold back her criticisms of him around the other doctors who might work with him. She even felt at one point that she needed to protect other women from his deceitfulness by making an impression on him to keep him from acting this way again. She drove to the hospital where he was working and presented him with a list of his character flaws in front of all his colleagues. He needed to be stopped, and she felt entitled to tell him so. Ruth probably knew she would be hurting Alex both personally and professionally by her actions, but she felt he deserved it. After all, in her mind he *was* a liar.

Ruth hurt Alex with her angry behavior. He was embarrassed and furious with her for doing what she did. She eventually moved on in her life, but not until she made him look bad in front of other people and made herself look somewhat unstable in the process. Ruth was hurt by their failed relationship, but she only made things worse by hurting Alex as well.

Hurt people hurt people.[8] Neither Alex nor Ruth were bad people, but they were both capable of hurting and being hurt. God warned us to "make sure that nobody pays back wrong for wrong" because he knows that returning hurt for hurt never helps. Ruth didn't help Alex learn anything useful with her hurtful behavior, and she only made it more difficult for herself to trust another man in the future. We can all learn something from Ruth's mistake. If you have been hurt by someone close to you, remember that you are in danger of becoming hurtful yourself.

10

People Pleasing to Avoid Hurt

One strategy to avoid hurt in life is to try to please everyone. In times of conflict, *people pleasers* try to placate instead of confront, and they are uncomfortable with dealing with anger directly. The myths that people pleasers believe are that feeling *fine* is always better than emotional discomfort, and that others will like you more if you make them happy.

On the surface, people pleasers appear to be concerned about everyone's feelings. But the truth is, they are really only concerned about their own. Avoiding conflict is their primary concern, even if it costs them genuine relationships with others. People pleasers are referred to as *nice* by those who have superficial relationships with them, but anyone who knows them very well doesn't really trust them. People pleasers don't realize that the only way to truly love others is to be willing to disappoint them. You can only trust someone if you believe they are willing to tell you the truth, even if it hurts. Trying to look good to others is not the same thing as loving them.

Diana is a nice person. She has many friends and a very active social life. Everyone at work thinks she is friendly because she is always willing to help people out if they need it. She is interested in what people have to say and very easy to talk to because she rarely has strong opinions about anything. She never talks about politics or religion, because she would never want to make anyone uncomfortable.

Diana is very active at her children's school. She has been the president of the parents' association, and she often volunteers to help out with school fund-raisers and parties. She tells her kids that she is doing everything at school for them, but they don't really see it that way. Her son would prefer to spend his afternoons playing games at home with his mom, but she is usually too busy getting things done for the next school event.

Because Diana has so many friends, she doesn't have the opportunity to spend very much time with any one of them. She tries to spread herself out evenly over all her friends so none of them feel neglected. But there is not enough time to go around.

"Hey, Nicole," Diana said cheerfully when she called one of her best friends recently.

"Diana, how are you?" Nicole replied.

"I know we said we would get together for coffee this morning, but I was wondering . . . could I just stop by your place instead?"

"Uh, sure," said Nicole, a bit confused. "I guess we can just have coffee here. Is ten o'clock still okay?"

"Well, I'm running late," Diana said with a pressured tone in her voice. "Could we make it eleven? I'll have about twenty minutes or so."

"Okay," Nicole replied, trying to mask her hurt feelings. "I was looking forward to getting out, but I guess a few minutes together is better than nothing. See you at eleven."

"Great," Diana replied, obviously relieved. "Eleven will be perfect."

"See you then," Nicole said and slowly hung up the phone.

Diana always runs late. She doesn't mean to be disrespectful of others' time, but she can't say no when she is asked to do something, and she can't leave whomever she is with very easily for fear of hurting their feelings. In her mind, Diana is trying to do what she thinks will make people happy. When someone needs her to do something, she says yes. When someone is with her, she stays until they are ready for her to leave.

Without realizing it, Diana had made her best friend, Nicole, feel unimportant and was causing her children to resent her involvement at their school. People who don't know her very well think she is an amazing woman to be able to do all that she does. But those closest to her get their feelings hurt often. Diana hasn't realized yet that trying to please everyone ends up pleasing no one who is important.

Trying to look good doesn't produce good relationships. People pleasers are more invested in trying to avoid disappointment than they are in achieving good relationships. Good relationships tolerate disappointment rather than avoid it. If you are trying too hard to avoid hurting everyone's feelings, then you can end up becoming a people pleaser. It's better to disappoint several people who aren't very close to you than hurt the few who are.

11

The Dangers of Denial

Denial is an attempt to strip away hurt from reality. It is a psychological defense mechanism used to protect you from painful feelings.[9] If you tell yourself that you don't feel any pain about something, you might be able to convince yourself, and others, that your suffering has stopped. No one wants to suffer. Denial can be a self-righteous way of pretending that you don't.

It is important to know that denial *is* a necessary defense mechanism at times. You can't feel all your pain all at once, or all the time. It would be too much. So sometimes you distract yourself from your hurt with denial. But if you are unaware that you are using denial, it can be dangerous. It is possible to cause even more hurt with denial than the hurt you are trying to avoid, especially when your denial comes in the form of "a righteousness of my own."

Daniel is a very outspoken Christian. He attends church regularly and is a very visible member in the worship services. Everyone at church knows him because he stands out as a self-appointed authority figure and knowledgeable person.

Daniel is frustrated with his pastor because he has not given Daniel any positions of responsibility in the church. Daniel knows the Bible well and is constantly counseling others on how to achieve greater maturity. Daniel believes he should be teaching classes or preaching occasionally at the church, but his pastor believes these positions of responsibility should be given out only after great consideration, because the Bible says, "Not many of you should become teachers, my fellow believers, because you know that we who teach will be judged more strictly."[10]

Daniel is a good man, but he didn't always live that way. He grew up in a very abusive household, married a woman who was an alcoholic like his mother, and struggled with a life of crime and addiction before he became a Christian. Daniel has suffered a lot in life, and he often talks about how grateful he is to God that those days are behind him. He is married to a kind Christian woman now and holds down a stable job. He talks about his past as a witness to how God can heal us from sin. But Daniel is in denial about how much of his past is still with him today. His denial comes in the form of "a righteousness of my own" that makes his pastor feel that Daniel is depending more upon his own strength that comes from the denial of his problems than relying upon God's strength that comes from humbly confessing them.

Over time, things became tense for Daniel at work when his boss found things wrong with Daniel's performance. After a series of mistakes that Daniel tried to minimize, he was eventually fired. Daniel was indignant about his boss's criticism of him, and he felt humiliated about how he was terminated. He believed it wasn't fair, but there was nothing he could do about it. Rather than seeking help for his pain openly from God and others, he tried to cover it with self-righteous denial. He tried to deny the pain of his own shame for being fired by blaming everything on his boss.

Daniel was so distressed about being fired from work that he was overwhelmed with painful feelings of embarrassment and failure. The feelings of hurt were so intense that he was tempted to use drugs again. And he did. Even though he knew it was wrong, Daniel couldn't help it. He turned to the god of his addiction to make his pain stop, instead of the God of his life to help him endure it.

The next several months were a nightmare for Daniel and his wife. He disappeared for days at a time, she was forced to spend their savings to keep from losing their home, and she was terrified that he might even become violent with her if she tried to stop him from his self-destructive behavior. Daniel was reliving his past, and he was dragging everyone who was close to him down along with him. He was no longer just hurting himself; he was damaging everyone who loved him, as well.

Daniel eventually stopped using drugs and returned to a life of sanity. His wife is glad that he is back at home, but she doesn't trust him. It may take years before she can do that again. Daniel is back at church, but his pastor is still uncomfortable with his emotional and spiritual stability. Daniel still talks about God's grace, and how grateful he is to be a Christian who is forgiven for his sins. But his pastor would like him to talk more about repentance and humility. I don't believe the pastor will be asking Daniel to assume any positions of leadership or teaching for a long time.

Because he suffered greatly in the past, Daniel wants to believe that God can erase suffering from his life now. This is denial, not faith. God doesn't want us to deny our suffering; he wants to give us the strength to deal with it. This is the spiritual principle behind the Alcoholics Anonymous[11] admonition to "take it one day at a time." From this perspective, God does not remove suffering from life, but he can give you the strength to deal with it daily. To be in denial about your suffering and problems is only having a righteousness of your own. Turning to God and others to deal with it is a better plan.

Some psychologists are uncomfortable with the principles of Alcoholics Anonymous. The emphasis in AA upon turning to a Higher Power, whom Christians name as God, to deal with your suffering doesn't fit with how some psychologists think about health. I disagree. Admitting that some things have power over you is not the same thing as believing that you are a powerless person. Realizing that you are not God, and that you need someone outside of yourself to help you, is a sign of strength, not weakness. Trying to heal yourself with a righteousness of your own is usually just denial.

12

The Solution to Suffering

Whether or not you suffer is not a choice. *How* you suffer is. You can choose to suffer silently or cry out loud. You can suffer by looking for the meaning behind it, or you can accept it as it is. There are many approaches to suffering. But no matter what approach you choose, you must learn to suffer well if you want to become a better person because of it.

On September 11, 2001, I rose about 5:30 a.m. to have an interview with a radio station. This was to be a phone interview, so I was able to receive the call at my home in Los Angeles from the radio station some 3,000 miles away in New York. I collected my thoughts, opened a Diet Coke (I was going to need the caffeine), and placed myself by the phone.

At a couple of minutes before 6:00 a.m., the phone rang. It was the producer of the talk show. Everything was set. She transferred me to the host of the show, and we were about to begin. But the interview never happened.

"Have you heard?" the host said as she picked up the phone.

"Uh, I'm sorry," I said in a puzzled voice. "Heard what?"

"Someone has blown up the World Trade Center," she replied in a still, shocked tone.

"What?" I replied.

"Yes. We just received news that the World Trade Center has been blown up. Actually, I'm somewhat frightened right now because my husband is in the city and I don't know exactly where."

I didn't know what to say. This seemed too incredible to actually be true. *How* she was speaking to me sounded very believable, but *what* she was saying didn't.

"I'm sorry. But would it be all right if we postponed our interview so I can try to locate my husband?" she asked.

"Of course," I replied. "This can wait. You need to be talking to him right now, not me."

I hung up and turned on my television to find the North Tower of the World Trade Center billowing with smoke. This seemed like a bad movie, not the morning news. And then, right before my eyes, I watched as United Flight 175 flew directly into the *South* Tower of the World Trade Center and exploded into flames. I was in shock.

That horrifying incident set a series of events into motion. Within the next hour and a half, one of the most important financial centers in America was leveled to the ground, killing over 3,000 unsuspecting people. Billions of people all over the world awoke to find their headline news reporting this epic tragedy. The initial impact of terrorism had its effect. No one felt safe. Average people going about their average lives could be killed instantly, and there was nothing anyone could do about it. This could have happened to any of us. This had happened to all of us.

But then something took place that the terrorists had not counted on. People didn't recoil in their fear; no one wanted to hide from what was happening. People wanted to get involved. Friends and family members of lost loved ones rushed to the site of Ground Zero to begin their vigils that would last for days to support the search-and-rescue efforts. Lines started forming all over the country to give blood to the injured. Even in Los Angeles, on the opposite end of the country, people stood in line for five and six hours to give their own blood for people they had never met who might need it. Crime in New York City dropped off, strangers opened their homes to take in those who were in need, and political differences between leaders seemed to disappear as a country under attack rallied together to support itself in a crisis. People needed each other, and in their time of need, someone was there.

The tragic events of September 11 taught us something about suffering. Tragedy can happen to any of us, and suffering is unavoidable in life. But we can choose how we are going to respond to our suffering. If we shrink back into the isolation that trauma causes us to feel, then we run the risk of becoming bitter and despondent. But if we reach out to others in times of need, then we find that they not only gain strength to survive their suffering as a result of our help, but we become better people ourselves in the process.

I saw a poster once with a quote on it by the former secretary-general of the United Nations, Dag Hammarskjöld. He was a Nobel Peace Prize winner who dedicated his life to international relations and diplomacy. The quote was, "Don't pray for peace, pray for strength."[12] God did not promise you a life without suffering. But he promised you that he will give you strength in it if you ask. You may not be able to lessen the intensity of your suffering, but you can make it more tolerable by turning to God and others in it. Then you will discover the real solution to suffering: *Don't try to suffer alone.*

13

Is Suffering Abandonment by God?

One of the oldest diseases on record is leprosy. It results in a disfigurement that is so distressing that leper colonies have been established throughout history to separate those with the disease from the general population. At first it was thought that leprosy caused body parts to simply fall off, leaving the afflicted person deformed and weakened forever. Now we know leprosy is a disease that attacks the nervous system and inhibits the sensation of pain. It locates itself in the cool extremities of the body, such as the fingers, toes, and limbs. Without sensitivity to pain, lepers injure themselves and are not able to respond immediately with the proper medical attention. This results in infections and the undetected deterioration of the body.

Leprosy is a good example of a difficult truth about life—*pain is necessary for survival*. Without pain we would not be able to respond quickly to emergency situations with appropriate action. Pain is a survival mechanism for us physically, psychologically, and spiritually. We must have pain in our lives in order to live well.

This difficult truth about life was addressed on a spiritual level by Martin Luther, a German theologian, dedicated Catholic monk, and university professor during the sixteenth century. He was a monk for several years before he experienced a personal spiritual renewal through his own study of the Bible. Excited about how an authentic relationship with God could transform lives, he tried to address a number of difficult issues concerning Christianity that might be hindering people in their relationship with God.

One of Luther's concerns was that many people did not seem to understand the role of suffering in spiritual maturity. To him, the crucifixion of Christ was not the bloodthirsty act of a vengeful God as the atheists argued, but the ultimate demonstration of the only way to find an authentic relationship with him. Luther wanted people to understand that "the true reality of God and of his salvation is 'paradoxical' and hidden under its opposite."[13]

To explain this, Luther referred to the Scripture passage in which Moses asked God to allow him to see the glory of God, but God refused and hid Moses behind a rock as he passed by, explaining that "you cannot see my face, for no one may see me and live" (Exod. 33:20). No human being could stand to look directly into the face of God's glory, as it would be too great for any human to bear. Instead, God allowed Moses to "see my back; but my face must not be seen" (Exod. 33:23). Luther concluded from this that the authentic presence of God would not be found by seeking success and glory in this life; it would be found by looking for him in our suffering. The times in your life when God will seem most real to you will be when you are looking at his back, not pursuing his glorious face, because finding God in the midst of suffering clarifies the reality of his presence the most.

Luther calls this the theology of the cross. Jesus suffered and died, not as a result of a failed ministry at the hands of people who hated him, but as a participation in suffering to show those he loved how to find the true presence of God. Seeking glory in this life will not give you the most meaningful existence, but looking for God in your times of suffering will. Luther admits this will be experienced as a "stumbling block" to some and "foolishness" to others, but it is this theology of suffering that makes the problem of pain tolerable. Suffering is not abandonment by God; it is the path to his authentic presence. It is up to us to look for him there.

The most important thing God has given you to make you better instead of bitter as a result of your suffering in life is *the presence of God*. When you are in pain, you can turn to him and ask him to be with you in it. We know psychologically that traumatic suffering is tolerable if we do not have to go through it alone. God does not want you to have to do that, either. He has given you the gift of himself to give you strength in times of need.

PART TWO

Guilt and Shame

14

The Difference between Guilt and Shame

Guilt is the bad feeling you get for doing something you should not have done. It is about what you did. You went too far, and now you feel bad about what you've done. Shame is the bad feeling you get for not measuring up to who you think you should be. It is about who you are. You didn't go far enough, and now you feel bad about who you are.

Guilt can play an important role in your happiness. God made you to feel bad about certain actions, and guilt can bring painful things into the light to help you make better choices. But shame is the pain of doubting your self-worth. Shame seeks to hide itself and make you feel privately defective. This is contrary to what the Bible tells us, which is that you are "fearfully and wonderfully made." God created your guilt to help you live up to the wonderful person you were created to be, even when your shame makes you doubt that you have it in you.

Ian's wife left him after six years of marriage, and she now has full-time custody of their two children. He sees the kids every other weekend and tries to be the best father he can be under the circumstances. Ian came to therapy because he was confused about why his wife divorced him and he just couldn't make sense out of his life.

"I paid the bills, I never cheated on her, and I tried to be a good father," Ian bemoaned.

"It just doesn't feel fair," I said.

"Life isn't fair," he snapped back. "I mean, I know that. If only we had moved to that new house when she wanted to. I just didn't know how big a deal that was to her. I guess it was a mistake to be so worried about finances all the time."

"You're feeling pretty guilty about it," I said.

"Of course!" he said angrily. "I know she would still be with me today if only she had gotten her way about that house."

"So you think not getting the house was the deal breaker?"

"I'm sure of it. That was the only thing she ever got really upset about," he concluded in exasperation.

Ian was plagued with guilt about his failed marriage. He pointed to specific things that he should have done differently. Most of the time he focused on the house he didn't buy, but sometimes it was about how he argued with her about money or how he played too much golf on Saturdays. The specifics changed a bit at times, but Ian was pretty sure that he did too many things wrong in his marriage, and that was why he was divorced today. That's the core of guilt feelings: having the conviction that you did something wrong and now you have to pay for it.

But as time went on, we discovered that Ian's problem wasn't really with guilt. Sometimes guilt can be used as a defense against something worse. There was something deeper, more painful, that he didn't want to face, so he was preoccupying himself with feelings of guilt instead. What Ian really felt in his heart wasn't that he didn't *do* something right for his ex-wife: it was that he wasn't *being* something right for her. If it was about what he *did*, he could change that. But if it was about who he *was*, well, that was a different matter. Ian was wrestling with shame.

Shame is often more difficult to deal with than guilt. It's doubting your self-worth and feeling defective as a person. But using guilt as a defense against shame makes things even worse because it keeps you stuck. If you really have questions about your self-worth, then it's best to address them directly and not cover them over, no matter how painful a task that might be. Ian and I found that even though he didn't like it, dealing with the shame he felt about who he was turned out to be an important part of our work in therapy.

Ian doesn't talk much about the "one that got away" these days. After several months of looking at this with me, he can see that not buying the house is not as important to talk about anymore. What we do talk about is how he feels about himself. He has doubts sometimes, and he feels genuinely guilty about several things, but more than anything else, Ian now speaks with a kind of humility that comes with honest self-reflection. He used to mistake feeling bad with being bad, and they aren't the same thing. Now he can feel guilty about some things in his past and not have to feel ashamed of himself for it. As he puts it, "You know what they say: *God doesn't make junk*." He means that even though he isn't perfect, at least he is willing to look honestly at those imperfections and try to learn something about himself.

Talking honestly about himself with another person has helped Ian with his shame. He still *feels* bad about his divorce sometimes, but that doesn't mean he *is* bad anymore. The way I like to think of it is that he believes he is *fearfully and wonderfully made*, even if sometimes he doesn't act like it.

15

Guilt That Leaves Regrets

There are two basic forms of guilt: guilt that comes from love, and guilt that comes from fear. Guilt based upon love is the bad feeling you get from doing something wrong, which makes you want to make things right again. Guilt based upon fear is the bad feeling you get when you are afraid you are going to get punished. The reason you fear punishment is that fear-based guilt is triggered by shame. People who get trapped in guilt based on fear don't just feel they did something bad, they feel they are bad and deserve to be punished because of it. Guilt based on love is focused on the good things you need to do; guilt based on fear is focused on the bad things that you have done, and the punishment you fear you deserve.

Guilt that comes from fear is often not that helpful. It doesn't restore broken relationships; it merely protects you from some retribution you might deserve. This type of guilt often lasts for a long time and sometimes doesn't ever come to any resolution. It is a way of punishing yourself because your hidden shame makes you feel you deserve it. But because this self-imposed punishment does not actually solve anything, the bad feelings of guilt based upon fear can go on for a lifetime, sometimes even until death.

Maria is a humble, dedicated Christian woman. She tries to be helpful to others whenever she can, and like Martha in the New Testament,[1] you can always find her working in the kitchen at church retreats and gatherings. She grew up in a conservative religious home and always tried to live by the teachings in the Bible. She hardly ever got into trouble as a child, and she prides herself on keeping the highest moral standards possible as a woman today.

Despite her efforts to be good, Maria often feels bad. No matter how hard she tries, Maria always seems to find something that she could have done better. She tries not to let others know, but her feelings get hurt frequently. She often feels others are critical of her and that her efforts to be helpful are largely unappreciated. Her favorite verse in the Bible is "faith without deeds is dead,"[2] which is why she works so hard at trying to be good.

"I just don't understand why so many Christians are so lazy," she bemoaned to me.

"It's frustrating when other people really don't care," I said.

"That's right. And most people don't," she replied. "Otherwise they would work harder at following what the Bible says."

"It is hard to be a Christian," I said.

"A lot harder," she went on. "I mean, if I weren't a Christian, then I could do whatever I wanted and it would be okay. But I know God is watching me. And I don't want him to be any more disappointed in me than he already is. I confess my sins to God daily; but I don't know . . . If I died tonight, I don't know if I would make it into heaven or not."

Maria lives her life based upon a fear of punishment. She doesn't live a bad life, but it isn't a very joyful one. She married a good man, but she isn't happy with her marriage. She feels constantly hurt by his failing to be the man she thinks he should be, and she feels horrible about herself for being so critical of him.

After courageously working on herself in therapy for a while, eventually Maria came to an important realization. She wasn't actually trying to be good; she was just trying to avoid being bad. She never felt truly satisfied with anything because she wasn't seeking satisfaction; she was only trying to avoid painful feelings of failure. Maria suffered from guilt based upon fear, and that is not what God intended. Godly guilt helps us feel bad about the things we do; Maria's guilt was based upon her underlying shame for feeling bad about who she was. The kind of guilt that God intends leads us to restored relationships and leaves no regrets. Maria was living with a lifetime of regrets, and it wasn't doing her much good.

Maria still struggles with guilt, but because we have exposed her shame's lie that she deserved to be punished, it isn't the kind of guilt that was consuming her life before. She tries to take the emphasis off of her fear and failings and put it on her efforts to restore relationships with God and others. Now when she feels guilty, she doesn't think about what she did that was wrong; she tries to think about what she can do to make things right. She now sees guilt as an indicator of a need to talk to someone about hurt feelings. If she hurts God or someone else, then she may need to talk to them about it. Feeling bad about herself wasn't doing anything constructive. Trying to restore hurt relationships is.

16

Guilt without Regrets

Some people come to therapy expecting therapists to relieve them of their guilt. They think they shouldn't feel guilty and perhaps therapy will help them see that their problems are not really their fault but their parents'. This is based upon an incomplete understanding of guilt. Some things are your fault, and feeling guilty about them is a healthy thing.

Guilt that comes from love is the bad feeling you get when you have done something hurtful and you want to make it right. The aim of this type of guilt is not self-punishment, because there is no underlying feeling of shame to make you think you deserve it. Instead, it motivates you to do something to restore a broken relationship. Guilt based upon love is not intended to last a long time; it is an uncomfortable feeling that results from violating your conscience and it spurs you on to take some action to make amends for your mistake.

Guilt that comes from love stimulates you to think about things differently. The biblical word for this is *repentance*. In Greek the word is *metanoia*, which means a "change of mind." You must come to some new realization that causes you to do something different and go in a new direction. Guilt that comes from love is a healthy thing that reminds you that your relationships matter. It motivates you to solve some problem that you have with God, someone else, or even yourself. In the end, guilt based upon love leaves you with no regret.

Brian is a successful, attractive man who considers himself to be confident and psychologically enlightened. He is well-read and respected by everyone who knows him for his success in the business world. He was open to coming to therapy, but he really felt he should be able to solve his problems himself. Eventually he decided to see what he could learn from a professional psychologist.

"I don't believe in looking backward," Brian announced in our first session.

"It feels good to be able to live in the moment," I replied.

"Right," he went on. "I have no regrets. I don't regret anything that has ever happened to me, because it has all gone into making me who I am today. There's no point crying over spilt milk."

"I see. So, how have you dealt with life's disappointments?"

"I don't let it get to me. If you let yourself feel bad about stuff, then you are giving it power over you," he declared confidently.

"So, feeling bad about something is a weakness?" I asked hesitantly. I had heard this type of reasoning before, and I usually found people who think this way to be somewhat inflexible.

"No one can make me feel anything, and I'm not responsible for anyone else's feelings," he stated as he sat forward in his chair. "If I create bad feelings in myself, then I am allowing disappointment to take control of me. I'm in control of my own life, and I'm not going to allow bad feelings to conquer me."

I could see we were off to a difficult start. Brian saw all guilt as guilt coming from fear. There was no room in his life for guilt coming from love. He hated fearful people, and he saw all guilt as something that fearful people felt, not confident people like himself.

Therapy doesn't always work. In the case of my therapy with Brian, I don't think I was very helpful. I tried to help him see that there are times when feeling bad about what you have done is a good thing. It's not a weakness to admit that you were wrong, and it's not allowing disappointment to control you if you express regret over hurting someone. It's actually a sign of emotional maturity to be able to say "I'm sorry."

But Brian never saw it that way. He kept insisting that other people's hurt feelings were their own issues and that the only reason women cried was to be manipulative. He would get angry quickly if I tried to explore any hurt feelings he might have, and he left therapy feeling good that he had tried it but that it didn't really help him that much.

My greatest disappointment in my work with Brian was that I could never get him to see that he was living exactly the life that he hated. I came to see that Brian hated guilt and fearful people who felt it because he was basically a fearful person himself. All feelings of guilt triggered Brian's hidden feelings of shame, and he was too afraid to acknowledge those painful feelings. This made it impossible for him to even conceive of any guilt based upon love. He had come from a very disappointing childhood, and although he had many acquaintances, he had virtually no close friends. His beliefs about people being strictly responsible for their own feelings kept everyone at a distance, and in the end it kept me there, too. Even though Brian was dedicated to living a life without regrets, his refusal to acknowledge guilt based upon love was creating regrets in everyone else close to him. Without healthy guilt, he was unable to deal with the injuries that come with normal relationships by using it to guide him to make the necessary repairs. It resulted in Brian being a rather lonely man. This, unfortunately, was quite regrettable.

Guilt based upon love motivates you to repentance, or a change of mind. It causes you to see something you have done in a new light. With this new understanding, you can change your course of direction and go on a new path. Some guilt is an important part of healthy relationships. Acknowledging this feeling, and using it to make amends for hurt you may have caused others, leads you to a life that *leaves no regret* for everyone involved.

17

Humility Is the Opposite of Low Self-Esteem

Some people confuse humility with low self-esteem. They are not self-sacrificing out of love for others; they do so out of a lack of love for themselves. God really doesn't want people to live that way.

The Bible tells you not to think of yourself more highly than others; it doesn't tell you to view yourself with disdain. The apostle Paul instructs you to think of yourself with *sober judgment*. Psychologically, this means to be self-aware, or to live with an accurate view of your strengths and shortcomings. This sober self-awareness equips you for service to others in a way that is pleasing to God.

Pat came to therapy because she was confused. She had been raised in a Christian home and believed in God. But her experience growing up in her family made her question if the Christian life was one that she really wanted to live.

Pat's mother is a committed Christian and lived by the motto that JOY comes from putting Jesus first, then Others, and then Yourself. While this sort of made sense to Pat, she didn't see her mother as truly happy living this way. It was impressive that her mother was so self-sacrificing and never boastful, but Pat could tell that she wasn't really putting others first because of her overflowing love for them, she was doing it out of a lack of love for herself. Her mother called it humility. To Pat, it seemed more like humiliation.

As we worked on Pat's view of her mother, Christianity, and herself, we came to some interesting conclusions. Humility isn't putting others first because you don't believe you deserve that spot. Humility is viewing yourself with *sober judgment*, and then choosing to serve others out of love. Pat's mother was confusing humility with low self-esteem. She loved God, but she didn't believe she deserved to be loved herself. Pat can see now that living a Christian life doesn't require you to feel bad about yourself, as if you were morally defective, and then put others first out of fear. As she is able to talk honestly about her feelings with me, and more frequently with God, not only is she feeling better about herself, but her feelings about her mother and God are getting better, too.

Pat was confused about what it means to be humble because she was afraid to call attention to herself when she was a child. Her mother was overwhelmed with raising six children, and Pat's needs and feelings only got in the way of her mother's already difficult task. Pat learned to be quiet about what she needed and to view her feelings as unimportant, because the message she got from her mother was that this is what God wants us to do. Pat's conversations with me helped her see that her mother didn't get her definition of humility as much from the Bible as she did from coping with a very demanding life. The biblical definition of humility isn't to have low self-esteem; it is to view yourself accurately and choose to serve others because of how confident you are that you are an intrinsically valuable person who is created in the image of God.

Pat's greater self-awareness is giving her better clarity on a lot of things. She is able to appreciate her mother as the godly woman that she is, even if some of her theology is more informed by her self-image than by Scripture. Her new understanding of humility frees her to openly talk about her needs and feelings honestly, and a surprising thing is happening. Rather than becoming more selfish (as her mother feared), she is finding a new compassion for others growing out of the good feeling of being precisely who God created her to be. Pat is much more attracted to living a Christian life now as she can see that humility is not the result of a weak view of herself, but actually the result of a strong sense that God loves her exactly as she is, including the most intimate concerns in her heart. Who wouldn't find it easier to let others go first once you felt that way?

18

Self-Awareness versus Self-Consciousness

Can you have too much therapy? Or, at what point is self-reflection no longer helpful? The answer is: when you are no longer interested in learning anything new about yourself. Therapy is designed to produce self-awareness. If this isn't your goal in being there, then it probably isn't doing you much good.

There is a difference between self-awareness and self-consciousness. They both involve self-reflection, but with self-awareness you are using what you find to facilitate growth in yourself and connection with others, and with self-consciousness you are not. Self-awareness is a dynamic part of the process of being a vital and growing person. The more you are open to looking at yourself, the more you are open to learning about others. Self-consciousness is a fearful state of stagnation in which nothing new is being learned and connections to others are being thwarted. Because they both require self-examination, they can look similar, but they are two very different things.

William made it very clear to me in our first session that he was nervous about therapy. His sister-in-law was also in therapy, and he wasn't happy with what he saw.

"I don't want to do a lot of *navel gazing*," he announced to me.

"I see," I replied.

"No offense, but I don't believe in lots of therapy." His back stiffened and his chin shot out.

"Okay." I had the feeling he was about to explain some things to me, so it was probably better if I just let him get to it.

"My sister-in-law has been in therapy for seven years, and she is so self-focused that it's hard to be around her," he said as he rolled his eyes. "I mean, she *overanalyzes* everything. Nothing is ever simple for her. I'm afraid to even have a conversation with her because I just know whatever I say, she's thinking, *So what did he* REALLY *mean by that?* Everything isn't always about her, you know."

"She sounds exhausting," I interjected.

"No kidding. If that's what seven years of therapy does to you, then I'm dropping out way before that happens to me," he declared.

Even though I wanted to say, "Just think about how bad she would be *without* therapy," I didn't. What I *did* say was, "Based upon your experiences, I can understand how you might be afraid that therapy will change you, and it may not be for the better."

"Well, it's not that I'm not open," he said in a somewhat softer tone. "I just don't like people who are too self-absorbed."

What William (and his sister-in-law) didn't know was that there is a difference between self-awareness and self-consciousness. Actually, the more self-aware you are, the less self-absorbed you become. Self-awareness frees you from having to be self-focused. It is only when you are afraid that you don't really know yourself, or you don't like what you *do* know, that you become self-conscious.

The more we talked about it, the more I was convinced that it wasn't her therapy that was the cause of his sister-in-law's self-absorption; it was her shame. Shame turns self-reflection into self-consciousness. Shame causes you to wonder if everything being said is somehow a negative statement about you. Each time William's sister-in-law asked, "What did you really mean by that?" she wasn't asking a question; she was making a statement. She was saying, "I know what you really meant by that, and it was something negative about me!" Her reflections on herself or others were rarely designed to learn something new; they were designed to confirm something negative she already believed to be true. This is how shame prevents self-reflection from facilitating self-awareness, and only turns it into self-consciousness.

Eventually William benefited from his own self-reflection in our therapy together. He came to be less defensive the more we looked at the unexamined aspects of his life. Although we didn't discuss it technically, he found that his greater self-awareness was healing him of his own unexpressed shame. Like all of us, he had secret pockets of misgivings about himself that felt better after we took an honest look at them.

Although William participated in therapy for quite some time, he didn't feel as bad about it as he feared he would. Unlike his sister-in-law, he doesn't think everyone talking *to* him is actually talking *about* him. Just as the Bible instructs us, he learned that people who *measure themselves by themselves* are actually self-conscious and not very wise. His greater self-awareness has freed him from any of the self-consciousness that he sees in his sister-in-law. He doesn't measure his self-reflections, or the comments made by others, by himself, so he is able to be truly open to learn new things and become more self-aware.

19

True Self-Esteem

The opposite of shame is true self-esteem. This is a feeling of value and worth for being who you are, someone created in the image of God. True self-esteem comes from feeling encouraged for your efforts and accepted for your attributes. It frees you from self-consciousness and empowers you to be self-aware. True self-esteem is a sign of psychological maturity.

Psychologists have discovered an interesting thing about true self-esteem. Just as shame causes you to become self-conscious, true self-esteem frees you to give attention to others. If you are self-aware and feel good about yourself, then you have energy to consider the good of others. Psychologists have looked back over the course of history and pointed to the few men and women whom they consider to have achieved moral maturity and true self-esteem. People like Jesus, Gandhi, and Mother Teresa made the list. Quite the opposite of what some might assume, even though they lived what we would consider to be superior lives, they did not act as though they were superior to others and they were not self-absorbed. Instead, psychologists found that people with true self-esteem are actually humble, living lives of service to others.

Dr. Lee Edward Travis was a well-known psychologist for the better part of the last century. His textbook on speech pathology was the standard textbook for courses in that area for many years. He was the first scientist to measure brain waves in America, and he was the founding dean of the graduate school from which I graduated. When I first met Dr. Travis, I didn't know anything about him other than the fact that he had been the dean and now he was teaching a course in his semi-retirement. He was in his eighties, but he was still alert and interesting, so I thought I would benefit from his wisdom by taking a seminar from him.

I enjoyed the time I spent with Dr. Travis. He was very knowledgeable and stimulating, and he allowed us to think about questions that were outside of the box, like, "Is there a receptor site in the brain for spirituality?" and "If dolphins can communicate to each other, can we learn to talk to them?" His accomplishments and knowledge truly made him a great psychologist.

The seminar I took with Dr. Travis had only six students in it, so we had the privilege of getting to know him pretty well. We would read the assigned material and come with questions to discuss. He didn't lecture; we just talked. This type of instruction gave us the opportunity to experience graduate education from one of the masters.

Looking back on my course with Dr. Travis helped me discover something about true self-esteem. I remember standing in his office some weeks after our course was completed with one of the other students. I noticed a picture hanging on the wall of Dr. Travis with two other men, and I was curious about it. Since Dr. Travis wasn't around, I turned to the other student and asked, "So, who are those guys with Dr. Travis?"

"You don't know?" the student responded with a look of confusion on his face.

"No. I assume they are old friends or colleagues by the smiles and closeness they appear to have between them," I responded with embarrassment.

"Why, they are two Nobel Laureates," he said indignantly.

"Really?" I gasped.

"Sure. Dr. Travis has friends in pretty high places," he said.

I was stunned. I had been sitting in an intimate conversation with a man who personally knew people who won the Nobel Peace Prize, and he had never mentioned it. I wondered what other amazing aspects to his life existed that he felt no need to bring up. Instead, what I did remember was that each time we talked, Dr. Travis seemed interested in only one thing—*me*. I went away from each exchange with this great man feeling great about myself, because he made me feel that way. This was a man who had true self-esteem. He knew who he was, and he felt so good about it that he was free to devote his attention to others, even graduate students who hadn't lived long enough to have much to say about life at all. It was then that I realized I had been in the presence of not only a great psychologist but a great man.

It was through experiences with people like Dr. Travis that I developed a test to help you know when you are in the presence of true or false self-esteem. On the surface, they can appear similar at times, so it is not always easy to tell. The test is, "How do you feel about yourself around them?" If you are in the presence of true self-esteem, you feel encouraged and *built up*. But when you are in the presence of false self-esteem, you feel diminished and put down. Those with true self-esteem have a quality of humility that frees them to be of service to others. I know, because I had the good fortune to have met one in the person of Dr. Lee Edward Travis.

20

False Self-Esteem

It is not possible to have too much true self-esteem. You were mistaken if you ever described a conceited person with something like, "Oh, he's that way because he loves himself too much." True self-esteem does not produce irritating people like that.

The people who act that way actually have *false* self-esteem. False self-esteem masquerades as confidence, but people who have it are actually not confident at all—they are arrogant. False self-esteem is very difficult to deal with, because it is often associated with other qualities like attractiveness, intelligence, or material success. It is confusing because what you see on the surface is quite different from what is buried down deep inside. On the surface, false self-esteem proclaims to be strong, self-affirming, and in control. But down deep inside, false self-esteem is rooted in shame that isn't in control at all.

As I said earlier, shame seeks to hide itself. And one of the most deceptive disguises it wears is false self-esteem. False self-esteem can be noisy and call great attention to itself, it can be angry and demanding, and it can lead to great success in many careers. False self-esteem can be effective in accomplishing some very difficult tasks. But in the end it will never heal the shame that it is based upon. At best, it can only cover it over in hopes that no one will ever see it.

Rachel came to therapy after her rapid advancement in the business world. She had graduated from a prestigious Ivy League college and gone on to receive her MBA from one of the most honored business schools. She was on her way to becoming one of

71

the top executives in the country, and she was doing it as a woman in a man's world. Rachel needed to be confident, and she came to therapy to make sure she was.

"Only the strong survive in my business," she announced.

"It sounds stressful to have to be prepared for anything," I responded.

"Not only that, but you have to be one step ahead of everyone else when it happens," she said sternly. "I swim with sharks. They smell weakness like blood in the water, and they eat their wounded. I couldn't have done what I have done already in life if I displayed any weakness to the people around me. When I walk into a room, I have to believe I'm the best person in it, man or woman. That's why I'm a success in life. I know I'm the best."

"You've had to develop a pretty thick skin to survive those waters," I said.

"Oh, it's not that I don't feel things. I'm very perceptive. It's just that I don't let things get to me. Men don't respect emotional women. They respect strength. So I've made sure that I'm stronger than any man around," she said firmly as she looked me straight in the eyes.

"Your approach has served you well thus far. I guess you're here to find out if you can learn anything new about yourself to make sure you can continue to be a success in the future." I could tell she was in her "I'm the strongest person in the room" mode, and I wanted to see if she was going to be able to learn anything from me. I knew that therapy was only going to help Rachel if she could be vulnerable, and that was not something that had ever been attractive to her before.

"I'm always learning new things. That's why I'm here. I have to stay ahead of the pack," she said, softening. I watched as she sat back in her chair, and I felt hopeful that perhaps something good could come out of our work together.

Rachel had fought and scraped her way to the top. She was a survivor. On the one hand, her definition of confidence had served her well. Believing she was better than others got her far in a competitive environment. But this same attitude that had served her well thus far might be standing in the way of where she wanted to go now. Rachel didn't have true self-esteem. All I had to do was look at her personal relationships to determine this. She'd never had a successful intimate relationship with a man. Men didn't love Rachel; they feared her. She had associates and companions, but she wasn't mutually intimate with anyone. Her false self-esteem served her well in helping her succeed in a competitive business world, but it was causing her to fail in her personal life. And now it was time to question if it was even going to serve her in her professional life in the future.

Jim Collins is a business consultant who put together a team of researchers to study the most successful companies in America over the past one hundred years.[3] They found twenty-eight companies that beat the stock market average by seven times or more over a fifteen-year period. These companies weren't just successful; they *sustained* their success. Collins and his team discovered that the truly great companies with continued success had what they called *Level Five* leaders running them. The characteristics of these leaders were not what they expected. Surprisingly, the leaders of these successful companies were defined by two characteristics: *humility* and *willpower*. In the comparison companies that shot to success and then fizzled, they found CEOs with gargantuan personal egos or false self-esteem. They were arrogant, called attention to themselves, and loved to be read about in the papers. On the other hand, *Level Five* leaders had an unwavering resolve to do what must be done for positive long-term results, never blamed others, and were characterized by a compelling modesty. The truly successful leaders of companies with lasting success have true self-esteem.

Rachel had something to learn from Jim Collins. False self-esteem has short-term benefits, but truly successful people build *lasting* success out of true self-esteem. Gargantuan personal egos and feelings of superiority do not build the type of businesses that last. True self-esteem does. Fortunately, Rachel was open to looking at herself in therapy. As time went on, we could see how her false self-esteem was not really built upon feelings of confidence. The truth was, she felt insecure at times. Sometimes she was frightened that she would be eaten by the sharks with which she swam, and she was keeping up a good front against them with her arrogance and façade of superiority.

I wish I could tell you that Rachel had a miraculous transformation in her approach to life because of her therapy. But swimming with sharks made it impossible for her to feel safe enough to give up her defenses completely. However, she is growing. She isn't as concerned about being better than everyone else as she is about being better at who she is herself. She doesn't have to act superior to compensate for her fears that she might not be strong enough to survive. Her therapy is helping her feel good enough about herself to not have to do that as much these days. She is learning in her own life what Collins discovered in his research, that "everyone who exalts himself will be humbled, and he who humbles himself will be exalted." Contrary to what she thought before, Rachel sees humility now as a sign of strength under control, and at times her quiet confidence speaks much louder than the noisy false self-esteem she had before. Now Rachel is developing true self-esteem that will help her be a lasting success in every aspect of her life, which includes her personal relationships that we are just taking a look at now.

21

Having Needs Doesn't
Make You Needy

Years ago I worked as a college minister at a large university. I spent
a good deal of my time talking to college students about God and
listening to them about their perspectives on life. This was when
I met Ryan.

"Religion is a crutch for people who can't deal with life," Ryan
asserted when he first learned that I was a minister.

"So, depending upon something greater than yourself means
you are weak?" I asked.

"You are weak if you have to depend upon some made-up old
man in the sky," he quipped.

"So, that's your picture of God?" I replied. Although we could
both feel the tension in our repartee, there was a kind of good-
natured sparring quality to it that made it seem almost fun.

"There is no God," he declared, his eyes widening. "The only
person you can depend upon is yourself."

Ryan believed he was the master of his own fate and depending
on others was stupid. He grew up with a harsh father and a mother
who was too busy to give him much attention. Ryan believed in
self-reliance, and no one was going to convince him otherwise.

In spite of his occasional arrogance and insensitivity to others, I liked Ryan. He was smart, well-read, and honestly seeking to
understand the meaning of life. But Ryan had a barrier to living a
truly satisfying life: he believed that *needing others makes you needy*.
Fortunately, his dissatisfaction with life and longing for something

more meaningful kept him coming back for dialogues with me. Over time, I was certain that Ryan would discover that he believed in self-reliance, not because he felt confident in his own goodness, but because he felt ashamed of having any needs.

Eventually, Ryan learned that his narcissistic lifestyle was really a cover-up for painful longings he just didn't want to acknowledge. He could never please his father, and his mother didn't seem to care. Early on in life, he learned that a great defense is a good offense, so because he couldn't get his needs met as a child, he adopted the belief that only needy people had needs. He, on the other hand, decided to become superior to needy people and assert that he didn't need anything other than himself. This overcompensation and inflated self-importance wasn't based upon his confident self-esteem; it grew out of his hidden shame.

Ryan learned the difference between guilt and shame. Shame seeks to hide itself; true guilt seeks to resolve. It took a while for Ryan to realize that he even felt shame. He was too busy trying to convince himself and everyone else that he was just fine the way he was. But once he realized that he felt ashamed (and weak) for simply having human needs for love and acceptance from others, a shift happened in his life. How he felt about others, and how they felt about him, started to matter. He wasn't as interested in self-reliance as he was interested in connection. And the idea that there might be a God who was greater than him was no longer such a threatening idea, especially if there was a God who cared.

Today Ryan talks differently about God. He is still somewhat argumentative, but he is not so convinced that he doesn't need anyone or anything anymore. Now, instead of trying to hide his shame for having needs, he is trying to bring out into the open any guilt he feels about his broken relationships. Hiding his shame only resulted in a narcissistic way of being that disconnected him from others. Asking for forgiveness for his guilt over any hurt he caused in relationships did the opposite. It gave him a chance to do something about the disconnection he felt from others in very meaningful ways.

Ryan's shame about having needs wasn't helping him live a meaningful life. He thought he was being wise and strong by asserting his independence. But he found out that "God chose the foolish things of the world to shame the wise; God chose the weak things of the world to shame the strong." When God first created Adam and Eve in the Garden of Eden, they "were both naked, and they felt no shame."⁴ We were created naked and dependent, which is nothing for which we should feel ashamed. Having needs doesn't make you needy; it points you to who you were created to be: a person who needs a relationship with God and others to be whole.⁵ Ryan's worldly wisdom declared it was foolish to be dependent upon anyone. He found out that admitting he needed others—and possibly even a loving God—wasn't really a sign of weakness but was actually the most powerful way to live.

22

Are You Useful or Valuable?

Self-esteem is based upon two things: feeling useful and feeling valuable. You feel useful based on encouragement for your accomplishments and hard work. You feel valuable based on being loved and accepted for who you are. It is important to have both of these in life. But one cannot replace the other.

A child raised in a home that was accepting—one that made that child feel loved as a part of the family, even if he or she didn't accomplish anything in life—might grow up to feel valuable. But that child could struggle with not feeling useful when it came to achieving goals and feeling productive. Likewise, a child raised in a home that had clear expectations for performance, but no unconditional love, might grow up feeling like a very useful person in the world, but he or she would not likely feel valuable.

Because guilt and shame are different, the cure for each is different. To heal your guilt, you must *do* something differently. You have done something wrong, and now you must make amends for it. I'm going to talk about the cure for guilt in just a moment. But to heal your shame, you must feel that you *are* different. You have lacked self-worth, and now you must begin to feel valuable. Because some people use their guilt to cover over their shame, they believe that they can merely decide to do things differently to heal their shame. But performance doesn't make you feel loved.

Courtney grew up as the favorite child in her family. She was younger, prettier, and more talented than her only sister, and everyone knew it. She did well in school and had a short but successful career as an interior decorator before she married a very wealthy businessman and began her own family. Everything Courtney had ever tried to do turned out well; at least it always seemed to be better than whatever her sister did.

It was very confusing for Courtney that the more successful she was, the angrier her sister was with her. After years of struggling with painful feelings of anxiety and guilt, Courtney finally came to therapy for help.

"I'm so embarrassed to be here," Courtney confessed.

"It's hard to ask for help," I said.

"Yes, but this seems so silly," she said, looking away. "I mean, I have so much to be grateful for in my life. And I try to be so generous to everyone, especially my sister and her family. But she keeps telling me that I am mean to her. No matter how hard I try,

I just seem to offend her at every turn. Am I really that horrible of a person?"

"Do you feel like a horrible person?"

"No, I don't think so. But I don't think she ever liked me. She tells me I'm spoiled and selfish. I've shared so much of what we have with her, given her loans, everything. It's as if she wants me to have sacrificed as much as she has in life. I've tried to be generous, but she still thinks I'm being unkind to her. I don't know, maybe I am."

"It sounds like you've tried to be very helpful to your sister," I said.

"I've tried so hard. I'm always thinking of what I can do to make things better," she said with a pleading tone in her voice.

"I can see that. But here's your problem. I can see that you have been very *useful* to your sister, but you are not very *valuable* to her," I said softly.

"Oh my gosh," Courtney whispered. "I never thought of it that way."

Courtney kept thinking that if she would only try harder, she could solve the problems in her relationship with her sister. But as Courtney continued to do more and better things, it only made her sister more envious of her, not grateful. Even though Courtney felt guilty that she had more than her sister in life, trying to *perform* for her sister wasn't making her sister feel loved. In fact, her sister eventually came to feel entitled to Courtney's efforts to make her life better. After all, they both knew Courtney had been blessed, and they both felt she should be sharing those blessings with her sister. The problem to be solved wasn't the guilt Courtney felt, for which she needed to make amends to her sister; it was the shame they both felt for not feeling loved.

Courtney eventually realized that she was making things worse by buying her sister things and feeling guilty that she had been blessed with more. She realized that performance doesn't make you feel loved, and no amount of success can ever make you feel accepted for who you are. Things are improving with her sister these days because of this realization. Sometimes Courtney will call her sister just to talk, or go over to her house for a visit without buying her something. Courtney realized that she can't sacrifice enough to make up for the differences between her and her sister, but she can do something else to close the gap. She can let her sister know that she loves her. And her sister is starting to feel grateful for that.

God said, "I desire mercy, not sacrifice, and acknowledgment of God rather than burnt offerings." He knows the deepest form of love is communicated through mercy and acceptance; and that no amount of sacrifice or performance can substitute for that. This is the kind of love that heals the shame of feeling useful but not valuable. Shame results from not feeling loved for who you are, so it only makes sense that love and acceptance are its cure.

23

The Cure for Guilt

Guilt usually nags at your conscience until you address it. It can be draining and difficult to deal with in life. Fortunately, if you decide you want to deal with your guilt, there is a pretty good cure for it: *forgiveness*.

Guilt that comes from fear needs to be acknowledged as fear-based, and the painful feelings of shame you have about yourself need to be brought out into the open where they can be addressed. In many cases with this type of guilt, the main person you need to forgive is yourself. Becoming more self-aware will help in that process of forgiveness.

Guilt that comes from love signals you that there has been a rupture in your relationship with God or someone else, and you need to begin a deeper process of forgiveness to achieve healing there. This type of guilt motivates you to restore broken relationships with God, others, or yourself. Even though guilt based on love may feel bad, its goal is actually very good.

There are two levels of forgiveness. The first is to *not return hurt for hurt*. This means that when someone hurts you, you forgive them. You don't retaliate; you leave that up to God. However, there are people you have forgiven who still give you that sick feeling in the pit of your stomach every time you think of them. If you have forgiven them, then why do you still want to avoid them? The answer is that you have not achieved the second level of forgiveness: *reconciliation*.

Reconciliation is deeper and more difficult. It involves participation by all the hurt parties. The offending person must have a change of mind, or repentance, and then come to see how much hurt has been caused and take responsibility for it. The hurt person must come to believe that the offender truly does know how much hurt has been caused, and that he or she is sorry for it. Now reconciliation can take place. Once this mutual understanding of pain has been achieved, guilt based on love can be healed.

Antonio is a brilliant medical doctor. He invented a medical procedure that saved numerous lives, and he enjoys a very successful life in America. But things have not always been good for Antonio.

Antonio was abandoned by his father when he was just a boy growing up on a farm in Mexico. He had to take over his father's responsibilities to support his family, and as soon as his brothers and sisters could care for themselves, he came to America to seek a better life. Because Antonio was able to get a scholarship to a good school, and because he worked so hard, he eventually was awarded another scholarship to medical school, where he graduated with honors. Antonio was truly a success story, having come from very humble beginnings to rise to a position of status and national recognition. But everything was not well with Antonio.

"I can't help feeling bad sometimes about my father," Antonio admitted to me.

"It hurts to be so disconnected from your dad," I replied.

"It's not only that," he continued. "I have been blessed with so much. I have everything a man could want, except for one major thing—a father to be proud of me."

"That is sad," I said.

"What's sad is that I have not spoken to him for nineteen years." He sighed. "I hated him when he left Mom and us. I swore at him when he left and told him I never wanted to speak to him again. And now that I have gotten my wish, I regret having asked for it. I mean, he's still my dad."

Antonio was coming face-to-face with a problem that I see in many of my adult male patients. Many men have either a distant or a bad relationship with their fathers. It's a silent epidemic. This creates a lot of problems for men, like workaholism or an inability to be close to other men. In Antonio's case, it resulted in the feeling of guilt. Even though his father was the offender by leaving his family, Antonio felt guilt for angrily chasing him away. Men need their fathers to be proud of them, and they can't get that if their fathers are not around.

As is typical of Antonio's character, he figured out what he needed to do and decided to do it no matter how hard it was. But this was harder than anything he had ever done before. Antonio had decided to find his father and talk to him about how hurt he was. He didn't know what his father was going to say, or if his father would even care, but Antonio knew this was something he needed to do for himself. Antonio had decided to attempt a reconciliation with his father.

Antonio found his father living in Mexico. He called him up and arranged to meet with him. At first the meeting was awkward, and they both got defensive as they recounted the circumstances surrounding his father's abandonment of the family. There was a lot of anger, and crying, and hurt that was expressed by both of them. But Antonio would not let it go. He kept talking to his father for many hours until he got what he came for. Eventually Antonio was convinced that his father understood how hurt he had been by his leaving, and how difficult this had made Antonio's life. But Antonio could also see that his father had been riddled with guilt for the entire nineteen years they had not spoken to each other. Once Antonio could see that his father's guilt was genuine, and that he, too, desired to repair their relationship, Antonio felt something he had never felt before. Antonio felt forgiveness for his father that was based upon love.

Today Antonio has a pretty good relationship with his father. In many ways they don't have much in common, but they do have something that neither of them could find anywhere else in the world. They have a reconciled relationship between a father and a son. Antonio found that in forgiving his father, he experienced forgiveness himself. At times Antonio, or perhaps his father, will come across something they feel guilty about in their past relationship with each other. But now they can do something about it. They can talk about it and ask for forgiveness.

PART THREE

Anger

24

What Is Anger?

Anger is energy to solve a problem. This may be surprising to you, since anger is often confused with violence, hatred, rage, revenge, and many other things. But anger is a necessary force given to you by God to mobilize you in times of need to take action. There are more references to God's anger than his love in the Bible, so it is obviously an important emotion for you to understand and make use of in your life.

In his letter to the church at Ephesus, the apostle Paul clearly made a distinction between anger and sin. But he went on to say that anger was not intended to last all day, suggesting that the purpose of anger is to motivate you to take action now. Like the red warning light on the dashboard of your car, anger alerts you that you have a deeper problem and motivates you to figure out what that problem is. In most cases, anger points you to one of three underlying emotions: hurt, fear, or frustration. So the next time you are angry, ask yourself which of these three feelings might be causing your anger. This will lead you to the problem you need to solve.

Christopher and Cassandra came for marriage counseling due to the painful distance that each of them felt in their marriage. They were both successful, career-oriented people who were very much in love when they first met, but now they had twelve years together and a six-year-old boy that made them want to work out their marital problems.

Although they could be polite in public, when they tried to talk about issues of any substance at home, it would result in hurtful comments being made by both of them.

"Why can't we talk about finances like other adults?" Cassandra pleaded.

"Because I hate it when you blame me for not making enough money," Christopher snapped back.

"Well, I hate you for shutting me out and making me feel so alone in this marriage," Cassandra sobbed.

Both Christopher and Cassandra knew they were angry. I didn't have to tell them that. But what they didn't know was *why* they were angry. Christopher thought he was angry because Cassandra was too demanding, and Cassandra thought she was angry because Christopher was so cold. But as our therapy together went on, we discovered that these things weren't the real causes of their anger.

After several sessions, I got Christopher and Cassandra to stop using their anger as a weapon in their marriage, and instead use it as an indicator that they were feeling something underneath it. They could both understand that when their son said "I hate you" to either one of them, he was merely trying to communicate that his feelings were hurt; they knew that he didn't really mean that he felt hatred for his parents. Telling your parents that you hate them hurts their feelings, which is a primitive way of sharing your hurt with them. But when they as adults said "I hate you" to each other, it had a more damaging impact, even though it was the same form of immature communication that they saw exhibited in their six-year-old son. What they discovered was that they didn't actually hate *each other*, but they each hated the painful feelings brought up in the marriage. Trying to get the other person to change was never going to work, but learning how to change their feelings did.

Christopher was able to tell Cassandra that he was angry because he was hurt by her criticisms of him; it brought up how he felt growing up with his father. Cassandra was able to tell him that she wasn't disappointed in him as a financial provider; she just needed to talk about her fears concerning their finances. She told him that she was angry because she was afraid he was going to abandon her, and that reminded her of the many lonely years she spent as a child feeling unloved.

Once they stopped talking about their anger and started talking about the hurt and fear *underneath* their anger, things began to change in their marriage. The anger that Christopher and Cassandra felt pointed them to deeper, more vulnerable feelings that they needed to deal with in their marriage. The anger in their marriage wasn't the problem; it was only the symptom.

Anger isn't a sin. But if you don't identify the hurt, fear, or frustration that is causing it, then it can lead to serious harm. The biblical instruction "Do not let the sun go down while you are still angry" is good advice. Your anger is energy to solve a problem, so don't let the sun go down before you solve it. Don't waste a lot of time being angry; use the energy of your anger to solve your deeper underlying problem. The red warning light on the dashboard isn't the problem, but it means there is something underneath the hood that needs your attention.

25

The Angry Defense Mechanism

Anger is a common defense mechanism. When you do something wrong or you feel exposed, a frequent reaction is to get mad. Most people prefer to feel anger rather than shame or fear. It pushes others away from them when they feel the need for self-protection.

A large part of my work as a psychotherapist is dealing with defense mechanisms in my patients. The term we use for that is *danger analysis*. People tend to get defensive when they feel they are in danger. To work effectively with defense mechanisms, therapists must understand what is causing the feeling of danger and work at seeing things from the perspective of the patient. Telling the patient to stop being defensive is rarely helpful. In fact, it tends to make them even more defensive. The therapist's job is to step into the shoes of the patient. Confronting defensiveness outright creates more danger—seeing things from the other's perspective usually lessens the threat. Once this happens, the patient might be willing to surrender the defense mechanism, because now that we understand each other, it is no longer needed.

When I worked as a college minister, I would speak to large groups of college students and was a fairly visible person on campus. We welcomed all students to our gatherings, which meant students with all kinds of problems sometimes attended.

I will never forget a student named Patrick. He was a good-looking, intelligent person, but he had odd mannerisms and seemed moody. He demanded attention from others, but he had no close friends. Eventually I was able to identify Patrick as a very troubled person. I didn't know it then, but today I would diagnose Patrick with a serious mental disorder.

Patrick would move in and out of reality, become quite paranoid at times, and even go into rages that could be quite frightening. The most troubling thing about Patrick's mental problems was that he would sometimes see me as the cause of his pain, because I was the leader of the group. Sometimes I was a trusted captain in God's army watching over him, and sometimes I was the enemy.

One day, just before sundown, I was taking a bulk mailing to the post office. I had to walk down the dark alley next to the post office to get to the back of the building where bulk mailings were accepted. I have no idea why, but this particular evening I was walking alone, with my arms full of letters, and who do you think I ran into? Patrick. As we approached each other, I could see his eyes widen with recognition, but by the time we were within speaking distance, I could see his face turning red and the muscles tense in his neck.

"I'm glad you finally came to me," Patrick breathed with clenched teeth.

"Uh, it's good to see you, Patrick," I said, not having any idea what he meant.

"You know what I would like to do right now?" he said as the veins began to bulge out of his neck.

"I'm sorry?" I asked as my heart began to race.

"I'd like to bash your brains in on the pavement," Patrick blurted out.

Now I was really scared. I had no idea what to do. I couldn't call for help; no one was around. I didn't dare try to fight him, as I could see the adrenaline pumping through his veins from where I stood. In a panic my mind raced, and suddenly a verse from the Old Testament came to mind: "A gentle answer turns away wrath, but a harsh word stirs up anger."

"I can see how much pain you are in right now, Patrick. And I just want you to know that it pains me to see *you* in so much pain," I said softly. I wasn't feeling calm, but somehow the words came out rather gently.

Instantly Patrick's face changed. A normal color returned to his face. Then he looked me in the eyes and said, "Well, you have always been my brother." And at that he turned and walked away.

I didn't know much about mental illness back then, and I certainly didn't have any idea about how to deal with anger as a defense mechanism. But I am thankful that God gave us wisdom in the Bible for how to deal with difficult emotional situations, and I was especially glad for the wisdom of that passage on that day.

Confronting angry people is sometimes necessary in life. But confronting angry defensiveness usually makes it worse. If I had responded out of my own fear and confronted Patrick, I would have created a power struggle between us that might have been disastrous. Instead, I relied on the wisdom of the Bible and tried to gently see things from his perspective. Once I did this, I was no longer a threat to Patrick, and his defensive anger was no longer necessary.

Psychologists understand that defense mechanisms are responses to danger for the purpose of self-preservation. Anger can be one such response. Learning to gently see things from the perspective of the other can help you deal with anger when it is being used as a defense. If you can see how you might be dangerous to someone who is angry with you, and you respond appropriately, you may see the defensive anger fade away. It isn't always easy, but with God's help you may find out for yourself how "a gentle answer turns away wrath."

26

The Anger of Hope: Fighting to Make Things Better

I come across two kinds of anger in the marriage counseling that I do.[1] The first is the anger of *despair*. This is when people have given up and are so hurt that their anger stems from futility and powerlessness. These people are very difficult to help. They are mad, and they simply want out.

But there is a second form of anger that is actually more common in the marriage counseling I do—the anger of *hope*. This is when people get angry because they want things to be different. This is the kind of anger that says, "This marriage is important to me, and I'm going to fight to make it better." This anger is just as intense as the anger of despair, but it motivates people to fight for a connection out of a belief that things shouldn't have to be this bad. The anger of hope inspires people to change.

Luis and Olivia came for marriage counseling because Luis had an affair. It happened about a year before, and they were finally admitting to themselves that they weren't getting past it. Luis was frustrated with the constant bickering between them over the smallest of things, and Olivia just didn't feel safe. Luis had betrayed her with someone they both knew, so it was even worse than a one-night stand. This was personal, and it still hurt.

"I can't take any more of these stupid arguments," Luis protested. "I mean, is it really that big of a deal to have the kids do their studying in their rooms instead of at the kitchen table?"

"The only reason we argue is because you are so controlling," Olivia snapped back. "If you wanted someone who would just go along with everything you wanted, then you married the wrong person. My opinions aren't always wrong, you know!"

"I'm not trying to control you," Luis replied. "I would just like us to be able to discuss things without having a fight."

Luis and Olivia were caught in a cycle of conflict that they couldn't get out of. They had discussed his affair when it first happened. Luis confessed his mistake and asked for Olivia's forgiveness. She said she didn't want a divorce, and she hasn't wanted to talk about it much since then. They were both trying to move on, but it just didn't seem to be happening successfully. They felt stuck, and they needed help.

As our counseling went on, the gridlock in their marriage became clearer to all of us. Luis and Olivia understood that Luis's decision to have an affair had been a terrible response to the problems they were having with communication and intimacy. They talked about it, recommitted themselves to their marriage, and were now trying to move on. But sometimes commitment alone isn't enough. After a terrible injury to a marriage like an affair, something more is needed. Luis needed to respond to the depth of the pain that he had caused Olivia. That had not happened yet, and that was why Olivia was still hurt and mad.

Olivia was humiliated by the affair and felt terribly rejected because of it. She was still angry, but she didn't want to talk about it, partly because it was so painful to discuss and partly because she was afraid her anger would just drive Luis away—again. But not talking about her anger wasn't making it go away. She needed more than just *time* to heal; she needed Luis to grasp the depth of her pain and respond to it in a way that made her feel safe. She didn't trust that his commitment was enough to keep him from having another affair. That hadn't worked the first time. If he understood how devastating this had been for her, and she could believe he truly felt bad for causing her so much pain, then perhaps she might be able to trust that he would not do it again.

It wasn't easy, but we switched the focus of our marital sessions off of the argument of the week and returned to the subject of the affair. Olivia was angry because she didn't feel safe and she needed to hear things from Luis that would help her trust him again: not promises of fidelity, but expressions of genuine pain over what he had done. Fortunately Luis took it like a man. We spent several sessions with Olivia trying to express her pain and humiliation, and it wasn't always pretty. As she was able to express her hurt (instead of attacking his character), and as he was able to authentically respond with his own pain in response to her hurt (instead of defending himself), things began to change. Everything wasn't instantly better for Luis and Olivia, but the bickering over small disagreements dropped off. At least the fighting now made sense to everyone, and both Luis and Olivia will tell you that they think their marriage is stronger today.

Luis and Olivia learned what the Bible means when it says, "Better is open rebuke than hidden love." Anger of hope is designed to make things better, and the wisdom of the Bible tells us that this should be expressed in the open so that underlying problems can be worked out. This type of anger is designed to confront situations that need it, resolve unfinished business, and reconnect broken relationships. Anger of hope is not designed to alienate; it is energy to solve problems so we can heal.

27

Hatred: The Anger of Despair

It is not good to allow anger's energy to go on for too long without being used for its intended purpose. Prolonged anger turns into hostility, and hostility that goes on too long becomes hatred. Hatred is hardened hostility that is very difficult to change. This is the anger of despair.

Kyle came to therapy because of the problems in his marriage with Amber. People often start therapy because of problems in relationships, and in this instance I could understand why. He wasn't sure if she was interested in therapy, so he came by himself.

Kyle and Amber were married for ten years but never had children. Neither of them thought they had the kind of marriage that would be good for children. They were both successful in their individual careers and had married hoping to find success in their personal lives as well. Unfortunately, they both felt they were failing in this area.

Feeling more like a success at work than at home, Kyle gradually spent more time at the office. This contributed to Amber's feeling of rejection by Kyle. She felt let down by him so often that she now expected everything he did to disappoint her. She felt hurt in the early years of their marriage over so many things that she now felt unsafe around Kyle and rarely talked to him about anything of importance. This added to Kyle's feeling that she didn't like him and that everything he did was wrong no matter how hard he tried. The marriage between them was cold and distant, and they were both extremely unhappy.

I learned over the years that it is impossible to help someone who is not in the room, so I asked Kyle to invite Amber to join us for marriage counseling. I thought Kyle's marriage was in critical condition, so that was where treatment was most needed. Reluctantly, Amber agreed to join us.

"I'm not sure why I'm here," Amber offered in our first session.

"I thought it would be good for me to get your perspective on the problems between you and Kyle," I responded. "If I only hear from him, then I'm limited in helping with the pain between the two of you."

"It should be clear to *you* what's needed," Amber said as she stared directly into my eyes. "Clearly he doesn't know how to treat a woman. Being subjected to such an *evil* man would cause problems for anyone," she said coldly.

"Evil?" I asked. "How so?"

"It's evil to crush another human being and destroy their self-esteem," she responded. "And it's evil to hate your own wife," she said sternly, still staring straight at me.

"But I don't *hate* you," Kyle jumped in. "It's just impossible to talk with you about anything."

"Yes, you do," Amber snapped back as she turned to face him. "And there's no point in lying about it now. Your words mean nothing to me. I have years of your behavior to prove it, and that's all the proof I need!"

Things were bad between Kyle and Amber. I worked as hard as I could to keep them from hurting each other in our sessions. I believe people need to express their anger in counseling, but only if it's anger of hope. Anger of despair is destructive. I spent the next few weeks *catching bullets*[2] that they fired at each other and trying to get them to deal with the years of underlying hurt. I tried to lift them out of the ruts of character assassinations and defensive hostility that seemed set in stone in their relationship. I tried to get them to see that fighting for a connection was better than attacking each other in retribution over past hurts. But in spite of my best efforts, their mutual feeling of failure overcame them. Amber's anger of despair won out. She didn't want a better relationship with Kyle. She just wanted him to go away.

Perhaps if they had come years ago, Amber's anger might still have been the hopeful kind. But she had lost sight of any hope of things getting better, and now could feel only contempt. She hated Kyle and felt hated by him, and nothing seemed to release her from this perspective. Sometimes people wait too long before coming for help. Then they run the risk of falling into the anger of despair.

The Bible warns us that there are times when people have "lived in malice and envy, being hated and hating one another." This is the destructive anger of despair. Anger is not meant to go on and on without being used for its designed purpose—to solve underlying problems. If you are experiencing the anger of despair in your life, seek the help of a professional to convert it into the anger of hope. Your anger signals you that there is work to be done. It is your job to figure out what that work is and then get the help you need before it is too late.

28

Sometimes Grief Comes Out as Anger

Sarah came to see me because of her anxiety. At least that was why she thought she came. She was irritable most of the time, exhausted, and lived with a knot in her stomach that just wouldn't go away. She was a young widow who had lost her husband in an automobile accident. Her life was very stressful now, and she was trying to put it back together in the best way she knew how.

"Ever since Cory died, my life just hasn't been the same," Sarah said.

"His dying so young was tragic," I replied softly.

"I know, I know," she said, looking away. "I heard all that in the grief group I went to. That group was lame."

"I know you felt frustrated with the group. There's no one *right* way to grieve," I said.

"How could they get it?" Sarah said, looking back at me. "There was no one in the group under sixty! How could anyone get it? It's just wrong," she said as her eyes teared up.

Sarah wasn't anxious; she was mad. She was mad at God for allowing this to happen, mad at Cory for abandoning her, and mad at everyone else for making her feel so alone. Losses are difficult to deal with, especially when they are forced upon you when you are not prepared. Sarah wasn't expecting to be a widow at thirty-two, and she wasn't prepared to be a lonely, angry woman in the prime of her life. Being around other people wasn't helping Sarah. Everything they said made her feel misunderstood and alone, and it's worse feeling lonely in a crowd.

Anger is a part of grief. For some people, it's a big part of it. The good news is that it doesn't last forever. It helps to keep talking about it, especially if you can find at least one person who can tolerate it and not rush you through it.

Grief is the natural response to loss, and anger is a natural part of the process of grief. We call grief a *process* because it usually follows a pattern of denial, anger, bargaining, depression, and then acceptance. The stages of grief are not exactly the same for everyone, and once you have passed through a stage, it doesn't mean you won't go through it again. It's just that over time, if you keep processing your grief, you usually come to a place of acceptance of your loss. It's important to understand that being angry about your loss is just part of the process.

The Bible tells us that some "anger lasts only a moment" and that "weeping may stay for the night, but rejoicing comes in the morning." Facing our anger facilitates the process of grief. There is a time to be angry and weep, but this is God's way of preparing your heart for the rejoicing that will eventually come. It's hard work, but grief is the way you make room in your heart for future love.

You'll be happy to know that Sarah is starting to feel less agitated. After many sessions of talking about her anger and loneliness, she is beginning to experience some other feelings that she thought she had lost forever. She is interested in hanging out with some of her old friends again, she is sleeping better, and she is thinking about going back to school. Cory's death still seems wrong to her, but she is not as angry about it. She has some pointed questions she wants to ask God when she gets to heaven; however, she is not as mad at him in the meantime. Because Sarah was committed to processing her anger and grief, she is starting to accept her life now and what it could be in the future.

29

When Anger Is Disguised as Flattery

Flattery is not always what it seems. In fact, it can be a cover-up for hostility. This might sound strange, but there are people who are very indirect with their anger, so they look for ways to express it that are disguised. One disguise for anger is flattery.

Jacob is an intelligent, well-educated man who is happily married but dissatisfied with his career. He sought out psychotherapy to help him address this dissatisfaction with his professional path in life. Jacob could be a success at many things if he applied himself, but he can't seem to find a direction that he can commit himself to. As a result, he is working as a substitute teacher until he can figure out which of his many options he wants to pursue.

"You were smart," Jacob commented in one of our sessions.

"How so?"

"Because you went straight to graduate school and launched off into a successful career without messing around for years," he said flatly.

"You'd like to feel further along by now," I replied.

"Yeah, sure. But look at you. You've got a PhD, a successful practice, a good family, and I bet you even own one of those houses up on the hill that cost a fortune. You've got it made," Jacob said with an odd smile on his face.

This type of exchange had been common in the first several months of my work with Jacob. On the surface it sounded like he admired me and possibly wanted to be like me someday. But I am always suspicious when my patients think I am wonderful so early on in our relationship.

In psychotherapy it is common to idealize one's therapist, and this can be an important part of the process of therapy. It is usually a good thing to have a therapist you can look up to and respect. It helps establish trust in the relationship and makes the work go better. But I didn't feel Jacob was idealizing me. It felt more like flattery. The difference is that when you idealize someone, you feel good about being in their presence. Healthy idealization produces a sense of security and safety. This is what most children feel for their parents, and it often gets replicated in psychotherapy. But Jacob didn't feel better being around all the great qualities he saw in me; it made him feel worse. He didn't actually like the fact that I was so successful in his eyes—he resented it.

This type of flattery comes from seeing in someone else what you think you deserve to have for yourself but don't. This creates a feeling of inadequacy and hostility that is expressed as flattery. Jacob wasn't really complimenting me; he was flattering me because each time he looked across the room at what he thought was the successful life that he wanted but didn't have, it made him feel bad. Flattery was his way of dealing with it.

The wisdom of the Bible tells us "those who flatter their neighbors are spreading nets for their feet." It will trip you up and keep you from getting where you need to be in life. As we took the focus off of what Jacob imagined to be my ideal life (or the ideal life he fantasized about for himself) and put it on who he was as a man now, our therapy changed. Jacob didn't need to keep feeling bad about the things he didn't have; he needed to feel better about what he did have now.

Jacob is feeling better about himself, and he is getting a better idea of what he wants to do with his life these days. He is not as concerned about fantasies of success as he is with developing a better appreciation for what he has to offer today. Being angry about what he didn't have was keeping Jacob stuck. Developing an appreciation for what he does have now is starting to set him free. And not surprisingly, Jacob isn't tripping over his flattery of me as much as he used to in the past.

30

Do Some People Have a Reservoir of Rage?

The most explosive form of anger is rage. It is an intense eruption of anger that is threatening and can be violent. Rage is automatic, and it gives you the feeling of power in response to vulnerable feelings like hurt or shame. It instantly moves you from a vulnerable, submissive position to a dominant one. Rage is a way of screaming,

"This is mine!" in the face of the threat of someone taking something from you.[3]

Some psychologists think humans have an innate aggressiveness that is a fundamental part of our nature. They think we inherit an inner rage that equips us to fight to the death for our survival when needed. As persuasive as this might be when you think about all the wars and violence that humans have perpetrated upon each other, I don't think this is quite right. I don't see humans as inherently aggressive; I see us as filled with rage when we are threatened.

One of the most frequent requests we get at our counseling center is for our anger management group. There, people learn where their anger comes from, how to see it coming, and how to respond in helpful rather than hurtful ways in situations where they tend to get very mad. Robert was one of the many people seeking help for his anger management problem. The tools he learned in the anger management group were useful, so out of his interest to live a more satisfying life, Robert decided to work on his issues in individual sessions with me.

"My wife says that I have only two speeds," Robert confessed to me.

"Just two?" I asked.

"Right. Anger and apathy. She says she only sees me express two feelings. Either I don't really care about things, or I get really mad."

"Wow. That leaves a whole lot of emotions in the midrange that you just skip over."

"I don't know," Robert continued. "I mean, I was raised to fight hard in life. My dad was tough on us kids and expected us to make something of ourselves. I work hard and I play hard, and I try to not sweat the small stuff."

"Does that work?"

"I guess not," he said sadly. "I can't seem to keep from getting upset about things, sometimes even small things. I keep thinking it's all the pressure I'm under, but now I'm thinking I need to get a better handle on this anger thing. I learned in the group that I need more than just two speeds."

Robert's curiosity about his emotions was a good sign. People interested in growing usually can. Robert and I both became interested in expanding his emotional life, and we discovered some important things. Although Robert was successful at his work, he didn't always feel confident. There's a difference between competence and confidence. He was an aggressive businessman, but he often had painful personal feelings that he kept hidden. He wasn't even aware of it, but he often felt that people didn't like him or that they were trying to take advantage of him. He rarely paid attention to these feelings as he tried to focus on what he needed to do to be successful. But ignoring those feelings was playing a major role in his anger problem.

Robert's anger was coming from somewhere. At first he thought it was coming out of some hidden reservoir of anger stored up inside him, like a dam waiting to burst. But eventually we could both see that his metaphor wasn't right. In each explosive instance when he became furious with someone, we could trace it back to painful feelings about which he was unaware. For instance, Robert hated feeling insecure; it made him feel weak. So he covered those feelings over with a powerful rage that made him feel potent and in control. The problem was that over the years, this strategy for controlling weakness was now in control of him. Each time he became filled with rage, he would feel temporarily better, but later he would feel bad about how he had conducted himself. This feeling of shame for being so out of control would make him feel even more insecure and predispose him to become filled with rage again the next time something triggered him. This cycle of rage leading to shame leading to more rage can be very addictive. Robert's rage became his drug of choice to cover over his shame, which only made him need more and more of it as time went on.

After several months of working on this, Robert is still somewhat reactive at times, but his rage-filled outbursts are less frequent. Now he can *slow himself down* and try to identify the painful feelings that he was covering over with rage before. Like an alcoholic swearing off alcohol, Robert is trying not to turn to the medication of rage to make his painful feelings go away. He is not as much in the grips of his rage as he used to be, and his wife is commenting on how happy she is to see that he has several more "speeds" of emotion for them both to enjoy.

The Bible does not refer to all anger as sin, but it does have a lot to say about managing explosive anger when it comes up. The admonition that "everyone should be quick to listen, slow to speak and slow to become angry" is a good one. Anger may not be instinctual, but it is very common and can come up very quickly. To manage it wisely, you must listen closely to its origins in your heart and not say the first thing that comes into your mind. When it comes to dealing with rage, follow the biblical wisdom of simply slowing down. You will find, as Robert did, that you have a variety of underlying emotions that you don't want to ignore.

31

Was Jesus Ever Aggressive?

Aggression has a bad reputation. But I think this is unfair. We typically think of aggression as an unprovoked attack or act of hostility. But not all aggression is bad. There is an *assertive aggression* that is the force needed to push back against opposing forces that are violating boundaries. It is intimidating, sometimes injurious, but not predatory. Assertive aggression can be found in the animal kingdom as an important survival mechanism, even among humans.

A friend of mine asked me to take a river rafting trip with him down the Zambezi River in Africa several years ago. I'm glad I decided to go down the South Fork of the American river near Sacramento instead. I learned later just how dangerous that trip down the Zambezi might have been.

Shortly after my river rafting excursion in California, I happened upon a documentary about George and Eddie, a father and son who took a river rafting trip down the Zambezi. Because I'd almost gone down that same river, I was fascinated by the story. After navigating around hippopotami, snakes, and wild animals for several days, the exhausted travelers stopped to refresh themselves along the riverbank. The guide instructed everyone to stay in water shallow enough to see the bottom for their own safety. But without realizing it, Eddie drifted slowly into deeper waters.

Suddenly, Eddie plunged beneath the waters with a splash.

"Eddie!" shouted George. "Stay where I can see you!"

Waiting for the typical guilt-ridden reply from his hyperactive son, George felt tense with the silence that followed.

"Eddie!" George shouted again. "Get back over here!"

The next few seconds of silence seemed like an eternity.

Then George had the most horrific moment of his life flash before his eyes. There, just a few yards away, a huge crocodile burst through the surface of the water, and he watched in terror as he saw Eddie flip over and over in the creature's jaws.

Without even thinking, George plunged into the water and swam as fast as he could straight toward the crocodile. With conviction that only a father can have in the face of losing his son, he grabbed the predator and began pounding it with his fist, scream-ing, "Let go of my son!" with every strike.

Amazingly, George was able to save Eddie's life that day. Stunned by the force of George's attack, the crocodile released Eddie and swam away—but not before severing George's right arm just above the elbow. Later, when he was asked what he thought he was doing, George merely replied, "There was nothing else to do. I have no regrets."

There is a force in life used to push back intruders when they vi-olate your boundaries. I call that force *assertive aggression*. George's assertive aggression saved Eddie's life, and even though he plays golf one-handed today, he has no regrets for using it against that crocodile on the Zambezi. Your boundaries, or those of someone you love, may be violated at some point, and you may need to aggressively push back intruders to the place where they belong. Jesus did.

When Jesus saw money changers violating the sacred space of the house of God with their self-serving enterprises, he became angry. Then he got aggressive. Jesus pushed back the money changers with an assertively aggressive force because they were violating the boundaries of the temple and someone needed to put them in their place. The Gospel of John even records him with a whip in his hand. There is a time and a place for assertive aggression, and Jesus gave us an example of it. It may require quick thinking and wisdom on your part to know just when to exhibit assertive aggression, but God has given you the capacity to use it when you absolutely need it.

32

Violence: The Destructive Form of Anger

Assertive aggression is the force used to protect boundaries. Violence is the force used to violate them. The healthy use of assertive aggression pushes others back to where they belong. Violence goes too far.

Every newspaper, radio, and television news report is filled with examples of violence. There is no doubt about the destructive impact of violence upon our world. But there are subtle forms of violence that are also a cause for concern. Violence is the violation of other people's boundaries without regard for their well-being, and it happens in many ways.

Kathryn is a devoted and loving mother of her nine-year-old daughter, Brittany. She is proud to be the mother of such a clever and confident child. Kathryn grew up as the only child of two unhappily married parents. As a result of their constant fighting, she was frightened and shy around other people. Kathryn is relieved to see that Brittany will not have to suffer the same insecurities that she did as a child, because Brittany is so outspoken and sure of herself.

As a two-year-old child, Brittany would push away the other children if they were interested in the same toys she wanted. This is not unusual behavior for a child of this age. What was unusual was that Kathryn's response was one of secret pleasure. She didn't correct Brittany's behavior or even see it as an inability to share; she saw it as the behavior of a child who could take care of herself in the world. *No one is going to take advantage of my daughter*, Kathryn thought to herself.

As Brittany grew older, the other children would complain that she was too bossy, so she learned to prefer the company of adults instead. She could engage adults in conversation that made her feel special and mature for her age. Children her own age didn't seem to like her that much.

Kathryn views Brittany as self-confident because she almost always gets what she wants. Brittany is strong-willed and will argue her case until everyone else gives in. But the truth is, Brittany is not just persuasive; she is manipulative. She doesn't always tell the truth because getting her way is more important. She doesn't just protect herself; she takes what she wants from others without much thought of how it will make them feel. Unfortunately Kathryn isn't just teaching Brittany to be assertive about protecting her own boundaries; she's actually teaching her to violate the boundaries of others.

Because Kathryn was passive as a child, she longed to be more assertive growing up. As a result, she encouraged Brittany to speak up to get her needs met. But Kathryn never learned the difference between aggression and violence, so she couldn't teach that difference to Brittany, either. Brittany has few friends her own age and is thought of as precocious and devious by the adults who know her. Sadly, Kathryn's goal for her child could not have been more different.

The Bible has a lot to say about people who take advantage of others. This type of self-focus does violence to both parties in the exchange. The proverb "Do not envy the violent or choose any of their ways" is a psychological warning against the pitfalls of violating the boundaries of others. Taking what you want without regard for the needs and feelings of others does not produce a better life. There may be temporary satisfaction in gaining power *over* others, but it is never as lasting as the satisfaction that comes from having a powerful relationship *with* them. Being violent not only hurts others, but it damages you as well.

33

Why Everyone Feels Disgust

Disgust has been observed all over the world by psychologists who study emotion.[4] Interestingly, you have the ability to suspend your feeling of disgust for loved ones, which is a sign of personal commitment to them. I remember the look of disgust I saw on the face of a young babysitter the first time I tried to show her how to change the diaper of our one-year-old child. To me it was just a part of taking care of my child. To her it was definitely disgusting.

While you can be disgusted by physical things, the most common cause for disgust is in reaction to something you find morally objectionable. Disgust is the emotion you feel in response to something that repels you or makes you feel *fed up*. Being angry over a long period of time can also result in feelings of disgust. When this happens in a marriage, it can be a very dangerous thing.

Jack and Elizabeth were stuck. Their marriage of twenty years was in trouble, and they knew it. Their two children were almost raised, and they both felt the urgency of looking at the problems between them. Soon the kids would be gone, and they would be left with only each other to deal with on a daily basis. This didn't sound good to either one of them.

"I just can't take this anymore," Elizabeth said as she folded her arms across her chest.

"What do you mean?" I asked.

"This!" she replied, pointing to Jack. "I've had it with the excuses and the broken promises. I mean, how much longer do I have to put up with this?"

Jack said nothing as he turned to look out the window, shaking his head from side to side.

"I can see that you're angry, Elizabeth," I jumped in. "So why don't we try to deal with that?"

"Oh, I'm beyond angry," Elizabeth retorted. "I *was* angry for the first fifteen years of our relationship. *Now* I'm just disgusted."

Jack and Elizabeth were wedged in a gridlock they couldn't get out of by themselves. Like commuters on a busy freeway at rush hour, they were trapped together trying to get somewhere, but everything around them was keeping them from making any progress. This had been going on for so long that it was hard to tell if there were any loving feelings left between them. They hadn't made love for a very long time, and they were both wondering why they were even still together.

Jack and Elizabeth had fallen into a very common, but toxic, marital pattern. She was disgusted with him and communicated her distaste harshly. Jack was so disgusted with her that he simply refused to respond—which in marital counseling is what we call *stonewalling.*[5] There was gridlock because her harshness led to his stonewalling, and his stonewalling led to her harshness. Neither one was responsible for starting it, but both were responsible for keeping it going. They both were disgusted with each other; they just had different ways of communicating it.

Over the next several months, the marriage between Jack and Elizabeth improved. We started by identifying the toxic pattern of relating that was keeping them stuck. They were equal contributors to the gridlock, so they were mutually responsible for changing their part in it. Elizabeth learned how to communicate her feelings without being so harsh and critical, and Jack learned how to respond and speak up about all the feelings he was having inside. Then we had to find the feelings that were buried underneath the years of disgust. Elizabeth found out that she didn't really think

Jack was disgusting; she was disgusted with the way they were *treating* each other. When this changed, she found out she had other vulnerable longings for connection and love that had been there all along. She had just been too disgusted to bring those feelings out into the open.

Jack found out that he had lots of things to say. His years of stonewalling gave Elizabeth the impression that he was so disgusted with her that he didn't have any feelings about her at all anymore. But nothing could have been further from the truth. He had lots of feelings about Elizabeth buried under his hurt and disgust; it was just that he felt unable to do battle with her when it came to expressing them. He felt outgunned by her verbally, so he had learned to just shut up instead of getting into a verbal fistfight that he couldn't win.

Turning around the years of disgust between Jack and Elizabeth was hard work. Engrained patterns are difficult to change. They fall back into old habits from time to time, but they get out of their old patterns more quickly now. They both knew something was wrong in their marriage. They just had to learn that it wasn't the other *person* that disgusted them; it was the disgusting way they were *treating* each other instead.

God made you with a moral compass inside. You are attracted to good things and repulsed by things that are bad for you. The feeling of disgust is something that people all over the world feel from time to time. It is an important indicator of things you need to avoid in life. But when that feeling of disgust enters into a love relationship, then something is very wrong and very much in need of attention. If this happens to you, then it is a signal that you need help. Living with disgust can be toxic. If this happens to you, you may need help in identifying exactly what is making you sick.

34

Resentment Is a Problem You Have with Yourself

When anger is used as energy to solve a problem, you are motivated to take action and deal with an underlying feeling that needs to be addressed. But sometimes anger can be misdirected toward someone who is not really the problem, which can cause you to get stuck. Anger that is not used for its designed purpose can turn into a deep and deadly trap that is very difficult to get out of.

Every moral person gets angry in the face of wrongdoing. God created you to get mad at injustice. But resentment is the angry feeling you get when you feel demeaned by another person, and then you start to doubt your own worth. Resentment is your defensive protest to mistreatment by someone because you have been made to feel bad about yourself—so now you want to get even. The real issue you have with resentment is really with yourself, but you can never solve it if you continue to focus your resentment on someone else.

Fred was a gifted and experienced minister. He was hired to work on the staff of a fast-growing church with a dynamic young preacher who was successfully growing a new congregation and needed help. At first, Fred was eager to be a part of such a dynamic ministry, because there were so many exciting things happening at the church that he wanted to be a part of.

But over time Fred became frustrated with what he considered to be impulsive decisions on the part of the younger minister, and he grew increasingly irritated with him. Because the younger minister was so deeply loved by the congregation, Fred couldn't talk about his irritation openly, so it began to grow into an unexpressed resentment. Fred experienced it as righteous indignation for what he believed was the mishandling of God's church. But it was really resentment for feeling dismissed by the younger minister, despite all his years of experience.

"We need to pray for our preacher," Fred shared in his small group.

"Of course," several people responded.

"The stress of being in the spotlight is a difficult burden to carry," Fred continued. "He's falling into the trap of believing that the church is more about him than about God."

"Really?" someone whispered.

"Yes. And we all know where that leads," Fred said seriously.

Fred had developed a problem, and it was more than just with the younger minister. Fred's anger was not just righteous indignation in defense of God's church, it was resentment in defense of his ministry that he feared had little value there, and resentment creates more of a problem for the one feeling it than the person it is directed toward. Over the next several months, Fred gained several pounds, was ill often, and missed a number of important meetings. The younger minister knew that something was wrong and tried to talk to him about it, but Fred's resentment had grown to such a degree that he was too afraid to express it openly to the younger minister himself. He couldn't keep it in around others, but when the younger minister tried to talk to him, he would only smile with a disingenuous smile and look back at him with an awkward silence that communicated more than words.

Eventually those closest to Fred were so confused that they left the church, not knowing what to believe. The church board met several times with both Fred and the younger minister to try to resolve the problem, but they were unsuccessful. After months of agonizing over the issue, the board finally asked Fred to resign. No one was able to help Fred with his resentment because his anger toward the younger minister had gone on for so long that he felt too justified in his own mind to give it up. He felt demeaned by the younger man, and his resentment was a blanket of protection in which he wrapped himself to keep the younger pastor and everyone else out. He wasn't going to open up and expose himself to more hurt, but he was trapping himself in at the same time.

On the day Fred left town, the younger minister joined several other church members who wanted to say good-bye to him. In an attempt to get some resolution one last time, the younger minister stepped forward to give Fred a hug and wish him well. As he did so, the younger minister inadvertently stepped on Fred's foot as they tried to embrace. Fred laughed, and as he stepped back, he said, "Well, this is how I will always remember you, stepping on me."

The Bible has a lot to say about the dangers of resentment. It is destructive and the sign of a problem that needs to be resolved. It can lead to physical, emotional, and spiritual problems that can become quite serious. If you don't realize that the source of your resentment is your own doubt about your worth, you can get stuck in believing someone else is really the reason you are so angry. In cases like Fred's, resentment can become addictive in ways that make it very difficult to release. Resentment is anger gone wrong, and no matter how much you may be able to convince yourself you deserve to feel it, remember, "Resentment kills a fool."

35

Revenge Is Not Justice

There is a difference between justice and revenge. Justice refers to an ethical way of living, with respect and protection for each other and God's laws. Revenge is a vindictive form of retribution.

Revenge is motivated by resentment and based upon hurts that are unresolved. It focuses upon *balancing the scales* of pain, as if human hurt could be quantified and a fair price could be established. To the person seeking revenge, it appears justified and righteous. But revenge has nothing to do with justice. Revenge is about getting even.

Monica grew up as one of two children in a very wealthy family. Both of her parents came from generations of wealth and social status. They lived in an affluent area, and Monica and her older brother went to the best schools growing up. In many ways she was blessed in life, but this didn't keep her from feeling unhappy much of the time anyway. She didn't feel very close to her mother because she was not involved with her upbringing, and she felt close to her father only as long as she didn't displease him. Monica's father was a powerful man, and she knew she would never win a power struggle with him, so she made sure that never happened.

Unfortunately, instead of her brother becoming an ally in their disconnected family, they resented each other. Even though there was plenty of material wealth to go around, they were in competition for the scarce emotional resources available to them. Because her brother was older, she had to be shrewd to get what she wanted and she lived in fear of his physical and emotional retaliation, which could come at any time.

Monica's upbringing was a confusing one. If she appeared to be too powerful, she would be rejected by her father or mistreated by her brother. So because of their privileged financial status, she felt she had a higher status than anyone outside of her family, but she felt she had a lower status than anyone within it. It was the crisis of her father's imminent death that brought Monica to therapy to sort all this out.

"I can't believe he did it," Monica said in disbelief.

"Did what?" I asked.

"Manipulated my father again," she said. "I can't believe a man as smart as my father can be so naive as to fall for my brother's obvious exploitation. Putting him in charge of that trust was incredibly stupid. Are all men completely egotistical?"

"You don't trust your brother," I said.

"Of course not," Monica said emphatically. "He's a selfish dolt, and I don't intend to let him get away with it. I explained my position to my father, but it was useless. He never listens to me. But I'm not a stupid woman. I have my own attorney working on plans to correct the situation. Wait until we get to the reading of the will. Then they will all be in for quite a surprise."

"It's understandable that you're pretty hurt at the way you were treated by your family."

"Hurt? Oh no. I'm good and mad about it, and I think that's a good thing. I mean, I'm not blaming myself for the problems between me and my brother. No, he is self-centered and cruel, and I think it's pretty healthy of me to be angry with him and not myself right now. Don't you?"

I sometimes face a dilemma in psychotherapy when my patients ask me to agree with their perspectives when I think they are feeling more than what they are acknowledging in the moment. Part of Monica's anger was attributed to the grieving process she was going through because of her father's impending death. But her anger was more than just the beginnings of her grief or a healthy self-protection from her older brother. It was related to something bigger in her life.

Monica was conflicted about whether or not she was supposed to be a powerful woman. Her father made her feel powerless around him, and her relationship with her brother only served to confirm it. She did feel powerful at times, but her automatic response to her own powerfulness was to repress it. She feared conflict in her family, so she adopted a powerless position with them. Yet she hated doing this because it felt insulting. In her attempts to avoid rejection, she acted like she was powerless, and over time this made her feel demeaned. Repressing her power didn't make her family relationships better; it made her feel resentful.

It was difficult for me to agree with Monica that her anger at her brother was purely healthy. Imagining ways she could hurt him or legally punish him was only reinforcing her feelings of powerlessness and resentment. Talking about how she could get even with him or make him see what a horrible person he was would only make things worse. She didn't need to punish him; she needed to resolve some of her own issues with power and her doubts about her worth in the family. Focusing on her anger at her brother wouldn't help that.

Over time I was able to direct Monica away from her plans of revenge against her brother and onto her own unresolved pain. Monica did need to express her anger, but only because it led us to deeper feelings of hurt, powerlessness, and self-doubt that needed to be healed. As we did this, the subject of her brother became less of a focus in our sessions and the subject of her own value as a woman came into view. We still talk about Monica's anger at times, but the object of her anger gets less of our attention now. Monica is starting to believe that she has worth in her father's eyes, both the one here on earth and the Father who sees her true worth from above. She no longer wants to give in to a power struggle with her brother by focusing on how she might be able to get even with him. Planning revenge on him was reinforcing her self-doubt and feelings of powerlessness, because it was confirming that he was the more powerful person who needed to be stopped. She is starting to believe she already *is* even with men in the world, and she's confident of her value even if others do not perceive it. Not surprisingly, she doesn't feel as much need for revenge if things don't work out.

36

Envy: I'm Angry at You Because I Feel Bad about Me

In the story of Cain and Abel in the Bible, God asked them both to bring him sacrifices as an offering to the Lord. Abel, who tended the flocks, "brought . . . fat portions from some of the firstborn of his flock" (Gen. 4:4), which was the very best he could offer to God of what he had. Cain, who was a farmer, brought in "some of the fruits of the soil" (Gen. 4:3), which was a sacrifice for him, but not the finest of what he had. So, God "looked with favor on Abel and his offering, but on Cain and his offering he did not look with favor" (Gen. 4:4–5). This made Cain angry. God, like any loving father, tried to explain it to him. "If you do what is right, will you not be accepted? But if you do not do what is right, sin is crouching at your door; it desires to have you, but you must rule over it" (Gen. 3:7).

At first Cain was jealous that Abel was more pleasing to God than he was. He wanted God's favor, too. But then he became envious of the goodness in Abel that he was unable to muster up in himself. This wasn't about pleasing God anymore; now it was about how bad Cain felt in Abel's presence. He couldn't stand how easily Abel was able to offer the best he had to God, when Cain couldn't find this type of self-sacrifice in himself. He hated that Abel seemed so good, which made Cain feel so bad. He was so angry that he committed the first homicide in history. Cain's envy was the very first motive for murder.

When God confronted Cain about the whereabouts of Abel, Cain had the interesting response of "Am I my brother's keeper?" With no apparent guilt, Cain seemed satisfied with the fact that he had removed the source of his shame. Cain didn't appear to be motivated by the desire to obtain God's favor (certainly, murdering his brother wasn't going to accomplish that); his only concern was to spoil the object of his envy. Cain felt no responsibility to his relationships with God or Abel—he just wanted his own pain to go away. This is the goal of envy.

There is a difference between envy and jealousy. Jealousy is the pain of fearing that someone or something of value will be taken from you. It seeks to remove a rival, and it involves three people in a triangle of competition. The goal of jealousy is to acquire the object of one's love. On the other hand, envy only involves two people, and it is the pain of watching someone else possess something that you do not. It is rooted in the shame of not being enough, and if you cannot acquire what you desire to possess, envy will seek to destroy the one stimulating your feeling of shame. The goal of envy is to make the painful feeling of shame go away.

Envy is a destructive form of anger. It is motivated by shame, and it does not seek anything good. It only seeks to avoid something that feels bad. Envy doesn't heal the shame that underlies it—it only covers it over with a vengeful hostility. It goes away only if the one feeling it can get whatever he or she needs to stop feeling inferior, or if the person stimulating the envy gets spoiled. Envy creates a selfish self-focus, like "sin is crouching at your door; it desires to have you, but you must rule over it."

Envy is a common emotion. You may have felt it at times. But don't be fooled into thinking that if you can hurt or diminish the person you are envious of, your life will be better. You may feel some temporary relief from damaging someone you envy, but just like Cain, your shame will still be there. The solution to your envy will never come from attempts to spoil another person; it can come only through healing your own shame within.

37

Jealousy Isn't Always Bad

There are two kinds of jealousy. There is a godly jealousy that is a desire to protect that which belongs to you and keep it safe. There is an ungodly jealousy that is a desire to possess that which is not yours. Both involve a triangle of love, and the fear that a rival will take someone or something of great value from you. Jealousy is not necessarily destructive, but it can be an intense form of anger that needs to be handled with wisdom.

Benjamin and Gabrielle have both been married before, and they want their second marriage to each other to be better than their first attempts at matrimony. Benjamin is a sensitive and soft-spoken man who is thoughtful but often shy around others. Gabrielle is an attractive and outgoing woman who is delighted to find a man so aware of his emotions and capable of caring for her deeply. They love each other and are grateful to have found one another.

But, as all couples eventually learn, love is not enough when it comes to making a good marriage work. In spite of their best efforts, sometimes Benjamin gets his feelings hurt by Gabrielle's carefree and animated approach to life, and at times Gabrielle feels disconnected from Benjamin when he is in one of his withdrawn moods. They try to talk about it, but sometimes that only makes things worse. Because of their love for each other, they wisely decided to come to marriage counseling.

"I was very hurt that we spent all that money getting away last weekend and you didn't even seem to be having a good time," Gabrielle stated.

"I thought *you* were having a good time," Benjamin responded defensively.

"I can't have a good time if you're moping around," Gabrielle said quickly.

"Let's see if we can figure out what happened," I said. I could see them falling into the typical trap of talking in terms of the *other* person's feelings instead of trying to express their *own*. "Let's start with you, Gabrielle. Instead of trying to talk about how Benjamin was feeling, why don't you let him know what *you* were feeling?"

"Okay," Gabrielle replied. "I was feeling all alone in an expensive, romantic hotel, and I was hurt that I was missing out on what could have been a good time with my husband."

"All alone," I said. "And when did you notice you were feeling that?"

"Saturday night," she went on. "It was very clear that Benjamin didn't want anything to do with me after that."

"All right," I said before Benjamin could respond. She was still trying to tell him what he was feeling, and I wanted him to express that himself.

"Benjamin, did you know Gabrielle was feeling all alone?" I asked.

"Alone?" he said sarcastically. "Right, like she was feeling alone. We were talking about some pretty important stuff, and as soon as the conversation wasn't going her way, she went into the other room and called her friend. I know they are just friends, but she made it clear she would rather talk to him than me. So I just stopped trying to talk to her. Isn't that what you wanted?" he asked, turning to Gabrielle.

Before she could take the bait for another argument, I quickly responded to Benjamin. "So, that must have hurt your feelings. Did you let her know that?"

"Well, no," he said. "I mean, I didn't want to seem petty."

"So, you were jealous?" I asked.

"I'm not that small," Benjamin said.

"But you wanted her to talk to *you* instead of her friend. You wanted to feel close to her, and you couldn't do that if she was talking to someone else," I insisted.

"Well, yes," Benjamin said, appearing to calm down. "But I don't want Gabrielle to feel controlled or anything. I only want her to talk to me because she wants to, not because I'm demanding it."

"I see," I said. "And Gabrielle, did you know that Benjamin was hurt by what happened on Saturday night? Did you know he still wanted to talk?"

"No," Gabrielle responded with surprise. "I thought we had finished that conversation. I feel so bad. I had no idea you thought that. I would rather talk to you than anyone. I was just so excited that I wanted to keep talking, and I thought you were done. I'm so sorry. Of course I can see now how thoughtless that was of me."

It took us a while, but eventually we did uncover the problem. Benjamin felt jealous when Gabrielle called her friend, but he thought jealousy was always bad. So he got angry and didn't want to talk about it. He thought expressing his jealousy would make him appear weak, so he ended up emotionally withdrawing instead. As it turned out, Benjamin's jealousy was actually a good thing in this instance. He felt a natural urge to protect the emotional intimacy he had with his wife, and he needed to speak up about it. And once he did, an interesting thing happened. She was glad. Gabrielle needed Benjamin to protect their connection and fight for it when it became threatened, even if she was the one threatening it by being impulsive or unthinking.

The Bible tells us that "jealousy arouses a husband's fury" (Prov. 6:34). This is a dangerous form of anger that needs to be handled with care. But not all jealousy is bad. Sometimes it is a warning that something precious needs to be protected. This is why God describes himself as a jealous God. He is willing to act to protect that which is his, and at times he wants us to do the same. It is not petty to want to protect your valuable relationships, and the anger that is aroused by the feeling of jealousy can direct you to do that. If expressed carefully, and in just the right way, sometimes expressing your godly jealousy is the most loving thing to do.

PART FOUR

Anxiety

38

What Is Anxiety?

Anxiety is unhappiness. It is related to stress, tension, and psychological discomfort. Anxiety is the upset feeling you get when you are nervous, worried, or feeling insecure. You can feel anxious for a few moments, or you can feel anxious for long periods of time. It can even become a habit, which might make you an anxious person in general.

Shortly after I entered graduate school in clinical psychology, one of the world's experts on anxiety, Dr. Richard Gorsuch, came to our faculty. He had coauthored the most widely used psychological test to measure anxiety. I was especially excited about this because Dr. Gorsuch was also the editor of the leading professional journal on the scientific study of religion. These were my two main research interests, so I transferred over to him as my advisor for my doctoral dissertation.

Under Dr. Gorsuch's supervision, I studied anxiety extensively and developed a research project to test the theories I developed regarding the relationship between anxiety and religion. Religion, I thought, should help people with anxiety. So I joined forces with a wilderness training organization and decided to see how religion affects one's experience of anxiety in extremely stressful circumstances. Armed with Dr. Gorsuch's test of anxiety, and another well-known test of religious orientation, I went out into the wilderness to find a group of people who might be experiencing intense forms of anxiety.

I'm not sure if you are familiar with wilderness training, but they do things like take campers into the wilderness and leave them in the desert overnight to see how well they can survive, throw them off of mountains with ropes attached to them (it's called rappelling) to see if they can let themselves down from extremely high heights, and other very anxiety-producing exercises to test their physical and mental abilities. This was the perfect environment for my research study.

I tested each participant before they went into the wilderness and then tested them again as soon as they came back. The results were, to say the least, very interesting. If you leave someone out in the cold desert overnight, or throw them off of a really high mountain, it makes them anxious. Really anxious. But quite to my dismay, your religious orientation doesn't matter. You can be really religious or not that religious at all, and it won't change a thing. If you are facing that kind of distress, you are going to be unhappy. No matter what.

But that wasn't the end of the study. I also tested each participant two weeks later and found another interesting thing. Those people who were intrinsically religious, which means religion was a personal and meaningful part of their daily lives, were not anxious anymore. Everyone else still was. If religion is important to you, it can help you make sense of the anxiety in your life, and even though you may become unhappy from time to time, you can return to a state of happiness much faster than those people who don't have a personally meaningful religion to help them do that. Religion does help people deal with their anxiety. It's just that religion doesn't *prevent* anxiety from happening to you; it helps you *deal* with it and restores you to a happy life.

God made the world to have anxiety in it. To pretend it isn't there is to be in denial about how God made the world. Anxiety isn't the problem; not having a way to make sense of it is. When the Bible says, "Do not be anxious about anything, but in every situation, by prayer and petition, with thanksgiving, present your requests to God,"

God isn't telling you never to feel anxious—he is telling you how to deal with it once you are anxious. You will feel anxious sometimes in your life, but you don't have to stay that way. God offers himself as a resource for dealing with anxiety. As the participants in my study found, making use of that resource is a profoundly healthy thing to do.

39

Why God Created Anxiety

Anxiety is a warning signal that stress is about to take place. Just like stressing your muscles is necessary for them to grow stronger, stress plays an important role in how you develop emotionally, as well. Anxiety lets you know you need to deal with some real or perceived struggle in your life. Facing anxiety-producing situations gives you the confidence to deal with difficulties in the future. Once you have suffered and persevered, you know you can do it again.

God is more interested in your character than in the absence of suffering in your life. I know you probably prefer it the other way around, but you didn't get to make the world. The other animals are only interested in avoiding pain; you, on the other hand, are more complex. It is only by facing your suffering that you develop character. And each time you choose to strengthen your character by facing your pain, you develop the hope that you can manage your life even better if trials should come your way again.

Jim came to therapy after a painful divorce. He had never been in therapy before, and he really didn't want to be there now, but he just couldn't stop feeling so bad about his breakup with his wife.

They had known each other for only a few months when they got married. The fact that his friends told him he might be rushing into a commitment with a woman he didn't really know all that well didn't bother him, because he was so in love with her that he wanted to spend the rest of his life getting to know her, and he wanted to get started right now.

But things didn't last. After only six months of marriage, she decided that she had made a mistake, and she left him. She didn't give him much of an explanation other than that she just wasn't in love with him anymore. Jim was devastated. His vow had been to be married for life, and now he was being forced to break that vow. He felt awful.

Jim was one of those men who didn't really "get" therapy at first. He was a hardworking, successful businessman who was raised in the Midwest with a strong work ethic and good values. He believed all he needed to be a good man was to be honest and hardworking. Talking about how he felt was never really important to Jim. He always thought actions spoke louder than words anyway.

"So, what do you want me to do?" Jim blurted out after one long silence between us in an early session.

"I'm interested in how you're feeling right now," I replied.

"I *feel* like I don't know what you want me to *do*," he said in an exasperated tone.

"So, you're frustrated?"

"Of course!" he snapped back. "I've never been more frustrated in my life. I thought I could trust my feelings when I married Julie, but look where that got me. And you're asking me to trust that talking about how I *feel* is supposed to do me some good now? I just don't see how that's going to benefit me."

"You could talk about how disappointed you are, or how angry you are that she gave up on the marriage so quickly," I said.

"Complaining is for sissies," he said as he tightened his lips.

"So, talking about your hurt is *complaining*?"

"It is where I come from," Jim said firmly.

"Then we have a disagreement," I said calmly. "You want me to help you get rid of your painful feelings, and I want you to talk about them. We are at cross-purposes here."

Jim looked over at me with a puzzled look on his face. He didn't know what therapy was all about, so it didn't surprise him that he didn't know what he was doing. But he just couldn't grasp where I was coming from. No one had ever wanted him to talk about his feelings before. His parents wanted him to be seen and not heard, his teachers wanted him to be good and not cause trouble, and his boss only wanted him to produce, and he didn't want to hear about how difficult it was to do it. No one was interested in how stressful his life was before, so he didn't know how to respond to me because I seemed to be interested now.

Men like Jim eventually do pretty well in therapy because they believe in perseverance and hard work. At first, this works against them because they don't see the value in talking about their feelings. But because they refuse to quit until the job is done, they often stay in therapy long enough to finally see the benefit of facing their feelings openly. Jim was one of those guys.

If we sat there long enough, Jim couldn't help feeling how unhappy he was. He was nervous and worried about what it said about him that he had made such a horrible mistake, and he felt insecure about ever getting married again. He was stressed out at work. He was tense most of the time and almost never felt content. Jim was filled with anxiety, and he needed to talk about it. Fortunately, once a week he did exactly that with me.

Some men go through a confusing divorce, bottle up all their hurt feelings, and simply go on about their lives. Those men often make many of the same mistakes again. Men like Jim are different from that. Jim faced his anxiety with me week after week. He "complained" and wrestled and even cried about it. That's right, he cried. Jim persevered with me and came out the other side a slightly different man. Jim is still the same honest, hardworking man that he always was. But after many months of talking about his feelings with me, he has a different view of what it means to be a man of character.

Now Jim knows the benefit of facing his painful feelings about the stressful events in his life, and how talking openly about them changes how he feels about himself. Jim still has anxiety about his future sometimes, but now he has a lot more hope about his ability to deal with it. Jim has learned that talking openly about his anxiety is a part of how "suffering produces perseverance; perseverance, character; and character, hope."

40

Stress Won't Kill You— But Distress Will!

Hans Selye was a world expert on stress.[1] He spent his lifetime studying its effects on our health and what we can do about it. Dr. Selye came to some important conclusions about stress. First, stress is the natural by-product of activity in life. Even good activity, like your daughter's wedding or the birth of your child, produces stress. Stress is not a problem; it's a sign that you are living an active life. Second, to remain healthy you must also have release.

Selye has identified the cycle of stress. Activity leads to stress, which if followed by release, leads to being prepared for more activity. This is the healthy cycle of activity, stress, and release. The problem comes when you do not have adequate release. Then, activity leads to stress, which then leads to distress. *Distress* is a problem. All kinds of physical and emotional problems are related to distress, and if it goes on long enough, it can even lead to an earlier death.

Marcus came for therapy because of the intense emotional pain in his life. He was a brilliant writer who had received awards for his movie scripts, even though his academic degrees were in the field of mathematics. Marcus could grasp complex aspects of the world and put them down on paper in ways that were quite compelling. But as brilliant as Marcus was, he couldn't figure out one thing. Although Marcus could create wonderful lives for the characters in his movies, he couldn't figure out how to be happy himself.

Marcus couldn't help noticing things. He would pick up on how people felt even if they never said anything about it. He could figure out how things worked when everyone else was confused. His mind just seemed to race faster than most people's minds, and even though he often understood others perfectly well, he rarely felt that anyone could understand him. Because Marcus had a powerful intellect that worked overtime noticing and figuring things out, he was never able to slow down. Marcus never felt relaxed, and he almost never experienced what Dr. Selye called release. After months of looking at the constant requirements that Marcus had placed upon himself, to be perpetually vigilant and pay attention to everything in life, we came to an important turning point in our work together.

"I can't stand feeling like I don't fit in anywhere," Marcus said as his eyes filled with tears.

"Does it feel like you fit in here?" I asked.

"Other people aren't like you," he protested. "They don't want to hear about how life feels to me. It's as if they don't feel things the way I do, or they don't want to. How could so many people be so cut off from how they feel?"

"It's exhausting trying to find ways to connect to others. You're constantly looking and constantly being disappointed. You've been disappointed so many times it makes it hard to have any hope that you will ever find connections," I said.

Marcus and I had worked on this many times before. It's true, he was more sensitive and aware than most people. But I didn't believe this was preventing him from connecting to others. A bigger problem for him was that he was constantly "on guard," always working at how to find what he needed. He had become unnatural in his approach to others, and he was trying too hard to make things work in relationships. Marcus couldn't allow his relationships to unfold naturally. Marcus was perpetually distressed, and this was getting in his way.

"I am so exhausted," he said, looking up at me. But now his expression changed from a sad, teary countenance to almost a smile. He had a look of discovery on his face as he said, "You know, I read a book this week by a business consultant. I was doing some research on my next script, and they conducted an extensive research study on what makes top athletes better than all the rest. What they found was that the top golfers and tennis players don't really have better skills than the people just under them. I mean, once you get that high up in a sport, everyone is really good. But what did distinguish them from the guys who never make it to the absolute top is that in between their shots they do something to relax. I think it was Arnold Palmer who chatted with his caddy between shots and didn't even think about the game. And the other greats all did something like that, something to give themselves a tiny break before they geared up again for the fight."

"That sounds like an important lesson," I said.

"I never do that," he blurted out. "I'm constantly thinking about what's coming next. I've always thought the harder you work at something, the more likely you are to succeed. But now I'm thinking it doesn't really work that way. I have to find some way to give myself a break."

"That sounds pretty good to me," I said.

I was encouraged. Marcus was finally seeing that he could do some things differently to help himself connect with others. It's not natural to live life without release in between stress and activity. That leads to distress, and that thwarts a healthy life, both physically and psychologically. Marcus needed to relax, and perhaps now he was coming to the realization that this could help him be more effective in life. Marcus couldn't find the love he needed in life because he couldn't be loving to himself first.

God designed us to live powerful lives. Stress is the natural by-product of that. But to live life the way we were created to do it, we must also have *love*. You can't leave that out and be healthy. In the case of Marcus, that meant doing something loving for himself. He was trying to live a disciplined and powerful life without any emphasis upon release and love. Hard work is good, but it isn't enough. God gave us everything we need to live a powerful life, but we must not leave anything out to achieve it. "For the Spirit God gave us does not make us timid, but gives us power, love and self-discipline." Power, love, and self-discipline work together just like stress, release, and activity. You can minimize distress in your life if you realize how they are all equally important aspects of the cycle of stress.

41

Obsessive-Compulsive Anxiety

Legalism depletes life. Even though most people agree with this statement, some people can't stop themselves from being legalistic. When people become fearful or anxious, they cling to the "letter of the law" to protect themselves. We are all subject to doing this from time to time. But there are some people who are so anxious that they cling to the letter of the law all the time.

Obsessiveness is an extreme form of clinging to the letter of the law psychologically. It means you can't stop thinking certain thoughts, and you think about them in a very legalistic way. It's not that you *want* to think the thoughts; you *have* to. To your mind, it's the *law*. It is as if your mind is at war with your reason. You know it isn't reasonable to keep thinking about these things, but you can't stop it. Because of your anxiety, you must follow the letter of the law. You obsess over and over again about certain thoughts, because you are anxious and you have to think about them in just the right way or you will become even more anxious.

Compulsiveness is an extreme form of clinging to the letter of the law behaviorally. This is when you can't stop doing certain behaviors that you believe are the exact solutions to your anxiety. You are too uncomfortable not to do these behaviors, so you must do them over and over again to prevent your anxiety from getting worse. Just like with obsessiveness, it doesn't make the anxiety go away for very long; it just provides a temporary sense of relief.

Paula is tortured by anxiety. She was raised by a mother who would fly into rages over the smallest of things. Paula lived her childhood in constant fear that she would do something to send her mother into a rage. Because she never knew what that might be, she was anxious all the time.

Even though she no longer lives with her parents, Paula can't stop feeling anxious. She is afraid something bad is going to happen to her, and she needs to be prepared for it. Having to constantly protect yourself from danger is a very anxious way to live.

Paula has a number of rituals that she keeps to avoid making her anxiety worse. She washes her hands a specific number of times each day, she can't touch car doors with her bare fingers, and she has to check and recheck everything she does. Paula has to count the number of times she locks the door before she leaves her apartment. She doesn't really *want* to do it, but she feels too anxious if she doesn't. Then she counts the number of steps she takes to get to the street for the same reason.

Paula suffers from an obsessive-compulsive disorder (OCD). She has very specific thoughts that seem to pop into her head, and then she has to take very specific actions based upon certain rules that she has for herself. Although she knows it is silly, Paula believes she must do these things to keep something bad from happening to her.

Paula inherited her OCD, and it was not her fault. It wasn't the result of anything she did, but she has to struggle terribly to overcome it. Medications are helping her, but she still must follow certain thoughts and behaviors "to the letter" from time to time. Without the help of her medication and therapy, Paula's OCD would probably not get better. This form of anxiety rarely goes away by itself.

We don't really know what causes OCD, but we know people like Paula suffer terribly with anxiety because of it. They are forced to follow self-imposed instructions to the letter or they will be overwhelmed with intolerable anxiety. Paula feels compelled to follow her own mental instructions exactly, and she finds it impossible to trust that some harm won't befall her if she doesn't. The Bible tells us that "the letter kills, but the Spirit gives life." Following instructions to the letter doesn't produce life. Thankfully, through a combination of medication and a specific form of therapy, Paula is able to loosen her grip and stop clinging so tightly to the letter of the law in her life. The less she lives by the letter of the law, the more she is able to experience life as it was created to be.

42

How Disorder Causes Dissociation

One of the things the human mind does to protect itself is to dissociate. We all dissociate to some degree. In its mildest forms, it's similar to those moments when you are driving down the road, perhaps on a familiar route, and you catch yourself not really paying attention to what you are doing. You were on "autopilot," and you caught yourself, and now you have returned to being alert and aware of everything going on around you. Dissociation is when you slip out of conscious awareness and into another state of mind that is unaware of your surroundings.

Some people have endured extreme anxiety and distress in their lives. When this happens in childhood, they may turn to dissociation to help them survive. It is not something they have decided to do; it's automatic. Dissociation causes them to slip into another state of mind that distances them from their distress. It is like a hypnotic state in which the person is here and interacting with you, but part of their mind is somewhere else, somewhere hidden to keep it safe. In its most extreme form, dissociation causes multiple personalities to form within one person. This is very rare and only happens as the result of extreme childhood trauma, but God created the human mind to survive in our world of disorder and pain with some serious defense mechanisms when necessary.

Laura grew up in a poor area of town where several members of her father's family lived together in the same house. Her father and his two brothers regularly abused drugs, were frequently unemployed, and were often in trouble with the police. Laura was frightened and anxious about her unstable home life, especially because of her uncle. Over the course of her childhood, she had been sexually molested by him on many occasions, and she felt powerless to prevent it. She tried to talk about it to her parents, but they didn't believe her and punished her for making up such a horrible lie. Laura has many memories of feeling terrified of her uncle. He would threaten to hurt her younger sister if she told anyone about what he was doing to her. Because she was trapped in a horrible situation, the only way for Laura to survive was to keep all her fears and anxiety locked deep inside. Laura never talked about the abuse in her home to anyone else growing up. Her secrecy helped her survive.

While locking the distress of her childhood in her heart helped Laura survive her terrifying childhood, it wasn't working so well for her as an adult. Laura has never been able to trust a man enough to develop an intimate relationship, and she is overly attached to her pastor because he seems like the only man safe enough for her to trust.

Laura came to me for therapy because she knew she was afraid of men, and she wanted to work this fear out with a male therapist. She was very tentative about starting therapy with me, which I could understand once she explained her experiences with her uncle.

"I felt depressed again this week," Laura said with some embarrassment.

"Tell me about that," I said.

"It was another difficult week," she said, looking down. I knew Laura felt a lot of shame for feeling depressed. She thought she should be stronger and have more faith, but she couldn't help feeling depressed at times.

"Tell me what was going on." I knew she kept many secrets locked inside, and she needed to let them out.

"Nothing," she snapped back as she looked at me out of the corner of one eye. Then it happened. I had seen it before in Laura and in other patients. There was a glazed look in her eyes that made me feel she was looking out into space rather than at me. Even though I wasn't speaking, she was staring straight ahead as if she was straining to pay very close attention to something. I couldn't tell if she was frightened or confused, but I knew something had just happened. I had hurt her somehow, and she had just slipped out of the room, leaving her body behind.

We sat in silence for several minutes as I tried to connect with her gaze. She was looking at me, but then again she wasn't.

"Laura?" I said softly.

"What!" she said as she snapped her head in my direction.

"What's going on?" I asked.

"Nothing," she said as her eyes widened. "I told you, I didn't do anything. It's not my fault."

"Did you feel I was being critical of you?" I asked.

"It's not my fault, I told you. I didn't do anything. Sometimes I just feel bad, that's all," she said quickly.

We experienced many moments like this over the first few years of our therapy together. Laura would be sitting in our session, and then I would do or say something that revived intense anxiety and fear in her, causing her to dissociate. She would mentally leave the room. Years later, she actually walked over to the corner of my office and crouched behind one of my large office chairs and explained to me that this was where she used to go. She found a mental hiding place to make it safe enough to continue our sessions together.

Laura is an example of what happens to children who are raised in ungodly ways. The Bible tells us that "God is not a God of disorder but of peace." The chaos, anxiety, and fear that surrounded Laura as a child resulted in her need to dissociate to protect herself. In the orderly and safe environment of my office, we began to restore a sense of peace to Laura's life today. It took several years, but together we created the kind of life that God intended for children to have; one that Laura had not experienced until now.

Laura rarely dissociates today, at least not any more than the rest of us do. A combination of her therapy and a loving church family has helped restore her to a life of order and peace. God did not make us to live with the disorder that overwhelming anxiety and fear cause. Thankfully, he gave us ways to survive it if we have to.

43

Post-Traumatic Stress Disorder

Prior to the 1970s, we thought psychological problems were either inherited or developed during early childhood. After we observed closely what traumatic stress can do to an otherwise normal adult, especially in wartime environments such as the Vietnam War, we came up with a new category of mental disorder: post-traumatic stress disorder (PTSD).

All of us have to deal with the ordinary stresses of life, but some people have to suffer through unusually traumatic events like war, rape, or witnessing someone die. Traumatic events such as these can cause any of us to suffer from PTSD. Nightmares and flashbacks are common, along with psychological numbing, hypervigilance, and an exaggerated startle response. PTSD can be very debilitating, and people who suffer from it are in need of professional help.

Emma was referred to me by an attorney. She was a twenty-two-year-old, single woman who was in graduate school. Emma had been at a party with some friends a few weeks earlier and left by herself to go home at about midnight. While driving home, she was pulled over by what she thought was a policeman who had flashing lights on his car. An officer stepped out of the car and approached her. He was wearing a uniform and instructed her to get out of her car. Emma was frightened and tried to comply with all of his requests. She knew she had been drinking alcohol, and she was afraid she was going to be arrested for drinking and driving.

After a series of questions, the officer told her he was going to arrest her. He handcuffed her and took her to a large house in the area. It turned out that he wasn't a police officer at all, but a security guard who had access to several large homes in the area. The man forced Emma to have sex with him, and then he let her go. Emma was so terrified that she did whatever he asked for fear of losing her life. It was a horrible event for Emma—one that she will never forget.

It was easy to see that Emma was suffering from PTSD in our first session. She couldn't sleep, and when she did she would often wake up with a nightmare of being raped all over again. She was afraid to go out after dark or drive by the place where she had been pulled over because these things reminded her of that night.

In the beginning she would just sit staring down into her lap, unable to tell me anything about how she felt because everything just felt "numb" to her. It didn't matter how softly I spoke to Emma; if I said anything to her, she would almost jump out of her seat. This exaggerated startle response is common to PTSD.

"How are you doing right now?" I asked almost in a whisper after several minutes of silence.

Emma jerked her shoulders and shot me a look of utter surprise.

"Sorry," she said. "I guess I was just thinking."

"About what?" I asked.

"The other day," she went on, as she looked back down into her lap, "I was driving my car to work. It was in the middle of the day, and I swear I saw a police car turn on his flashing lights behind me. My heart jumped into my throat. I was terrified. *Not again*, I thought. *Should I pull over? Should I drive to the police station? What should I do?* But then, when I looked back again, there was no one there. Am I going psychotic? Do you think this has made me go crazy?"

Emma was staring wide-eyed at me now. I knew she was frightened, not only by what happened, but also because she was afraid she was losing her mind because of it.

"You saw a car with its turn signal on, and you thought it was a police car. Of course you were terrified. You were frightened for your life just a few weeks ago by a man in a police car, so of course you are going to be on the lookout for one again," I said.

I knew she was suffering from hypervigilance, a condition that causes trauma survivors to be so vigilant in an attempt to protect themselves that they actually see things that aren't there. It isn't psychotic, but it feels crazy to the one suffering from it.

"So, you don't think I'm losing my mind?"

"No, I don't. I think you are doing what anyone would do in your situation," I replied.

PTSD is nothing to be ashamed of, but everyone who has it feels shame anyway. We live in a world where bad things happen to good people. We can't keep this from happening, but we can deal with it once it does.

Because of several months of conversations like the one I just described, Emma is doing much better these days. She has a new relationship with a boyfriend she is beginning to trust, the nightmares are not as frequent, and she is better able to tell me how she feels about things. This has taken many months of going over the events of that night in detail, and working on her feelings of anxiety and fear, but Emma is getting better.

Emma suffered from PTSD as a result of a traumatic event that happened to her and changed her life. It wasn't her fault, and it didn't matter what good care she had taken of herself before that time. Some trauma is simply too much, and if we are forced to go through it, we will suffer. The Bible tells us there are times when "even the bravest soldier, whose heart is like the heart of a lion, will melt with fear." Traumatic moments can happen to any of us. But there is help available if one ever happens to you.

44

Why Do You Have Panic Attacks?

A panic attack is an extreme form of anxiety. It is a sudden, overwhelming fear that seems to come out of nowhere, causing your heart to race, making it difficult for you to breathe, and making you feel like you are going to faint. Your hands will sweat, you will get dizzy, and you may even think you are going to die. A panic attack is so terrifying that many people are rushed to the hospital thinking they are having a heart attack.

As awful as it is, a panic attack is not dangerous. However, most people who have them develop an intense fear of ever having another one. In fact, panic attacks often lead to other serious problems like depression, phobias, substance abuse, and medical complications. Having a panic attack once in a while usually isn't a problem, but some people develop a persistent fear of panic attacks and can end up having them all the time.

Delia saw several therapists before she came to see me. She had suffered from panic attacks for years, and she was miserable. She had multiple panic attacks daily, and her life had come to a virtual stop because of them. She moved back home to live with her parents, she quit her job, and she felt hopeless about her future.

"I can't stand it anymore," Delia said, with her hands quivering as she adjusted her sunglasses. She often refused to take her sunglasses off for the first several minutes of our sessions.

"It's awful, and embarrassing, to have to live with this all the time," I said.

"It's a nightmare," she said. "I just want it to stop. I can't even go on the freeways anymore for fear that I might have another attack and can't get off. You've got to help me get this under control. I just can't take it."

"When was the last time you had a panic attack?"

"On my way *here*," she said desperately. "I had to stop at a red light. That always scares me. What if I start to have a panic attack? How will I get out of traffic? I mean, sometimes I can't even tell when they are going to come over me. I just never know when it's going to happen. I hate this," she said as she started to cry.

Delia had a serious problem, but it wasn't exactly what she thought it was. The obvious problem was the intense anxiety she felt. It is all-consuming to have panic attacks daily, and of course anyone would want them to stop. But *trying* to get them to stop was actually making things worse for Delia.

Over time, Delia began to see that intense anxiety was not her only problem. Her *fear* of her panic attacks had become just as big a problem as the attacks themselves.

Delia would be driving down the street and stop at a red light. She would feel anxious because she had to stop. This bit of anxiety made her afraid that she might have a panic attack. She *misinterpreted* this fear as the beginning of a panic attack. She would then try to stop the attack from coming on, which of course made her more anxious. It takes effort to suppress anxiety. And within a few seconds, she was on her way to another panic attack. This cycle of anxiety and fear had become a regular experience for Delia—up to ten times a day. No wonder she was exhausted.

Delia eventually grasped what I believe to be a fundamental aspect of human psychological problems. Humans are meaning makers. We search for meaning in life, and we make meaning out of the life we have. Her problem was not only the anxiety she was feeling; it was the *meaning* she was attributing to it. She began to see that every time she felt anxiety didn't mean she was going to have a panic attack. Some anxiety is a helpful signal that stressful events are coming—you have to be aware of what it means. If you do, then you will "call understanding your intimate friend."

Delia still has panic attacks, but we count them monthly now instead of daily. Delia can see that her biggest problem was not with her anxiety; it was with what she believed about it. It was not easy getting Delia to see her problems as a matter of beliefs. Medication helped her, so she was convinced that she had a physical problem. The panic attacks were real, and they seemed to be coming from somewhere outside of her, not generated by her own mind. But eventually she was able to see how her beliefs were playing a major role in her panic attacks, and that helped her greatly.

What we believe drives us at our deepest levels. If we are too concrete and fail to see our underlying beliefs, then we can end up with serious problems like Delia did. Fortunately she had the wisdom to seek out a new understanding of her anxiety, which improved the quality of her life. If you are having panic attacks like Delia, you might want to focus less on the anxiety you are feeling and take a look at what you believe, too. If you can come to a new understanding of your anxiety and apply that understanding with wisdom, then, like Delia, you will be able to "say to wisdom, 'You are my sister,' and call understanding your intimate friend."

45

Living Lives of Quiet Desperation

Jonathan came to see me because of his anxiety. He was troubled by the fact that he had a good life, but he couldn't stop thinking negative thoughts anyway. He is a handsome man, well educated and happily married. On the surface, you wouldn't think Jonathan would have anything to be concerned about, but appearances can be deceiving.

Jonathan was the only child of the chancellor of a highly regarded university, and his mother had a master's degree in philosophy, but she stayed at home full-time to raise him. His father had a very distinguished career, and Jonathan was very proud to be his son. Jonathan spent quite a bit of time with his mother, which made them very close. He remembers many philosophical conversations he had with his mother when he was growing up. I know he was grateful for the closeness in their relationship, but I'm not so sure *all* of those conversations were in his best interest.

"I just can't stop having these negative images," Jonathan shared with me in one of our sessions.

"Tell me about them," I said.

"It's terrible," he said. "I can't even watch the news anymore because I keep thinking that something like that is going to happen to my family. All the tragedy, car crashes, and murders. The world appears to be a really horrible place if you watch the news. Why do they have to show all that stuff?"

"The evening news is pretty grim," I said. "So, what does it do to you?"

"It makes me imagine horrible things happening to my own children," he gasped. "Why would I do that? I love my kids, and the worst thing in the world would be for me to not be able to protect them. We have such a great life. Why would I get such negative thoughts about something so precious to me?"

The human imagination expresses in images what it cannot express in words. Jonathan was having automatic negative images because he had negative feelings that he didn't know how to talk about. One of the goals of our time together would be to get to those feelings and express them, so they wouldn't have to come out in such troubling imagery.

Jonathan told me that even though he was grateful for his life, he lived with a vague feeling of unhappiness. He called it his *ennui*. He wasn't overtly unhappy, but he wasn't content, either. We traced the roots of his feeling back to his conversations with his mother.

Looking back on it now, Jonathan could tell that she was not happy that she had given up her career as a philosophy professor, and she was frustrated in her role as a housewife, so she adopted a philosophical nihilism in her perspective on life. She was skeptical about everything and believed that all human values and religions were baseless and ultimately meaningless. This might be an interesting conversation to have with other academics around the university, but it was not a healthy way to talk to your nine-year-old son. When young children are required to deal with things that are developmentally beyond their reach, their natural process of development gets thwarted. Although Jonathan's mother thought she was helping him develop beyond his years by exposing him to her philosophies, she was actually handing to him her own hopelessness and despair.

Jonathan is getting some freedom from his negative images these days, because we are getting to the root of his unhappiness. He wasn't really anxious about what was going to happen to him or his children; he was anxious about what had already happened to him long ago. He actually feels completely adequate to care for his family; it's just that he felt completely inadequate to take care of his mother's despair. He found that his *ennui* was the result of his attempts to avoid the unhappiness of his childhood, which was hampering his attempts to pursue happiness in his own family now.

Some people live lives of quiet desperation because they are not pursuing happiness; they are attempting to escape despair. As a result, they have lives for which they could be grateful, but they don't live them happily.

The Bible contains lots of stories of people with problems and difficulties. Many of the heroes of the Bible made poor choices and had tragedies to deal with, much like what Jonathan observed on the evening news. This is because the Bible is a real book about real people who lived real lives. It doesn't sugarcoat life; it describes it as having both joy and pain.

But God's perspective on life is a hopeful one. The Bible teaches us that values and religion are meaningful. You can choose which philosophy of life to follow for yourself. You can follow the nihilism of those who live lives of quiet desperation, or you can choose the hopefulness of the Bible. "'For I know the plans I have for you,' declares the LORD, 'plans to prosper you and not to harm you, plans to give you hope and a future'" (Jer. 29:11). Jonathan is choosing the latter more often now, and he is happier every day that he does.

46

Why People Worry

Worry is the illusion of potency for the impotent. It is a strategy for dealing with anxiety when you don't know what else to do. You worry when you are troubled and anxious about something, and you imagine what might happen or what might be done to deal with the situation. Sometimes worry is an attempt to imagine the worst-case scenario, and by preparing yourself for the worst you are ready to deal with the source of your anxiety. Worry anticipates a negative future in hopes of keeping it from happening. This, of course, is magical thinking.

Although worry is negative, you are not trying to be harmful when you do it. Worry gives you the sense that you are doing something about a problem, even when there doesn't appear to be anything to do. Worry gives you the sense that you are a good person because you are trying to do something about a bad situation by worrying about it. You don't worry because you are trying to be unhelpful; you worry because you feel powerless.

"I guess I'm just a worrier," Samuel said with a smile.

"Really?" I responded.

"Yes," he continued with a singsong tone in his voice. "I've always been that way. I can't help it. I just worry about the people I love."

"And does that help?"

"Oh, I don't know," he replied, still keeping a falsetto quality in his voice. "I know I shouldn't worry, but you know, it's hard not to care about those who are close to you."

Although Samuel insisted that he worried for the ones he loved, I wondered if he worried for other reasons. He knew intellectually that worry doesn't change anything, but he agonized over details of problematic situations for hours on end. At first I thought it gave him something to do now that he was retired. At least in his mind he was thinking about his loved ones, and even if he was being negative, he thought to himself, *Isn't it good to keep loved ones in mind?*

Over time I saw that Samuel's worry wasn't really born out of his love; it was the product of his powerlessness. Samuel was troubled about the difficult circumstances in his life and the lives of his loved ones, but he didn't feel that he had the power to make anything happen. It wasn't that Samuel *was* actually powerless, because he was intelligent and capable in many ways. It was that Samuel *believed* he was powerless. This was the root of his constant worrying.

God tells us that worrying is a useless activity. You can't "add a single hour to your life" by doing it. But in Samuel's case, it was worse than useless. It contributed to his belief that he was powerless, which perpetuated his tendency to worry. Samuel was addicted to worry because it made him feel good about himself temporarily, but it reinforced his feelings of powerlessness at the same time. Addictive cycles such as this are very difficult to break.

The next time you catch yourself worrying, ask yourself a question: *Do I feel powerless?* If you do, you might want to consider asking God to help you change that. He has a different view of you and what you can do about your circumstances that you might find helpful: "For the kingdom of God is not a matter of talk but of power" (1 Cor. 4:20).

47

The Antidote to Anxiety

Anxiety signals you to prepare for stress ahead. It is an important part of life. There is no cure for it. But because anxiety can be overwhelming at times, there is an antidote. An antidote is a remedy you can use to neutralize the effects of something that is toxic. It doesn't cure the problem, but it counteracts the negative effects.

This is an important distinction to make, because trying to *rid* yourself of anxiety generally makes it worse. You were not designed to live an anxiety-free life, but it does need to be within a certain range to be helpful. God designed the world so that you can live an active, powerful life, which brings both anxiety and joy. It takes some wisdom to know how to do this.

Sophia came to therapy because she suffered from irritable bowel syndrome (IBS). This is a medical condition that causes stomach cramping and abdominal pain, which results in constipation and diarrhea. Sophia was afraid to go to restaurants or attend large public gatherings for fear of having to go to the bathroom and being embarrassed. Although she pretended not to be, she was anxious about it almost all the time. She consulted several physicians about it and tried to have a positive attitude, but she still couldn't control herself. This was a humiliating condition that she never spoke about to anyone, so she thought she should come to therapy to try to deal with the distress it was causing her.

"It happened to me again last night," Sophia said with frustration.

"It did?"

"Yes," she said. "We were on our way to my son's house for dinner. We haven't seen him for quite some time, and I was so looking forward to it. I was afraid it was going to happen, and it did. I think I must have eaten something for lunch that didn't agree with me. I was perfectly fine, and then out of nowhere I had another attack. This is so frustrating!"

"What happened?"

"We turned around and went home. Thank goodness we had only gone a few blocks," she said sadly. Sophia was exasperated with how chronic her condition had become.

"I can't go anywhere if I don't know there is a bathroom right where I can get to it," she lamented. "I should have known not to try to go to a dinner party. We called and said I had another headache. This is so exhausting."

Sophia had a medical condition, and she was receiving good medical care from her physician for it. But her condition was being exacerbated by how she was dealing with her anxiety. Sophia had the fantasy that if she could rid herself of painful feelings, then she would be okay. Even though trying to make her anxiety go away worked temporarily at times, over time it was making her even more anxious. It was not possible for her to expunge anxiety from her life. Sophia needed to understand her feelings, not get rid of them.

After many months, Sophia and I came to a different approach toward her problem. We came to see that her physical problems were a concrete example of how she was trying to deal with her emotional problems. She saw her anxious feelings as disgusting, and she wanted to rid herself of them. Because this is not completely possible, her body took over and would try to get rid of everything else disgusting inside of her instead. Sophia needed to stop trying to fight her feelings, even the painful and distressing ones. She needed to see them as her friends, telling her something that she needed to know. Sometimes our friends warn us of stressful times ahead. This is not something to rid ourselves of; it is something to listen to and heed.

Sophia's IBS symptoms are much less frequent today. She still gets stomachaches, but when she does, she takes a different approach to them. Sometimes the cause is something she ate. But more often she is feeling something that she needs to pay attention to, not get rid of. The more she talks about her distressing feelings and faces them openly, the less physically distressed she feels in her body.

Sophia is grateful for this change in her life. But this is not the most important change she has noticed. More importantly, she is more joyful. She discovered that she has anxiety about lots of things other than her IBS; in fact, we rarely talk about it anymore. She has anxieties about her relationships and her career. She has anxieties about her retirement and her children. But the more we talk about these anxieties and face them, the stronger she feels about herself. Sophia found that facing the trials in her life made her a stronger person, while trying to rid herself of her anxiety was just making things worse.

God cares about your anxieties. He doesn't promise that they will ever go away, but he does give you a strategy for dealing with them. Your trials don't have to diminish your joy in life if you have the wisdom to face them openly with God and others. Don't try to rid yourself of your anxieties, but face them as opportunities to develop your strength of character. King David had the courage to present his concerns to God when he said, "Search me, God, and know my heart; test me and know my anxious thoughts" (Ps. 139:23). It is this kind of courage to look honestly at the root of your anxiety with the help of God and others that can most empower you to deal with it. This isn't intended to cure your anxiety, but it is an excellent antidote.

PART FIVE

Sorrow

48

What Does It Mean to Be Sad?

As I mentioned in the last section on anxiety, I have also found that whether you're suffering from a common sadness or a clinical depression, what you *believe* about your sorrow plays an important role in how much you suffer. Sometimes the intensity of your sadness doesn't determine the degree of your suffering as much as what it *means* to you to be sad.

Isabella is an educated woman who has a good job and several friends. She is very likable and kind to everyone she meets. She is involved in her church and successful at her job. But Isabella has a problem. She suffers from depression. She hates it, but at times her depression overtakes her life. When her depression becomes serious, she even thinks about taking her own life. She knows it isn't a godly response to her pain, but sometimes she just can't help thinking about suicide.

When Isabella first came to see me for psychotherapy, she had already seen several therapists for help with her depression. She tried very hard in each of her previous therapies, but she couldn't stop the feelings. She hated the fact that she got so depressed, even though she believed that God could deliver her from any circumstance.

"If only I could stop feeling this way," she said in one of our first sessions. "I know it isn't what God wants for my life. If only I trusted God more."

"So you see your depression as a lack of faith?" I asked.

"Of course," she replied emphatically. "I just need to try harder to be pleasing to God."

Over the next several months, we discovered that Isabella's problem wasn't a lack of faith or willpower but a lack of awareness about what she believed about herself for suffering from depression. Isabella not only hated feeling depressed, but she hated *herself* for being depressed. She saw her depression as a sign of spiritual weakness. Intellectually she could read the Bible and see that there is "a time to weep," but unconsciously she didn't believe that at all. In Isabella's thinking, to be as sad as she was revealed to everyone that she was a spiritual failure.

During our first several months of therapy, Isabella often became depressed and wanted to call me. But she fought off this feeling of dependency on me and tried to conquer her feelings of depression by herself.

"I shouldn't have to call Dr. Baker about this," she said to herself. "I should be strong enough to not feel so sad." But this strategy rarely worked. Isabella then became disappointed about the fact that her efforts to rid herself of her sadness were unsuccessful. Now she was saddened not only by her original depression, but also by her failed attempt to stop her painful feelings. This would escalate into intense feelings of shame and depression that spiraled into suicidal ideation. This downward spiral of sadness leading to disappointment leading to greater sadness was a vicious cycle for Isabella. This made her hate sadness. And for Isabella, her hatred of her own sadness became a bigger problem than the sadness itself.

After many months of working on her depression, Isabella still feels sad from time to time, but she experiences it differently today. We were eventually able to break her downward cycle of sadness leading to shame, which then only led to deeper sadness. Today, Isabella's depression isn't nearly as intense because she no longer hates herself for feeling sad. She understands that the intensity of her sadness isn't as big a problem as what it *means* to her to be sad.

The Bible teaches that there is a time to be sad. There's a time for every feeling. If we decide that having sadness means something bad, and we try too hard to get rid of it out of self-hatred, then we can get into trouble. The wisdom of the Bible is that there is a purpose for every feeling we have. In terms of our sorrow, if we work through the sad times, then we make room for the times to laugh.

49

Grief: The Sorrow of Saying Good-bye

One of the most common reasons for sorrow is loss. When you lose something or someone important to you, the natural response is to feel the sorrow of grief. The paradox of grief is that it feels bad, but it is actually good. It is the way you prepare yourself for future attachments. Grief clears room in your heart for future love. Because it feels bad, you may think something is wrong when you feel intense grief. But you are actually engaged in a healthy process of closure on a part of your life that you will no longer have with you. Grief is the sorrow of saying good-bye.

Grief is not clinical depression. The process of grief is to feel denial, anger, bargaining, depression, and then acceptance. But sometimes the process gets derailed, and you may get caught in the depression phase and not be able to get out of it. If this happens, you may need special help to get through your process of grief. Don't be afraid to ask for help if this happens to you. But if all goes well, the process of grief will take its natural course and you will eventually find your way to accepting your loss. This could last from a few weeks to a few years, but if you work through the process of grief, the sorrow of saying good-bye eventually lessens over time.

Jimmy was the eldest son in a strongly religious family with established cultural values. He grew up, became successful, and was looked to by the entire family to take care of his parents and his younger brother who suffered from a severe disability from birth. His life's mission was to make his parents proud and to serve God. He was a leader in his church and lived a frugal life so that he could support others less fortunate. He said, "I live simply so that others might simply live." He was generous and never complained about his life of service to God, his family, and others.

Two years before I met Jimmy, his mother became seriously ill and died of complications in the hospital. Then his elderly father died shortly thereafter. His mission in life now became to care for his brother and support him into old age. Jimmy moved his brother in with him and cared for him daily. He got him involved in church activities whenever he could and structured his life for him in a way that helped his brother improve and function at a higher level than he had ever done before. Jimmy was delighted with his progress, and he often thought that his parents would be proud.

Then, quite suddenly, his two closest friends died: one in a car accident and the other from a fast-acting form of cancer. His support system of fifteen years had been wiped out within a few months. Then, a month later, his brother died in his sleep.

Having never considered therapy before, Jimmy was brought to my consultation room on his knees.

"This is too much," Jimmy cried in our first session.

"I know," I said quietly.

"How could God let this happen?" he asked.

"I don't know," I replied.

"I've tried to share my grief with others at the church, but I can't stand to be told one more time that God is in control. It doesn't feel like it to me," Jimmy said indignantly.

"How could it?" I said.

"I don't care what their motives are. Christians are useless to me right now. I've been faithful and I tried to be obedient. How could God be so unfair?" he said as he wept.

Not all grief is as complicated as Jimmy's. But all grief hurts. He lost too many people and suffered from too much disappointment all at once. Jimmy felt like Job: "When I lie down I think, 'How long before I get up?' The night drags on, and I toss and turn until dawn."[1]

As awful as he felt, Jimmy's intense grief was actually a normal response to an abnormal situation. Anyone would have been brought to their knees in his situation. Anyone would have been depressed. It was not a lack of faith that brought Jimmy to my consultation room; it was the presence of pain that he could not bear alone.

Because Jimmy believed in a personal God who loved him and promised to care for him, he was struggling with how God could allow him to suffer so much. For God to be loving and to allow such suffering was a contradiction that caused Jimmy even more pain than the grief he was experiencing over his losses.

Intense misery disconnects you from the sense that life is meaningful, and it makes you feel very alone. Jimmy's intense grief made him feel that no one could understand, not even God. But somehow my being with him and listening to his pain helped Jimmy process his grief. Very slowly we moved along the process of grief together.

Although it took several months, Jimmy eventually improved. His depression lifted somewhat, and his despair was gradually replaced with the beginnings of a hope that he could have a new mission for his life. Jimmy is still struggling with intense grief at times when anything reminds him of one of his lost loved ones, especially his brother. But that is because his heart is still trying to process the loss of so much love in his life. And in doing so, Jimmy is preparing himself to love again.

50

Sadness of the Heart

Clinical depression is a serious form of sadness. There are two basic types. The first is called *reactive depression*. This form of depression results from circumstances in one's life that create a depressed mood. This can range from a mild sadness to an extreme loss of pleasure, fatigue, and the hopeless feeling of depression. The second type of depression is called *endogenous depression*. This is when a chemical reaction in a person's body results in depression that may have nothing to do with one's circumstances at all. This form of depression also ranges from mild to quite severe. In either case, some form of antidepressant medication may be necessary in conjunction with psychotherapy to help you.

Clinical depression is a sadness that comes directly out of the heart. It is not a weakness or a lack of faith that causes this kind of sadness; it is a physical condition that is simply the result of your particular biology and circumstances. You are not responsible for causing it, but you are responsible for seeking help.

Noah is the strong, silent type. He is hardworking and honest, the kind of guy you know you can depend upon. He stays in good physical shape and likes to read to keep himself informed. Respect is important to Noah, and everyone who knows him holds him in high esteem.

Noah has had a difficult life. He was adopted as a child, and his adoptive father was strict and often unkind. Noah couldn't wait to move away from home, so as soon as he turned eighteen, he left. Out of sheer determination, Noah made a success of himself in life. He overcame his difficult upbringing, but it wasn't easy.

Although Noah has been able to conquer most of the difficulties in his life, there is one thing that he has been powerless to defeat. Noah suffers from a lifetime of clinical depression. For as long as he can remember, he has struggled with insomnia, agitation, and overwhelming sadness. He often feels depressed and hopeless, and despite his accomplishments, he struggles with feelings of worthlessness and excessive guilt. He's fought off a lifetime of constant fatigue and frequent bouts of losing interest in doing anything that might make him happy in life. It is often hard for him to concentrate when he feels this low, and he even gets thoughts of suicide when the feelings get really bad.

Noah has tried almost every antidepressant medication ever made. Very few of them have been helpful. Fortunately, he finally found one that relieved his symptoms. He tried to go off his medication several times, but he became extremely depressed each time. Because Noah is adopted, he doesn't know anything about his biological parents, and he doesn't know if any of his relatives also suffered from depression. He just knows that in spite of years of therapy and hard work on trying to combat his depression, he just can't make it go away for good.

Noah's condition is somewhat unusual. Most people who need antidepressant medication feel better over time and can eventually stop using it. Noah can't. There are those people whose biology makes it necessary for them to take medication for a long time in order for the chemical imbalance in their brains to get corrected. In Noah's case it took several years. I am hopeful that through our work together he may someday not need as much medication as he does now. But for now, the medication helps him feel good enough for us to do our work. Without it, he wouldn't be able to function at all.

Endogenous depression is an inherited form of clinical depression. It is nothing to be ashamed of, but most people who have it are anyway. For people like Noah, it is a physical condition that they were born with, and it isn't their fault. Fortunately, we can do something about it. God made each of us in a mysterious and wonderful way. It is important for you to understand exactly how God has made you individually, especially if you are someone like Noah who suffers from this form of sadness of the heart.

If you suffer from clinical depression like Noah, then you need professional help. This is a disease that can be treated, and even in the most difficult cases, a combination of psychotherapy and medication usually helps. Don't try to force yourself to feel better; seek out the help you need to actually get better.

51

Wrestling with Sad Thoughts

Depression causes you to misinterpret things. You can't help it. When you become depressed, your thoughts turn negative. No matter how hard you try, you think in depressive ways that will make you even more depressed. Depression is hard enough, but having to wrestle with your thoughts can make it almost unbearable.

There are a few negative tendencies that come up frequently when you feel depressed. The first is *catastrophizing*. This is when you turn a small mishap into a calamity in your mind. Something that is simply unfortunate becomes an unmitigated catastrophe. Depression makes things seem worse than they actually are.

The second thing you might do is *personalize* things. This is when someone says something that is not directed toward you personally, but you take it that way anyhow. Everything doesn't relate to you, but when you are depressed you can't help thinking that it does. Taking things personally makes them hurt more. Of course, this doesn't help your depression.

Two other things you might do are *jump to conclusions* and utilize *all-or-nothing thinking*. This means you are making assumptions that other people might not be making, and then you are making things extremely black and white when they aren't. Concentration is difficult when you are depressed, so you may be tempted to think in shorthanded ways about things. But shorter is not always better. You may think you know where other people are going with their thinking, but let them finish so you don't jump to any conclusions. There are a lot of nuances in life, but depression makes it harder for you to sort them out. If you are feeling depressed, you may be wrestling with your thoughts in ways that you wouldn't if you weren't feeling so sad.

Amanda came to therapy after her father died. She was close to him, and even though she had moved away from home years ago, they stayed in close contact. It is a sad thing to lose someone close to you. Fortunately, Amanda's relationship with her father was a good one, and although the pain of losing him was intense, it wasn't complicated with a lot of regrets or unfinished business. Amanda needed to do her grief work and process her feelings surrounding the death of her father, which would take some time. But because she had a good relationship with her father, this type of grief work is usually straightforward and resolved over time.

As it turned out, Amanda's problem wasn't really with her grief over her father's death. She eventually came to accept the loss of her father and moved on to sad but positive feelings about him.

However, we did discover that she had a good deal of unfinished business with her mother, who was still alive. Her mother had been judgmental and punitive with her growing up, and now that her father was gone, she was forced to develop a one-on-one relationship with her. This turned out to be depressing.

"We used to call her the lizard lady," she whispered in one session.

"Who?" I asked.

"My mom," she continued. "My brother and I would call her the lizard lady behind her back."

"How come?"

"You know, lizards are kind of scary and coldblooded," she said. "You don't think of them as having any feelings. That's my mom."

Amanda had not only been deprived of the warmth and nurture she needed from her mother, but she had been invalidated by her for having these needs in the first place. She was a sensitive child who felt punished for being that way. I was so moved by the contradiction between her longing to be cared for by her mother and her mother's cold, invalidating response that I responded with a look of surprise on my face. *How could any mother be so unloving?* I thought to myself.

"You think I'm awful," she blurted out.

"I do?" I asked, still somewhat surprised.

"I saw that look on your face. I know what that means. You think I'm an ungrateful daughter for saying such terrible things about my mother after how hard she worked to take care of our family," she said, now in tears.

And that's how most of our sessions would go. She would offer an intimate insight into her feelings, I would have a reaction (sometimes ever so slightly), and she would assume I was personally attacking her and drawing catastrophic conclusions about her character in very negative ways. Amanda was depressed and she couldn't help thinking this way. It wasn't fun for either of us, but it was important that we work these thoughts and feelings through.

Amanda still jumps to conclusions about things at times, but not as much. We are able to examine her automatic conclusions and trace them back to her feelings and mine. Just because I was having a reaction didn't mean it had to be a negative one about her. Human interactions are rarely all-or-nothing and neither all good nor all bad. They are usually a mixture of both. After a while, she began to entertain a more flexible way of thinking. And as she did, she became less depressed.

God made us with the wonderful capacity for thinking. Life is more meaningful because of it. But when we are depressed, we wrestle with our thoughts in negative ways. This capacity for thinking can actually work against us when we are depressed, causing us to catastrophize, take things personally, and jump to all-or-nothing conclusions. Fortunately, we can use this same remarkable ability for thinking to work through the depression that causes us to wrestle with these sad thoughts.

52

Anger Turned Inward

Anger turned inward produces sadness. There are many reasons why you may not want to express your anger: it is not socially acceptable; you feel out of control; or perhaps you just don't like it. But if you are in the habit of not expressing your anger in healthy ways then you are running the risk of turning your anger inward, which can result in a deep form of sadness.

Charles grew up in a small rural town in Arkansas where arguments were often settled with fistfights. He didn't talk about it often, but he remembers one incident of getting into a disagreement with some neighboring boys that led to a fistfight, which escalated to throwing rocks, which escalated to BB guns, and finally ended with small-caliber rifle fire and the local sheriff intervening. But then Charles grew up and moved to a large metropolitan city where he became a successful engineer in a much more sophisticated society. Because he was good at what he did, he kept getting promoted to positions of greater authority. But just because you are good at what you do doesn't mean you will like managing other people who do what you do, too.

Charles was a shy man, and he didn't like having to deal with large groups of people. But because he kept advancing up the ladder of success, he was given more and more responsibility over others. This made his life increasingly stressful. When he would have conflicts at work, he couldn't settle them as he did growing up in the woods of Arkansas. He had to negotiate his feelings in refined, articulate ways. Charles just wasn't used to doing that.

Charles often came home from work mumbling to himself and shuffling around the house. After dinner he positioned himself on the couch in front of the television and sat there all evening smoking cigarettes until long after everyone else went to bed. He usually didn't say much, and no one in his family would try to engage him, either. They all knew he was mad, but no one knew what to do about it.

It's not that Charles would never express his anger—quite the contrary. He often exploded into a rage over the smallest of things. But he never felt any better because of it. You might think that "getting it off your chest" would help someone when they lived with a lot of anger inside, but it didn't. Charles needed to get to whatever it was that was hurting him, so his hurt would last "only for a little while," but that never happened. He fumed about the hurts and frustrations that angered him, never came up with a good way to express them, and ended most of his days almost bent over with a sadness that wouldn't go away.

I talked a lot about anger earlier in the book, but the point I want to make here is that anger turned inward leads to sadness. And the *habit* of turning your anger inward leads to depression. Charles was in the grip of this habit, and he never got out of it. He died at the age of sixty-five, just when he retired. He might have wanted it that way. He said once, "I don't want to grow old and be a burden on society." He felt sad about his life, and it was hard for him to enjoy it. He never learned how to express his anger in healthy ways, and the habit of turning it inward made him depressed, perhaps too sad to live a long and happy life.

When the apostle Paul wrote to the church in Corinth, he had some painful things to say. These things were designed to help his readers become better Christians, but sometimes he hurt and even angered them with his comments. Paul was aware that hurt and anger can lead to a productive sorrow if these feelings are "only for a little while." If they are turned inward chronically, then a more protracted sadness in the form of a severe depression can result.

53

Can You Have Faith but Lose Hope?

It is a tragedy to lose hope. It is different from losing faith. It's more depressing. If you have faith, you believe that something is possible. You keep trying because you know things can get better. If you lose faith, then you stop trying and you probably will even stop caring. Life may feel meaningless, but you probably won't care.

But hopelessness is crushing. You may still have faith that good things are possible and that you should keep trying because of it. But when you lose hope, then you stop believing good things are possible for you. It's torturous to have faith that God is good and loving but lose hope that his goodness and love apply to your life. You may still believe that God and help are there, but only for others, not for you. To have faith without hope is very, very sad.

Irene grew up waiting to leave home. She hoped if she could only survive until she was old enough to go to college, then her life would get better. Her parents were abusive and controlling. She couldn't wait to leave home. Then her *real* life could begin.

When Irene finally did leave home, things got better. She never had to see her parents again, and she could confront them from a distance about their inappropriate behavior. If they got angry and started to abuse her again, she would simply hang up. Being able to stop their abuse did make her life better.

Irene went to college, became a Christian, and graduated to find a good job in a nice area of town. Many things changed for her and almost all of them for the better. Irene had every reason to believe that she could be happy in life. But Irene wasn't happy. In fact, Irene finally came to therapy because she couldn't escape a chronic sadness that wouldn't go away.

"It's probably a sin to feel as bad as I do about my life," she said as she slumped down in her seat.

"You think it's sinful to be sad?" I asked.

"It is when you're a Christian who has a good job, owns her own home, and could make anything of her life she wanted. The Bible says all I have to do is believe," she snapped back.

"So you think your problem is a lack of faith?"

"Isn't it a lack of faith to know God and still feel this depressed?" she wondered as she looked up at me through the strands of hair covering her face.

"Not in your case," I said. "I don't think your problem is a lack of faith. I think you are suffering from a lack of hope."

"What?" she asked in a surprised tone.

"You have never stopped believing in God. You have just stopped hoping that what he has to offer applies to you," I replied.

Irene was suffering from what the ancient mystics have called the "dark night of the soul." She believed that God brings about good things in the lives of those who love him, but she had experienced so much disappointment in life that she couldn't allow herself to hope that those good things would happen to her. If she didn't let herself hope, then she wouldn't be disappointed again.

Irene learned to postpone happiness as a child. There was no hope that things were going to change then. Her parents were in control, and there was nothing she could do about it. Paradoxically, this strategy helped her survive her childhood, but it was getting in the way of happiness in her adult life. Prohibiting herself from hope helped her endure the chronic disappointment then. Prohibiting herself from hope was crushing the life out of her now.

As a result of our honest conversations about her feelings, Irene is gradually becoming less depressed. In her case, it isn't because she has greater faith, but because she is taking the risk to have greater hope. She sees that she isn't as trapped as she was as a child, and while it is risky to trust that she could really be happy, she is improving her quality of life by allowing herself to hope for it. Irene learned what it means to be "sorrowful, yet always rejoicing" in her life. She can be sad about the circumstances in her life, but still have a sense of joy that comes from the hope that things can get better.

54

Overcoming the Lie
That You're Worthless

Depression changes how you feel about yourself. It makes you think you should be able to "snap out of it" and makes you feel guilty for feeling so bad—especially when you don't seem to have any good reason for it. If you are in the grips of depression, you could be overwhelmed with excessive sorrow that distorts your perception of yourself in some negative way. Depression can make you feel worthless.

Worthlessness can arise in many ways when you are depressed. It can come from feeling useless and unproductive. Or it can come from not being able to do things up to the standards you think you should be doing. And even if you are able to keep doing things, you might still feel that what you are doing just doesn't have any value to anyone. Sure, you do your job, but does anyone really care about *you*? Depression can make you conclude that the answer is *no!*

Tom is an energetic and likable guy. He is a successful business-man at a medium-sized company, and he is very good at his job. His boss treats him well, and everyone respects him. Most of the people who work for him say they learn a lot from him, but they are often afraid they don't measure up to his standards for quality work. He is pleasant about it, but Tom doesn't feel people are as conscientious as he is about almost everything.

Although he doesn't look it, Tom is actually somewhat de-pressed. He suffers from what is called a *smiling* depression. He will look right at you with a *painted-on* smile on his face and tell you that he's "fine," but somehow you just don't believe him. He is anxious most of the time, making him look more agitated than depressed. But inside he is quite sad. It isn't because he isn't accomplishing anything; it's because he feels like nothing he does, no matter how good it is, really matters.

"I read a book the other day by that radio psychologist," he said as we started off a recent session.

"Really, which one?" I asked.

"The one about taking control of your life. He says if I start doing one self-affirming thing each day, I can improve my self-esteem. I just have to get focused," he said hopefully.

"How does that feel?"

"What do you mean?" he responded in a surprised tone.

"I mean, when you think about doing one self-affirming thing each day, how does that make you feel?" I repeated.

"I don't know," he mumbled. "I mean, I guess I'll feel better."

"Have you been doing it?"

"Yes," he replied.

"So, how has it been making you feel?" I wanted to know.

"Well, it makes me feel like I'm doing something. I don't know, I guess now that we're talking about it, I don't really feel any better yet. But maybe if I just keep trying it might make a difference . . . ," he said as his voice trailed off.

But it didn't really make Tom feel any better. He had tried many approaches to making himself feel better in the past, and those ended unsuccessfully, as well. Tom didn't really believe he needed to *do* things differently; he believed he needed to *be* different. His problem wasn't with what he was *doing*; it was with his *self-worth*.

The kind of sorrow that Tom was battling wasn't going to be changed by focusing on doing things better. He already was doing things pretty well in many areas of his life. This type of sorrow was going to be healed by feeling loved for who he was. He needed to feel accepted as a flawed, sad, and sometimes unlovable person. At least that is who he felt he was. Adding another thing to the list of things that he was doing would only get him more of the same thing in his life: appreciation for how well he could do things. But his feelings of worthlessness were only going to change when he felt loved for being the man he was. Would anyone find any value in him if he wasn't doing so much? He was afraid that a man as sad as him simply had no worth.

Worthlessness is one of the key aspects of depression that causes it to be so crippling to people. The intense feeling of sadness is hard enough to endure. But when you add to that the feeling of worthlessness, then excessive sorrow becomes overwhelming.

Tom started to feel better about himself, and not as sad, when he began to take the focus off of his performance and placed it on how he felt about himself. He discovered that if he could talk about his sad feelings with me and we could make sense out of them together, then he felt a little better about himself. If I could see him at his worst and we could find some value in exploring how he felt about his life, then maybe he wasn't worthless. Maybe he didn't have to perform for God and others to have value. Perhaps he had value for being who he was, having the character and qualities that he did, and even though he was often sad, he was still good enough to add some value to the world. Tom made room for the fact that while his efforts made him a useful person in the world, just being with me and telling me about who he was had value in his life, too.

The wisdom of the Bible is that the treatment for someone who is "overwhelmed by excessive sorrow" is "to reaffirm your love for him." This gives that person the feeling of being valuable. God knows there are times when you are overwhelmed by excessive sorrow, and the healing for the feeling of worthlessness that comes with it will not come from doing things better but from being loved for who you are.

55

Dealing with Loneliness

Jesus felt lonely. It's not a sin if you do. There is a disturbing difference between being alone and feeling lonely. Loneliness is a painful feeling of sadness that makes being alone feel despondent. Being able to be alone and feel content is a good thing. But feeling lonely can be miserable.

The capacity to be alone in a peaceful way is part of how we develop a secure sense of self. If you can be alone and feel okay about it, you probably like the person you are spending time with—you. But after a while loneliness stimulates you to seek out relationships with others. It reminds you that while being alone can be a good thing, you were not created to live that way forever. Your loneliness reminds you that you are a relational person. Just like Jesus, sometimes you might feel so lonely that you need to say to others, "Stay here and keep watch with me."

"I hate eating alone in my apartment," Kathy moaned.

"It feels different eating there?" I asked.

"Yeah," she replied. "I mean, I would rather go out to a restaurant and eat there than stay home."

"What does it mean for you to eat at home alone?"

Kathy didn't respond right away. After a few minutes of shifting quietly in her chair, she mumbled, "It means I'm a loser."

"Really?"

"Yeah. All the normal people have someone to come home to, but not me. Why does everyone else seem to find someone, but I can't make a relationship work? Eating alone at home makes me feel all screwed up," Kathy said, looking down at her feet.

Kathy actually liked being alone at times. She planned vacations alone, went to fun restaurants alone, and would often go to museums or walks on the beach by herself and have a pleasant time. If Kathy didn't feel lonely, then being alone was just fine.

But being alone doesn't determine whether or not you feel lonely. In fact, you can be in a crowd of people and feel lonely. And feeling lonely can range from an uncomfortable feeling to something quite painful. For Kathy, feeling lonely had become painful because of how it made her feel about herself. When Kathy felt lonely it made her feel unlovable.

Kathy feared loneliness, and fear and love don't go well together. When she felt lonely at home, she would become afraid that it meant there was something wrong with her. She would think, *I should be married* or *I should have more friends*, and start to doubt whether anyone really loved her—whether anyone *could* love her.

Kathy eventually saw that her biggest problem with loneliness was her fear that it meant something bad about her. Exploring this fear from many different angles helped change Kathy's problem with loneliness. She still has doubts about herself, but she doesn't automatically assume that feeling lonely means she is an unlovable loser. She doesn't like feeling lonely, but it isn't as immobilizing as it was in the past. Because she doesn't fear it as much as she used to, she can actually think of things to do to reach out to others when she feels lonely. That makes the feeling not as bad.

Being alone and even feeling lonely can be good things. You can contemplate things deeply when you are alone, and sort out your thoughts and feelings. And feeling lonely can be the sign that you need to reach out to others. Just like we need punctuation points in sentences to signal the coming of new meanings, loneliness can be the still moments (like punctuation points) between the meaningful activities of relating to others. Even Jesus had moments of loneliness that made him seek out the company of others. Your loneliness can do the same for you.

56

How to Deal with Suicidal Thoughts

Suicidal ideation is a serious problem for people who are clinically depressed. It is important to understand that depression can cause thoughts of hurting yourself and even thoughts of death. Depression can make people who don't really want to die consider suicide as an option to solve their problems.

A severe depression results in the loss of pleasure in just about everything. You can't sleep, you can't eat, and you can't think straight anymore. Everything feels bad, and you feel like there is nothing you can do about it. This loss of control over your own happiness can make the idea of taking your own life pop into your head. You aren't intentionally making yourself think this thought; it just comes to you. Tragically, thousands of people every year get the idea that if they were to take their own lives, they would be taking back the control of their lives from their depression. In their depressed way of thinking, if you kill yourself, you at least have control of whether or not you are alive.

Amy came to see me for therapy after many years of suffering from depression. She had seen several therapists before, but no one helped her very much. Amy is introverted, and she has very few friends. She had never had a serious boyfriend, and she had never been able to succeed in any career path. Amy often has thoughts that the world might be better off without her.

"I felt pretty bad this weekend," she whispered at the beginning of one of our sessions. Her hair was covering her face as she picked at the back of her hand in her lap.

"You were feeling depressed?" I said.

"Yes," she replied, not looking up.

"Did you think about hurting yourself?" I asked calmly. I had learned with Amy it was best to ask directly about suicidal thoughts. I wasn't worried about giving her the idea. I knew that severe depression causes suicidal ideation, and it is a bad idea to try to avoid it.

"Yes," she said again.

"What did you do?"

"I drove to the motel. You know, the one I go to," she said flatly.

"Did you take your pills?"

"I had them with me, but I didn't take them," she replied, this time looking at me with one eye between the strands of hair hanging down.

"I'm glad. You know our agreement," I said gratefully.

"I know. I promised I would call you first if I was going to take them. I just thought about it; I didn't do anything. I didn't want to have to call you, so I didn't take them," she said.

"I appreciate that. We're in this together, and I'm glad you are keeping your end of our agreement," I said, slightly relieved.

Unfortunately, this was not the first exchange like this between us in our early months of therapy together. Amy felt very out of control in her life. She had had very few happy memories or good relationships throughout her life. From childhood on, Amy felt like she was just an object to be used by others and discarded when they were done with her. To her, suicide was the logical solution to a lifetime of feeling powerless. She could control the pain by ending it once and for all. In her depressed and distorted thinking, psychological control was more important than physical survival. She wanted to have the last say about her life. She wanted some shred of control.

Through many months of psychotherapy and the use of some helpful antidepressants, Amy stopped going to the motel where she would consider taking her own life. And in time, her thoughts of suicide faded away altogether. After many sessions and many phone calls between us, Amy came to feel differently about her life. She still gets depressed, but she can see there are options other than suicide available to her. One of the things she can do is talk to me about her painful feelings, and together we can make sense of them. If I can understand her in her most confused and shameful moments, then Amy gets the sense that her feelings, and even Amy herself, have some value. Then, perhaps, suicide isn't the only solution to her pain. Sorting it out with another human being helps. Amy has learned there are ways of dealing with her painful feelings other than trying to stop them. The process of therapy has given her the sense of control that she so desperately needed to survive.

Suicidal ideation is a frequent problem for people suffering from severe depression. It is a misguided attempt to gain control over a painful life that seems to have no value or control. Thankfully, there are other options. God made us with the capacity to benefit from talking about our pain with someone we trust. By honestly sharing our most painful feelings with someone who can accept and understand them, we can find relief and comfort in ways that we cannot achieve by ourselves. We were not made to deal with life's most difficult challenges all by ourselves, and suicidal thoughts are a good example of this fact. If you ever suffer from suicidal thoughts, you should know that your depression is causing you to consider this as an option to your pain, but this is not your only choice. It may be difficult to imagine when you are depressed, but you can be helped, and there are people who know just how to help you.

57

How Jesus Dealt with Isolation

In one of the most difficult moments of his life, Jesus was so sad-dened about what was going to happen to him that he prayed to God to "take this cup from me" (Luke 22:42). However, even though he felt tortured and depressed, Jesus decided to accept whatever the will of God was going to be for him. And then a very interesting thing happened: God sent an angel from heaven to "strengthen" him.

Even the Son of God did not try to lift himself out of a serious depression by himself. He turned to God for help, and he got it. Interestingly, the help he *didn't* receive was for God to answer his prayer to "take this cup from me." That is the same prayer most of us pray when we are feeling really bad. You have probably prayed something like, "This is just too much. Please, God, take this agony away from me." But just as he did for Jesus, God probably didn't take your painful situation away. Instead, he sent you divine sup-port to help you get through it. The hard part is accepting the strength while you are in so much anguish.

Gloria hated feeling so sad all the time. She knew it made her unattractive to other people, but she just couldn't seem to help it. She tried to think positive thoughts, but she struggled with feeling down for many years.

"I need to improve my self-esteem," she told me in one session.

"You do?"

"Yes. That's my problem. The greatest love you have is the one right inside of you. You have to love yourself before you can love anyone else, you know," she responded somewhat defiantly.

"So if you just try harder to love yourself, you'll feel better?"

"That's right. I just need you to tell me how to love myself better. I mean, I have to do it, but if you could just give me some advice about what I'm doing wrong, I'll change it."

"I see," I said. "And how has this worked out for you in the past?"

"Well, I must be doing something wrong. I do try to love myself but I guess I need to try harder."

Gloria was half right. Her efforts to try to love herself were not working to make her feel better. She felt sad much of the time, and she needed to do something different to change that. But it wasn't that she needed to try harder to love herself on her own.

Gloria felt bad about herself, and she didn't want anyone to see it. If she got her feelings hurt, she would hide those hurt feelings and try to work it out on her own. Sometimes she got so sad that she wouldn't get out of bed for several days. She went into her apartment, closed the door, and cried for hours. Sometimes she cried off and on for days. Gloria's biggest mistake was that if she became very sad, she would *isolate* from others. Trying to hide her true feelings from others wasn't working. She didn't need to try harder; she needed to try something different.

After several months of working on this with me, Gloria isn't as sad as she used to be. She still gets sad, but it doesn't last as long and doesn't go as deep as it used to. It's not that she is trying harder to like herself more; she is doing something she never did before. She isn't isolating herself. She didn't like to do it at first, but when she talks about her painful feelings with someone she trusts, a surprising thing happens—she feels a little bit better. She finds comfort in having another human being understand the depth of her pain and help her sort out where all the feelings are coming from. Being sad, at least with me, doesn't have to make her unattractive. Sometimes it helps her get to painful memories and feelings that need to be understood better. She never felt this way before, but sometimes she even feels something good can come out of feeling sad.

Sadness and depression can make you want to isolate from others. You feel bad, and you fear others won't want to be around you because of it. While it's true that some people don't want to hear about your sadness (probably because they don't want to be reminded of their own), it's not true that isolating is a good choice when you are sad.

The next time you are feeling really sad, pray to God to help you with your pain. Remember what he did for Jesus. He didn't take the pain away, but he did send an angel to give Jesus strength. Look around; you might just find an angel in disguise.

58

When Sorrow Is Better Than Laughter

Everybody loves to laugh. Laughter opens you up to new things and helps you enjoy life. But there are times when laughter is used to cover over painful truths that are too difficult to face. Sometimes you are more honest with yourself when you are sad. It is hard for some people to accept this, but sometimes "sorrow is better than laughter."

David is a successful businessman and a loving husband. He was adopted as a child and has always been grateful to his parents for providing him with a good life. He started his own business and works hard at providing the best service to others that he possibly can. David would tell you that he doesn't have any real problems, but he decided to come to therapy for some "fine-tuning."

David ambled into my office for our first session with a smile on his face. He is a tall, good-looking man with a friendly manner.

"So tell me, David, how are you doing?" I asked as we both sat down.

"I'm fine," he responded cheerfully.

"That's good. So, tell me why you're here," I probed.

"You see, I'm like a Ferrari. I'm a top-quality machine that needs some fine-tuning to keep it running at its maximum capacity," he responded as he leaned back in his chair.

"I see," I said thoughtfully. "So even though your life is pretty good, there may be some benefit in taking a look under the hood once in a while."

"Right," he said. "Every good Ferrari needs a good mechanic."

I knew from the beginning that my sessions were not going to be easy with David. Not because he was a difficult person to be with—quite the contrary. He was always happy, constantly telling me jokes and quick to minimize whatever problems he faced. David was a fun guy, but not always honest with himself about how he really felt about things. He suffered from one of the most common ailments I see in men today: the inability to talk about sadness. For him, FINE meant "Feelings Inside Not Expressed." And that makes my job in therapy a difficult one.

David and I came to like and trust each other over time. Our sessions would start with him telling me about how well he was doing, and I was honestly glad to hear about his successes. But unlike everyone else in David's life, I was interested in something more than just his latest joke (which almost always made me burst out laughing) or accomplishment. I was interested in the things that made him sad. As difficult as this was for him, David would eventually get around to the painful areas of his life that he never discussed with anyone. Then, real therapy would begin.

David's life is different now. He doesn't drink alcohol as much as he used to, he doesn't get as angry when he is frustrated, and his wife tells him that she feels close to him than she has ever felt before. But David isn't different because I have given him better advice about how to manage his problems (he didn't really view himself as having significant ones anyway). David's life is different because he has another man with whom he can be sad. At points in our sessions now, we may come across a memory or feeling that hasn't occurred to him since he was a child, and he may even weep for several minutes. He doesn't try to laugh it off as much as he used to, and as a result we are able to understand how these old painful feelings are still affecting him today. By taking the time to face the sadness in his life, David is becoming a better man.

Sorrow isn't always bad. Sometimes it is the appropriate thing to feel. And there are even times when it is the only feeling that will put you in a frame of mind to understand yourself better. If you are honest with yourself when you are sad, you can grasp some of the deepest meanings about your life. Don't be afraid to be sad. If you are courageous like David, you will see that sometimes "sorrow is better than laughter."

59

The Things You Can Learn from Sorrow

Rhonda didn't want to go to therapy because she believed that all therapists do is blame everything on your mother. She loved her mother and was convinced that she had a wonderful childhood. She believed that rummaging around in her past would be a waste of time and, quite frankly, insulting to the good woman who had raised her.

But Rhonda came to therapy anyway. She felt forced to come because she was suffering from anxiety that was disturbing her and she couldn't make it go away. She had nightmares and became anxious in certain social situations, especially around men, and it was holding her back in life. She wanted to know how to deal with her problems, but without blaming everything on her mom.

"My childhood was great. I loved my mother, and I respected my father. There, we've covered my childhood, so I guess we can get on to the business of dealing with my current problems," she announced to me in our first session.

"It's good to see that you came from a loving family," I replied. "I may have a few more questions about your upbringing, but for now it's good to know that you grew up feeling close to your parents."

"Yes, I was very close to my mother. My father was away a lot, but I respected him for providing for our family," Rhonda went on, now with a little tension in her voice.

"So you were closer to your mother?" I asked.

"Sure, but that's normal. Moms did the raising of the kids when I grew up, and dads went to work. Everything was normal at our house," she said. But I wasn't sure if she was trying to convince me or herself.

After several months of resistance analysis (a technical term for getting behind the walls that people put up when they come for therapy), Rhonda and I came to understand some things about her that turned out to be quite helpful. She discovered that her anxiety around men did have something to do with her mother. She grew up very close to her mom, in fact, closer to her at times than her father was. Because her dad was away so much, her mother would often turn to Rhonda for companionship and emotional support. While she was delighted to have this special role in her mother's life, it also brought with it the unique burden of feeling responsible for her emotional well-being. Children feel anxious when they are responsible for their parents while growing up. This is a task for another adult, not a child.

Eventually we came to see that because of her relationship with her mother, Rhonda was afraid that an intimate relationship with a man was going to be another emotional responsibility that she could not fulfill. She loved her mother and felt very loyal to her. But she was unable to make her happy. It wasn't her role to make her mom happy, but she felt like a failure about it anyway. This made her feel very anxious whenever she became closely involved with any man. On an unconscious level, she feared that she would fail to make anyone happy in an intimate relationship, so the thought of entering into one with a man felt like a burden to her.

Although it took quite a while to get to this realization, once we did, two things happened in Rhonda's life. First, she became less anxious around men. Once she realized that it was her mother she was afraid of failing, it opened up the possibility that an intimate relationship with a man might be different. This made her feel better. But, second, Rhonda felt a deep sadness about her relationship with her parents. She was sad that her father hadn't been closer to her and to her mother, and she was sad that she had felt responsible for taking care of her mother in his place. She didn't blame her parents for how her childhood went, but she felt sad that it wasn't as great as she had always thought it was. In fact, there was a lot of sadness in her childhood that she began to talk about. Only this time she was only responsible for dealing with her own sadness and not her mother's.

Rhonda was only partly right about therapists, at least therapists like me. I do want to understand how your parents affected you, including the painful disappointments you may have experienced with them. But understanding how your parents may have failed you is not so we can blame them for your problems. It is so we can understand the origins of your problems to enable you to take responsibility for them now. The goal of therapy is wisdom. But as the Bible says, "With much wisdom comes much sorrow." Neither the Bible nor therapy can eliminate sorrow from your life, but they both can help you find the wisdom to deal with it.

PART SIX

Fear

60

How to Fear No Evil

You may have prayed in the past, "God, help me. I'm so scared. Please take these problems out of my life." And you may have even turned to Psalm 23, the most famous passage in the Bible on dealing with fear, to see the psalmist declare, "I will fear no evil." But *why* is it that we are to fear no evil? Because God promises to pluck you out of danger just before harm can fall upon you? As I mentioned earlier, God didn't do that for Jesus, so I doubt that happens very often in your life either. No, the most famous passage in the Bible on dealing with fear does *not* say, "I will fear no evil, for I know you will remove it from my path." It says, "I will fear no evil, for you are with me."

The reason you can fear no evil is not because God promises that evil will never happen to you. Anyone who has lived very long at all knows this simply isn't true. The reason you can fear no evil is not because God promises to take you out of the darkest valley; it is because God has given you a way to deal with evil once it comes upon you.

God comforts you when you encounter evil because what he offers you in your time of great trouble is himself. The word *comfort* is derived from two parts. The first is *com*, meaning "with," and the second is *fort*, meaning "strength," as in *fortify*. Comfort is God's strength with you in your fears. The comfort of God is that he promises to give you *strength* to deal with your fears, not *escape* from them.

In chapter 12 I described the terrorist attack in New York City on September 11, 2001. Every major newspaper in the world featured the story of the destruction of the Twin Towers that day. Within a few days of the tragedy, I was interviewed by a local television news station. I was invited to the studio where I was to address the subject. I was asked to submit a list of questions that I would like to address, but I wasn't prepared for the direction that my interview actually took.

The producers for the news station were aware that I had degrees in psychology and theology and wrote books integrating these two things. The anchors of the news were all set with both my background and the questions that I had prepared for them. But when the lights came on and we were in front of a live camera, the lead anchor looked at me and said, "We are delighted to have with us tonight Dr. Mark Baker, who is both a theologian and a psychologist. It is at times such as this that we are all led to ask the question, 'How could a loving God allow such a horrible tragedy to happen?' Dr. Baker, what is the answer?"

I was stunned. Brilliant theologians have wrestled with this question for thousands of years and failed to come up with a good answer, and I was supposed to come up with one on the spur of the moment in front of bright lights and a live camera sending out my reply to thousands of onlookers? I didn't know what to say. Should I quote Kierkegaard or Tillich? Or perhaps I should turn to a contemporary thinker such as Kushner or Yancey? What is the solution to the problem of evil in the world?

Then I remembered a conversation I had years ago with a friend of mine who is a Christian missionary to a Buddhist country. For years he lived and worked among people who didn't believe in the God of the Bible. Their approach to suffering was quite simple—it's a part of life. They didn't have a notion of personal redemption or forgiveness, so to them suffering didn't have anything to do with anyone other than one's own self. Suffering was something that you had to accept and work out within yourself. For Buddhists, there was no conflict between God and evil. Evil wasn't a concept that they found useful, because suffering was each person's own responsibility, and they didn't believe there was a personal God to complain to about it anyway.

At this point I turned to the camera and said, "For those of us who believe in a personal God, we don't have a really good answer as to why God allows evil to exist at times like this. But we do have a really good answer as to *what to do when it happens.* We can turn to God and each other for comfort. God did not make the world so that planes won't fly into buildings and innocent people won't get killed. Tragedy happens. But God made the world such that we do not have to go through it alone."

Trying to tell someone not to be afraid who has gone through a tragedy or who is about to face another one is usually not that helpful. But being with them usually is. Philosophers and theologians will continue to wrestle with *why* evil exists, but you and I have been given the answer as to *how* to deal with our fears of it now.

When stricken by senseless acts of violence or evil, we all respond with fear. Fear is not the problem; it's what you do next that might be. Do you withdraw and hide, or do you reach out and bond with others to find the strength to go on? Many Americans found the strength they needed in the face of terror by seeking out others. An important point that I will try to make several times in this book is that fear is tolerable if we do not have to go through it alone.

Fear is an essential element in life, a natural reaction to potential harm. There are many things you can learn about yourself by facing your fears, while attempting to escape them usually leads you in the wrong direction. God knows this. This is why God does not redirect you around the "darkest valley" but encourages you to march right through it, with him. "I will fear no evil" because I know how to deal with it. Fear signals you to remember how to best deal with crisis: *don't try to go through it alone.*

61

Why We Fear Vulnerability

It is interesting to note that Adam was naked in the Garden for quite a while without feeling any embarrassment about it. But once he ate of the tree of knowledge, everything changed. Once Adam became aware of his vulnerability, he was afraid. From that moment on, people have feared vulnerability.

Tom is a healthy guy. He works out at the gym, eats health food, and is always up on the latest fashions and trends. Tom went to therapy a couple of times, but only for a few sessions because he just needed to "check in" about a few things. He is very modern, sees all the latest movies, and reads most of the popular self-help books.

One of the things that strikes you when you meet Tom is how open he is. He is not afraid to talk about himself, which is very engaging. He is open about the dysfunction in his childhood and what it took for him to overcome it. He is not afraid to give you his opinion on things and is willing to hear your opinions, as well. Tom is a great conversationalist, and he usually stands out in the crowd. He almost always knows just the right thing to say.

The funny thing about Tom is that even though he is very open, there is still something about him that makes people uncomfortable. It's as if his openness is an invitation for you to be open with him as well, but you really don't want to be. He seems to have a good grasp of what it takes to recover from difficult circumstances, and you start to feel a little uncomfortable if you don't have the same degree of success in solving your own problems.

You see, Tom is open, but he is not vulnerable. He is open about the things in his life, but his struggles are all in the past and well under control now. To be open, one merely has to be disclosing. But to be vulnerable, one has to risk being hurt. This means admitting imperfections and problems that might be too embarrassing to share because they are *not* all under control. Vulnerability requires a level of honesty that Tom is not willing to reveal.

Tom is not willing to be vulnerable, because that would mean giving up his control and placing himself at risk of being hurt. In the end, people find Tom attractive but somewhat superficial. Like Adam in the Garden, Tom is afraid to be vulnerable. He may see the aspects of himself that are embarrassing or imperfect, but instead of being vulnerable about those parts of himself, he makes Adam's mistake—he hides.

There is a difference between openness and vulnerability. People who are open appear to be uninhibited, candid, and eager to experience new things. They may seem confident and even have a psychological sophistication about them. But it is possible to be open without being vulnerable. People who are vulnerable are capable of being hurt.

Openness is attractive, but we can only genuinely connect to others by being vulnerable. That means talking about our tender feelings, our places of insecurity, and the areas of our lives that we don't have figured out completely. Vulnerability means sometimes only knowing what you feel without having any good answers about what to do about it.

Being open is easy. We fear vulnerability. When we are vulnerable, we admit that we are dependent upon others. That's right: dependent. Vulnerability opens us up to depend upon imperfect people who might fail us, or a busy God who might have another agenda for us other than our own. We fear vulnerability because that is where we can get hurt. But it is also the only place we can be loved. You and I are confronted with the same choice that Adam faced. You can be naked and vulnerable, which opens you up to the possibility of being loved and cared for—or you can hide. The greatest life possible comes from choosing the vulnerable path to love.

62

The Confidence to Face Fear

How can you develop the confidence to face your fears? The answer to this is especially important when you are under attack. Your enemies will assault you, and at times you will see "the wicked advance" against you. But you can find the confidence to face these attacks when your stronghold is God, because the kind of confidence that comes from relying upon God is balanced in just the right way.

Healthy self-confidence is based upon a balance of two things: encouragement and acceptance. I said more about this in the portion of the book on guilt and shame, but put simply, encouragement is the feeling you get from accomplishing things, which makes you feel appreciated. But acceptance is the feeling you get from experiencing love for who you are. Encouragement is about doing; acceptance is about being. A balance of both is necessary to develop healthy self-confidence.

Nathan is a success story. He came from humble beginnings, put himself through college, and worked his way up to the top of his company. He is nationally recognized for his brilliance as a chief executive officer in a prestigious corporation. He has appeared on numerous magazine covers and is often quoted for his opinions on matters of business and economics.

Nathan didn't come to therapy because he wanted to; he did it because his wife said he had to. When I asked him why he was there in our first session, he said, "Because my wife thinks this would be a good idea."

"Really," I replied.

"Yes," he said somewhat indignantly. "I'm fine. She seems to be the one with the problem."

"Well, that's going to be difficult," I said cautiously. "Because, you see, she's not here. I can only help people who are actually in the room."

"Look," Nathan continued in his typically confident tone. "My life is great. I have two thousand people working for me who depend upon me being at the top of my game. I have built companies up from next to nothing to world-class organizations. I am respected all over the country for being the 'go-to' guy. I'm the one others come to to solve their problems. Being here is almost a contradiction for me. I'm the guy who knows how to make things work in life."

"I see," I said. "So your wife is mistaken."

"Yes, I think so. Well, I guess that will be up to you to determine. I mean, you tell me. Do I look like a guy who needs help to you?"

I have learned in my many years as a psychotherapist that this is usually a trick question. Nathan wasn't really asking a question; he was making a statement. He was telling me that he was very confident about what he knew to be true in life. He was smart and successful. He had learned how to make businesses run and to turn things from unproductive to productive with amazing skill. He was good at this. But he wasn't good at everything or he wouldn't be sitting in my office. The fact that his wife had convinced him to come to therapy was telling me something. His confidence was not complete. He wouldn't be there if he wasn't lacking confidence in something. He just wasn't sure what that was.

After some psychological arm wrestling, Nathan agreed to enter into a course of treatment with me. As our sessions went on, we discovered something in Nathan's life that I find fairly often with hard-nosed professionals in the business world. Nathan's confidence was out of balance. He was confident about what he could *do*, but he wasn't confident about who he *was*.

Nathan was certain about what he thought, and he was extremely decisive. But he was rarely able to articulate how he felt about things. His life was about making things happen, not about how he felt about it, or how he felt about anyone else for that matter. At the end of the day, he was paid an extremely large salary for accomplishing things, not making friends.

This created an imbalance in Nathan's life. Nathan had the encouragement to feel confident about what he could do, but he lacked the acceptance to feel confident about who he was. This resulted in a number of enactments in Nathan's life to overcompensate for what was missing. His office had to be the largest and most extravagant of anyone he knew, his vacations had to be the most exotic, and he could never admit to feeling insecure about anything. This need to overcompensate was driving Nathan to drink too much. At first it was the extra drinks he would have at business meetings. Then it was the extra drinks he would have when he got home at night. And finally it had grown to the need Nathan felt to have several drinks every night when he got home, usually in secret because he didn't want his wife to know that he *needed* to drink. Nathan was caught in the trap of trying to convince everyone, including himself, that he was completely confident. But someone who was truly self-confident would never have to do that.

We are still working at it, but things are starting to change for Nathan. He is able to admit that he doesn't know some things. He often doesn't know how he feels in tender moments, and he doesn't know what his wife wants from him when she feels hurt. He is also able to admit that there are plenty of times at the office when he has a pretty good idea of what to do, but he is still afraid that what he is proposing might not work out. He will only admit it to me, but it does bother him when his competitors are out to get him. He says it doesn't, but the truth is, it does. And when he can admit this, he finds out something that he never knew before—the difference between feeling appreciated and feeling accepted. He is realizing that only showing others your strengths gets you lots of appreciation in life, but you feel accepted only if you feel understood and cared for in the midst of your greatest weakness. This is the experience he needed to balance out his self-confidence.

Even if you were successful at everything you tried to do in life, this would not guarantee true self-confidence. You must also feel loved independent of your accomplishments. Of course, feeling lovable even though you failed at everything you tried to do wouldn't be enough, either. You must have both.

The psalmist David explained how God can give you the confidence to face your fears when you are under attack by others. He wrote, "The LORD is the stronghold of my life—of whom shall I be afraid?" If you rely upon God, you will feel encouraged when you succeed in life, and accepted by God even when you don't. This is the balance required for healthy self-confidence. Evil people prevail, and sometimes for a period of time. But in the end, their confidence is based on temporary self-gratification that doesn't last.[1] When God is your stronghold, you have the greatest possibility for complete confidence. You will feel encouraged by your accomplishments from time to time, but even in your weakest moments you will always know that you have the unconditional love of an omnipotent God. There is no better place to find the confidence to face your fears.

63

Healthy Fear

Fear is your teacher. You will learn some of your most important lessons in life from listening to your fears rather than trying to ignore them. Fear is the emotion you feel when you are in danger. It is automatic and often exists for a reason.

Because fear signals danger, we learn to respond to it without even thinking. Especially when we are children, we learn to fear certain aspects of our lives and file those lessons away in the deepest parts of our minds. Then, when circumstances arise that remind us of past fears, we respond spontaneously in self-protective ways. In psychotherapy we call these *defense mechanisms*: automatic, self-protective responses to danger. If you look back over the life of someone who has developed defense mechanisms, you will be able to see the purposes they served in protecting the person from past danger. The only problem is that what serves us in childhood can enslave us as adults.

Mary is a beautiful, intelligent, and successful woman who has every reason to feel good about life. She is happily married and content with both her personal and professional lives. However, in spite of how wonderful her life was, Mary had a strange reaction to sexual intimacy with her husband that bothered them both. She knew he loved her and that she loved him deeply as well, but each time they tried to be physically intimate Mary became very uncomfortable. All she could say was that it just felt "icky." Very wisely, Mary decided to come to therapy for help.

Mary was raised as the only daughter of two unhappily married people. Her parents married while very young and grew apart over the years. Her mother devoted her life to raising Mary, and her father was more interested in his career than the family. Although they never divorced, they lived in a cold and distant marriage for all of Mary's life. She didn't understand it, but Mary knew things were terribly wrong between her parents.

When Mary was about nine, she learned that her father was having an affair. This was very disturbing to Mary, but because her mother chose to stay married to her father, it seemed like something they should all learn to work out. At first, her parents fought about the affair, and her father promised to discontinue it. Unfortunately, he did not keep his promise. Mary learned later that, not only did he continue this affair, but it eventually led to a pattern of extramarital affairs that he carried on for many years.

At one point Mary's father began confiding in her about his relationships with other women. On one hand, she was flattered to be allowed access to such private adult information; on the other hand, she was repulsed by the nature of her father's immorality. This created a dilemma for Mary. She wanted to be her father's confidante, as she was finally getting his intimate attention. But she hated knowing the details of his sexual liaisons with other women. Tragically, her own sexual identity as a young woman was developing at the same time that her father was creating a terrible conflict for her surrounding sexual intimacy. Understandably, Mary developed two opposing reactions to sex: she was both excited by it, and she found it "icky."

Mary became sexually active as a teenager, and like her father, she had a number of sexual experiences over the next several years. She liked sex with men she hardly knew, but as the relationship became more intimate, the icky feeling would surface and she would have to end the relationship. She was drawn toward sex, but she feared sexual intimacy. Without realizing it, Mary learned as a child to both fear sexual intimacy yet be excited by it because of her relationship with her father.

In therapy, Mary realized the icky feeling she had in her marriage was a defense mechanism she had developed as a child to protect her from the inappropriate intimacy she had with her father. She feared her father's improper sexual behavior and his inappropriate use of her as an intimate confidante for his sexual confessions. To protect herself from her fears, Mary automatically felt icky when a relationship was both sexual and intimate. This had helped her distance herself from the sexually inappropriate intimacy she had with her father as a child, but it was creating distance between Mary and her husband that she didn't want as an adult.

Mary is developing a more comfortable sexual relationship with her husband now. Her conscious awareness of the origins of her icky feelings helped her develop a proper sexual intimacy with her husband. Her fear of inappropriate sexual intimacy with her father was appropriate for her as a child, and her defense mechanism of icky feelings was a helpful response to the very real danger she felt then. Mary's healthy fear protected her from danger as a child. She just needed to feel safe enough now as an adult to realize that she no longer needed to protect herself in that way.

Some fear is healthy. It signals you that danger is near, and you should heed it. The Bible tells you that you will need to "work out your salvation with fear and trembling." There is a healthy fear that will be your teacher in life. And just like Mary, you may have to work it out in order for you to learn the lessons you need to know.

64

The Fear of the Lord

One of the most important things fear teaches you is that you are not God. Thankfully, God is omnipotent and omniscient and running the universe so that you don't have to. What the Bible means when it says "the fear of the Lord is the beginning of wisdom" is that you need to respect your limitations as compared to the limitlessness of God. No matter how knowledgeable or brilliant you may be, if you do not know your limits, then you will inevitably be foolish. This is the beginning of wisdom. A healthy respect for your limitations will save you a great deal of regret.

Ethan and Veronica came for marriage counseling because they were stuck. They were both Christians, and committed to their marriage, but they knew they should not be struggling as much as they were. It was as if every disagreement ended in the same way, and yet nothing seemed to get resolved. They would have a disagreement that would lead to an argument, and Veronica would eventually just give up with, "Okay, Ethan, have it your way. I'm not going to keep arguing with you over this. It's just not worth it." The fighting would stop, but the distance between them would just keep growing.

The pattern of fighting between Ethan and Veronica is typical for many couples. They would disagree over the facts of some matter, and both would fight for their point of view, hoping to convince the other of the correctness of their position. Ethan was especially concerned about getting things right, and he was convinced that correct thinking leads to correct behavior. He was very fond of saying, "Good theology—good life," to emphasize this point.

Although Veronica is very intelligent and no pushover in her arguments with Ethan, she didn't like the distance and tension created by their arguments, so she would eventually just "drop her end of the rope" in the verbal tug-of-war between them. She grew up in a family that had its share of disagreements, but the value of harmony was too important to be sacrificed over petty arguments. She would fight with Ethan, but she hated disharmony more than she loved to be right; so walking away without getting in the last word was something she was willing to do to protect her marriage.

Ethan, on the other hand, was raised in a very chaotic family where differences always led to disagreements, and fighting was a daily occurrence. His father was either angry or gone, and his mother was constantly distressed and disorganized. He could rarely turn to either of them for comfort when he was upset, so he had to learn how to solve problems on his own. Thankfully, during his sophomore year in high school, a friend invited him to a youth group where Ethan became a Christian and found the comfort of God and the support of a Christian community that he desperately needed. Now his life made sense, and he could turn to the God of the Bible to solve any problem that came his way. Ethan committed himself to his relationship with God and dedicated himself to the study of Scripture, and he has lived with a sense of security that has been his source of comfort ever since.

But just because he became a Christian, it didn't mean Ethan was never going to have any problems. It also didn't mean that all the effects of his childhood were completely erased. Some injuries leave scars that last a lifetime. In Ethan's case, even though he found the greatest source of security in the world when he became a Christian, he never forgot what it was like to live in the chaos of his childhood. That had scarred him emotionally, and he never wanted to return to that way of living ever again. This left Ethan with a very strong sense of *right and wrong*, and he was very determined to live according to what was right in every circumstance he possibly could. However, because of the scar that the chaos of his childhood left, Ethan didn't realize that he didn't just want to do the right thing, he actually needed to be *in control*.

Every time Ethan had a difference of opinion with Veronica, it made him feel anxious. He experienced the differences between them as disagreements that needed to be confronted and resolved in order to feel safe. Partners in even the very best of marriages disagree a good deal of the time, but Ethan's marriage was reminding him of the chaos of his childhood, and that was something he could not let happen. He loved Veronica too much to allow chaos to creep into their marriage, so he would try to get her to agree with him to make the differences between them go away. Unfortunately, this was not just to ensure "right" living, but without knowing it, Ethan was also trying to control the chaos he feared coming back into his life, and the anxiety it was causing him. This, of course, did not go over well with Veronica. She was perfectly willing to agree to disagree at times, and she certainly didn't like feeling controlled.

It was an awful thing for Ethan that his parents were not in control of the world in which he was raised. That meant he needed to be. And it is a terrifying thing for a child to feel he has to be in control of his world. That job is just too big for any child. In a way, Ethan was forced to be the god of his own universe. He had to cling to his own ideas about what would make him feel safe, because there was no one bigger than him around to make life safe for him. Way down deep inside Ethan still believed that to feel safe in the world, he must be in control. Unfortunately he was trying to create a world in which no one, especially not Veronica, could actually live.

The marriage between Ethan and Veronica is getting better now. They are fighting less often, and when they do, they are actually resolving things. The most important reason for this shift is that Ethan is accepting his limitations and realizing that he is not God. What I mean by this is he is trusting that God is in control of the universe and that it will not fall into chaos if his wife disagrees with him. He can now see that his need to be right was triggered by an underlying fear of loss of control, and it saddened him to realize that Veronica felt controlled by him. That was never his intention. Ethan doesn't fear differences like he did before. He can see that all marriages have differences, and all differences do not have to lead to disagreements. It was foolish of him to think this before, and his healthy fear of God has given him the wisdom to see this now.

Some Christians confuse the fear of the Lord with being scared of God. They live as though, if they don't get things right, God will be mad at them. That is not what God wants. The Bible does talk about a fear of God when it refers to punishment for sin. But that is reserved for those who refuse him and choose evil ways. Those people would do well to be more afraid of the consequences of their choices. But for those of us who believe in God, the fear of the Lord refers to an awe of him that reminds us of our limitations. He is in control, so we don't have to be. That's not our job. And Ethan will tell you that accepting this truth has made him a very wise man.

65

Fear-Based Relationships

Fear-based relationships are caused by the fear of rejection. Humans are social animals, so needing others is a good thing. But it is not a good thing when you live in fear that you are going to be rejected by someone you need. People caught in fear-based relationships are not actually trying to get love; they are trying to avoid rejection. This is an important distinction to understand, because fear and love don't go well together in relationships.

Susan was raised in a strict religious home with firm rules about how one should behave. She tried to be a good girl, but no matter how hard she tried, she never felt like she lived up to her mother's standards. The atmosphere at Susan's house was often tense because of this.

One of the reasons Susan married early in life was to get away from home. She desperately wanted to feel loved, so she married her high school sweetheart and began her own family by the age of twenty. Susan was a beautiful girl, kindhearted and loving to children. She wanted to make her own home a warm and caring one, not like the critical and judgmental one in which she grew up.

But try as she might, Susan's home didn't turn out to be the loving place she had hoped it would be. She found herself disappointed with her husband's lack of attention toward her, and she couldn't help feeling hurt by him frequently.

"What do you think of the colors I picked for the dining room?" she asked her husband recently during the remodeling project of their new home.

"I think they look good," he said.

"Do you like the contrasting colors on the trim and the windows?" she asked.

"Sure. They're fine," he replied calmly. "How much did the paint cost?" he asked. He was typically concerned about the cost of things since he was the sole breadwinner of the family.

"About sixty dollars," she said proudly. Susan had shopped around and thought this was a pretty good price.

"Really?" he replied. "I thought we paid less than that for the living room."

"What!" Susan snapped. "Why is it that you always have to be so negative? Why do you have to criticize everything? Can't I ever do anything that is good enough for you? I'm constantly looking for some approval from you, and all I get is rejection." Then she stomped out of the room.

"What are you talking about?" he yelled back. "I didn't say it was your fault that the paint cost more. Can't I be concerned about the cost of the paint?"

What Susan didn't realize was that she wasn't actually looking for her husband's approval; she was expecting his rejection. By this point in her marriage, her husband's positive statements almost didn't register with her. He liked her choices, and he felt good about many of the decisions that she made around the house. But he did have negative reactions to things at times. And this is what registered with Susan. This is what she was expecting to hear, so when she did, it cut like a knife.

Susan was caught in a fear-based relationship. She was afraid that her husband was critical of her just like her mother was. He wasn't always saying it, but she was sure that it was there. So when he did say something negative, she was sure that this was evidence of what he *really* thought of her. As with all fear-based relationships, Susan was not really looking for acceptance; she was trying to avoid rejection. This was exhausting for Susan, as well as her husband.

Fear-based relationships are not looking for love; they are seeking to avoid pain. This usually alienates the other person, which will make you even more desperate. Things usually spiral downward from there. To avoid rejection is a task that has no end, because as soon as you have done something to escape the rejection you so desperately fear, you must start the very next instant working to avoid the rejection that could follow.

Fear-based relationships are like stepping into a snare because the more you struggle, the more deeply entangled you become in the problem. Trying harder to avoid rejection rarely works. You must do something entirely different to get out of that trap.

Instead of working harder, Susan needed to work smarter. Instead of trying to *avoid* rejection, she needed to try to *find* acceptance. What's the difference? Relationships that are based upon acceptance have trust. Fear-based relationships don't. Trust means believing in others and not interpreting their actions as meaning something negative about you. It means having faith in yourself and what you have to offer. And trust means creating a place that is safe for everyone's feelings. Building trust takes time, but it's actually less work than trying to avoid rejection.

God has given you a model for how to free yourself from fear-based relationships. He has told you that you should seek love rather than fear rejection because "fear of man will prove to be a snare." God's comfort to you in your relationship with him is that you can trust he will never reject you. With God you are safe. With that as your model, you should endeavor to seek love in all your relationships rather than fear rejection. Relationships based upon trust are always a good idea; fear-based relationships never are.

66

Why We Become What We Fear

Life would be so easy if you could simply identify those things that are dangerous and avoid them. Your fear would be your guide. If you fear it, you avoid it, and it will never bother you. That's it. But the human mind is far too complex to allow you to get away with such a simplistic approach to life.

The vast majority of mental processing happens outside of your conscious awareness. Childhood experiences, emotions, and unconscious beliefs play major roles in determining your choices. You might like to believe that humans are rational beings, but we are actually rationalizing ones. Most often, your unconscious feelings determine your choices first, and you come up with the rational explanations later.

The human mind operates on two levels. On the conscious level, you know what you are thinking and feeling and you are fully aware of your thought processes. But on a deeper level, your unconscious mind is operating outside of your conscious perception, processing thoughts and feelings completely outside of your awareness. This means that you have thoughts and feelings going on in your mind right now that you don't even know about. You may think you understand yourself very well, but you will never fully know the depths of your own unconscious mind.

This is why you cannot simply avoid your fears. Although this may be hard to accept, you rarely have a good enough understanding of yourself to know all of why you fear what you fear and what you should be doing about it. Too often, you fear something because you have some unfinished business with it that you are processing in your unconscious. Like a moth to a flame you are drawn, mostly unconsciously, toward this unfinished business. This is how you can become what you fear.

Hannah came to Los Angeles almost twenty years ago to make her fame and fortune in the entertainment industry. She was born in a small town in Kansas into a Christian family of hardworking farmers who believed the sign of a good person was the ability to work hard, be humble, and earn the respect of the community. But Hannah was a creative child, and she never felt that growing up to follow in her family's tradition of farm life was her destiny. While Hannah wasn't as interested in her family's traditions as her father would have liked her to be, she still loved and respected him. Despite her desire for her father's approval, Hannah felt somehow special, and she was determined to find out what her unique purpose was in life. Instead of coming straight home after school to help out on the farm, she tried out for the school plays. She knew this was a disappointment to her father, because he was always too busy to attend any of Hannah's productions. But she found the recognition that she longed for from her acting teachers. So after graduation, despite her father's objections, Hannah made her way to Hollywood, the last place on the planet that her father wanted her to go.

At first, Hannah was fairly successful in her new career as an actor. She found an agent who would represent her, and she was hired to play several roles in a number of movies. Hannah was living her dream. She no longer felt like a disappointment in her father's eyes, but instead felt like a success in the eyes of a growing adoring public. "Think of all the good I can do as a successful Christian woman in Hollywood," Hannah would say to her friends. But Hollywood is fickle. As Hannah is also fond of saying, "You are only as good as your last performance."

Sadly, Hannah is considered to be talented, but she is no longer considered successful in her career as an actor these days. At some point, Hannah was no longer getting hired for jobs as an actor. The opportunities for auditions tapered off, and she no longer has an agent to represent her. She still works in jobs that allow her the freedom to go on auditions during the daytime so she can continue to pursue her dream, but there has been a shift in her life. She is no longer the girl with great potential. She is now the woman who has to face her fears. It's just that the thought of going back to Kansas to face those fears would make Hannah feel like too much of a failure to do it.

Hannah left her hometown in pursuit of her dream for more than one reason. Of course, she found something that she loved to do and she wanted to pursue the opportunity to do it. But Hannah left home not just to pursue something; she wanted to get away from something. She was afraid that she was a disappointment in her father's eyes, and she never faced that fear. On some deeper level, she went to Hollywood to force her father to be proud of her. Even when she was successful, she was afraid that she was failing her father's expectations of how she was supposed to be succeeding as a woman in life. Hannah wasn't just pursuing a dream; she was trying to escape a fear. Unfortunately, we often become what we fear, especially if we are trying to escape it.

On the surface, you might think Hannah had unfinished business with her father, but that's not quite right. Her father might not have approved of Hannah's choice in career, but that wasn't the real issue with her. Instead, Hannah was afraid her father just might be right. Perhaps she *wasn't* cut out to be a successful Christian woman in Hollywood. This fear caused her to cling to her dream long past the point when it was possible to be fulfilled. Hannah wasn't just trying to be a success; she was trying to escape her fear that she was a failure.

If you are trying to avoid failure, then you can't ever know when to stop trying. Changing your course of action will always feel like failure. Trying to run away from something doesn't give you a clear direction of where you are supposed to be going, because running away from something is very different than running toward something.

You may say things like, "I never want to be anything like my father," or "The only reason I get so angry is because my wife is so difficult," but the issues that disturb you the most are rarely with the external world. The most troubling aspects of life are found within. And unless you stop blaming others for your fears and start examining your deeper feelings that underlie them, you are likely to be drawn toward your fears in ways you won't be able to perceive consciously. Then you will start sounding like your father and acting like the unpleasant spouse you resent.

If you feel deeply about something, you will be drawn toward it in the unconscious area of your mind. If you are not mindful, you can become what you fear. But the good news is, you can use the same complex mind to *resolve* your unfinished business that *draws* you toward it. You only become what you fear if you leave your unfinished business unexamined.

67

Fear of Death

Everyone has some anxiety about death. It's unknown and physically irreversible. You may know what you believe about the afterlife, but you've never been there. While it's common to feel anxious about death, there are those who live in fear of it. The permanence of death for them is terrifying. When this happens, it makes it very difficult to truly live.

Self-preservation is natural. But self-preservation *at all costs* keeps you from genuinely living. It is both psychologically and spiritually damaging to cling too tightly to your life. If you cling too tightly, you will likely become defensive and disconnect from others to protect yourself. Then you may develop a life that becomes enslaved by self-protection. If you try too hard to keep from getting hurt, you will build walls of protection to keep out the pain. But those same walls become prisons that keep you from getting out. Self-preservation at all costs makes people become unnatural.

Just because you really don't want to die doesn't mean you really want to live.

Katie sought out my help after her husband's heart attack. He had been experiencing tightness in his chest off and on for a couple of weeks, and a strange numbness around his mouth for a while, but he kept thinking he was just out of shape and never worried much about it. When he collapsed in the kitchen and was rushed to the hospital, doctors discovered that his major arteries were almost completely obstructed. He was fortunate to survive the quadruple bypass surgery that saved his life. Katie was both grateful and terrified.

"Thank God I was there," she cried in our first session. "I shudder to think what would have happened if he had been alone."

"That must have been awful," I said.

"Yes," she continued. "And we didn't even know it. I mean, he was on the edge of death for who knows how long, and we didn't even know it. It's so scary to think he could have died, or that any of us could die at any moment. You just never know when your time is up."

Katie was traumatized by watching her husband almost die. Coming face-to-face with death is a very sobering thing. It brought up a number of fears for Katie. She started thinking about her own death more.

Thinking about her own death caused Katie to become afraid of several things. She didn't like the thought of traveling to other countries anymore. She claimed it was because of the strain on her husband, but it actually had more to do with her own fear of flying. Katie also stopped going out at night. Again, she said it was because her husband might need her, but it was actually meeting a need of her own to shrink her life down to a smaller, more manageable size that made her feel safe. If she could live her life within the familiar boundaries that she knew so well, then she didn't have to think about anything happening that might bring up her fear of death.

As our sessions progressed, we discovered that Katie had been dealing with a fear of death her entire life. She hated scary movies as a child, fearing that she might end up like one of the murdered actors. She often worried that her parents might die and leave her alone and afraid. And as an adolescent, Katie would fantasize about what others would say if she were to come to an untimely death. Would they be sorry? Would she be able to know up in heaven if they were?

As an adult, Katie admitted to me that she often wondered if her life was worth living. Did she deserve to live the life she had, or would the world be better off if she wasn't even around? These unpleasant thoughts of death had been rolling around in Katie's mind for most of her life. And her husband's brush with death brought this all up for her.

But Katie and I eventually discovered she wasn't afraid of what was going to happen to her in the future; she was afraid of reliving things that had already happened to her in the past. Katie's fear of death was her way of condensing all the frightening things that disturbed her in the past into one identifiable event in the future that she could single out and worry about. It was just too difficult to list all the events of her life that frightened her or made her anxious in one way or another. She couldn't deal with the possibility that any of these things might happen to her again in her life. So she simplified the list of possible things that could make her afraid in life into one main event: her death.

The problem with Katie's strategy for dealing with her fears was that it wasn't helping her live her life very fully. Her attempts to protect her life were actually cutting her off from the enjoyment of it. She might live a longer life by being hyperprotective, but she wasn't enjoying the one she was working so hard to save.

Katie realized that she had erected many walls of fear to protect herself. If she feared something, then it couldn't get close enough to hurt her. If she feared something else, then she would always be watching it, and it couldn't get her either. Her fears were her form of self-protection. But she eventually came to see that these walls of protection were also her prison of isolation. Sure, she was safe from harm behind her walls of fear, but she was all alone with her fears inside.

Katie understands her fear of death differently now. Instead of worrying about what might happen to her in the future, we are talking about the things that have already happened to her in the past. We can't deal with the unknown in the future, but we can deal with the effects of what has already occurred. In talking about the painful and frightening things in Katie's past, something interesting is happening. Katie is enjoying her life more. Facing her fears and talking about them openly with another person is making a difference. Somehow they have less power over her. Scary things don't seem so scary when they are brought out into the light. And something else is happening since Katie is enjoying her life more. She isn't thinking so much about her death.

When the fear of death triggers self-preservation at all costs, you begin to starve. You may be protecting yourself from dying, but you are not getting what you need to truly live. Going to new and different places no longer sounds interesting, learning additional things appears too radical, and meeting new people feels boring. You need a connection to the world around you to keep your life vital and full. The fear of death can cause you to become immature and stunted in your growth. Then, the fear of death becomes the imprisonment of life.

In general, Christians have less fear of death. This is something that psychologists have measured with research using psychological tests. Believing that God has a wonderful place for you after you have finished your time on earth frees people enslaved *by their fear of death*. Being prepared for death frees you to embrace life. But being prepared to die doesn't necessarily mean you are willing to live. Not fearing death means you are ready to live life more fully. Now you must go and do it.

68

Overcoming Fear of Failure

Wasting human talent is the greatest waste of all. Although the original use of the word *talent* referred to a sum of money in the Bible, it's helpful to think of the word in contemporary terms. We have all been given different talents, but we all have equal opportunity to develop the talents we have been given. A spiritual truth about life is that it is not the quantity of our talents or wealth that determines a satisfied life, but what we do with what we have been given.

Developing their talents is a daunting task for some people. They are afraid to take the risks necessary for success because of their fear they might fail. This can be quite immobilizing.

Kevin came to therapy because he was frustrated with his dating life. He graduated from a well-known college and landed a good job related to his degree. Although Kevin is an attractive and articulate man in his twenties, he has never had a serious relationship with a woman that lasted for more than a couple of months. Even though he has every reason to expect to be a success in his personal life, Kevin is afraid this will never happen.

Kevin was raised in an upper-middle-class family with a stay-at-home mom and a father who was a successful executive for a Fortune 500 company. His father was a hardworking man who loved his family, but he was often away on business, and when he was home he was preoccupied with business matters that made Kevin feel he was unavailable. Kevin turned to his mother for emotional support as a child, but she was very reactive and easily angered, making it unsafe for Kevin to bring his problems to her. At an early age, Kevin decided he was on his own when it came to solving emotional problems in his life. For a young boy, this can create feelings of insecurity.

Because he was intelligent, he figured out most things by himself eventually, but inside he masked the fear that he wasn't doing it just right. Kevin was forced to think for himself before he was emotionally prepared to do so. Young children don't need to feel like independent thinkers; they need to feel safe. Kevin could come up with intelligent solutions to his problems, but inside he felt like his parents should be doing it. This created the misleading picture of a rather mature young man, acting quite self-sufficient in the world and not asking for help from anyone, while inside Kevin was a fearful little boy who was afraid his decisions might not turn out to be the right ones at all. Children like Kevin slip through the cracks at school because they don't cause problems for teachers; they get their work done and can even be perfectionists. But on the inside, children like Kevin are actually only pretending to be confident when they are covering over feelings of fear and insecurity that come from feeling too young and having to act older than they really are.

This strategy of being self-sufficient helped Kevin navigate his childhood circumstances pretty well, but it was failing to help him in his personal life as an adult. When it comes to relationships with women, he can decide which women he is attracted to, but he is riddled with fears that he might not measure up to the man they want him to be. After months of agonizing, he can ask a woman out for a date, but he is afraid to let her know too much about him for fear of disappointing her. This, of course, does not result in feelings of connection, and women often lose interest in Kevin or assume he is not that interested in them because of his emotional aloofness.

Kevin's fear of failure with women became a self-fulfilling prophecy. He was afraid women would find some weakness in him that would make him unattractive as a man, so he hid his vulnerable feelings from them, which in turn made him less attractive to women. Kevin worried over whether or not he was attractive enough, or witty enough, or successful enough to keep the attention of a woman. But none of these things were actually his problem. Kevin was afraid of being *found out*. He lived with an outward façade of confidence, while inside he was hiding his fear that he was somehow deficient. Tragically, his deficiency wasn't actually related to any of his present-day qualities as a man. He was actually just fine. His problem was that he was *afraid* that he wasn't.

Kevin's attractiveness to women and his success in his dating life began to change when he uncovered his fear of failure in relationships. Hiding who he was out of a fear of failing to measure up to expectations wasn't working for him. Taking the risk to actually fail by letting others know who he really was had a paradoxical impact upon him. Not only did he discover that showing his vulnerabilities made him more attractive to the women he was trying to get close to, but he also learned that what he had to share about himself wasn't all that bad after all. Of course, Kevin had weaknesses as a person and a man, but they were turning out to be well within the range of normal. He never knew this before because he was too afraid to find out. Kevin learned the spiritual truth that failure offers us more of an opportunity to grow than success does.

The fear of failure is often rooted in the belief that we have something to hide. The issue isn't really the possibility that we won't succeed in the future; it is the fear that who we already are is going to be discovered and found lacking. Hiding your talents to avoid failure brings limited effectiveness in life. It is only by risking failure that we find out that who we are is not perfect, but certainly good enough.

69

The Fight, Flight, or Freeze Syndrome

Most people have heard about the fight-or-flight syndrome. This is the basic response to fear. All animals have it. But the truth is that it is actually the fight, flight, or *freeze* syndrome.

When faced with a sudden fear, the first response is to freeze. This is when you stop in your tracks and evaluate the situation. First you freeze, and then you respond with either a fighting response or a fleeing one. This syndrome is automatic. You don't think about it; you just do it when you are afraid. You may not freeze for very long—maybe even less than a second. But sometimes you can get stuck in the freeze response for quite a long time.

Joe came to therapy because he felt overwhelmed at work. He was a good employee and well liked by everyone who worked for him, too. But Joe couldn't say no to his boss, so he often took on extra work just because his boss asked him to do it. By the time he came to see me he was not only doing his own work but the work of about two other people, as well. Joe needed to make some changes, but he felt stuck.

"I sleep at least eight hours a night, and yet I wake up every day so tired that it doesn't feel like I slept at all," Joe complained.

"You feel exhausted. All you do is work," I observed.

"These things have to be done," Joe said. "I know if I don't do it, then no one will. My boss is an 'idea' man, not a detail-oriented kind of person. He needs me to follow through with things or they won't get done."

"So what would happen if you didn't do his work for him?" I asked.

"I couldn't do that," Joe replied. "Things would back up, and then I would really have too much to do. I'm stuck in a bad situation, and I don't see a way out of it."

Joe was a dedicated and responsible person. His personal work ethic was to do what was expected of him, and then some. I admire a good work ethic, but I think something more was going on for Joe that he needed to understand.

Joe was stuck in his relationship with his boss, not just because he was conscientious, but because he was afraid. Joe wanted to do a good job, but the reason he wouldn't speak up to his boss about the unfairness in their working relationship was because Joe was afraid of disappointing him, which would make Joe feel like a failure.

Joe grew up with an absent father and a mother who was overwhelmed with the responsibility of raising five children pretty much on her own. He didn't feel close to his father, and he was afraid to ask much of his mother for fear that his needs would be too much for her. Joe concluded early in life that to ensure his place in the family as a good son, he would work harder than everyone else. Whatever he lacked in natural talent, he could make up for in effort.

Joe came to realize it wasn't really his boss he was afraid of disappointing, it was his parents. Joe was still living as though his parents were alive today, and he lived under the constant fear that he might slack off and disappoint them. Joe did have to confront someone, but his boss wasn't at the top of his list. We wrestled with countless memories of things he had done to win the acceptance of his father and shoulder the burdens of his mother that only left him feeling inadequate because he could never do enough. After hours of struggling with the feelings he had about himself and his parents, Joe started to see himself differently. Perhaps it wasn't

Joe who was the disappointment, but his father and mother, who placed too much responsibility on him and failed to nurture him into a confident manhood.

Joe no longer works for his former boss. After wrestling with his fears of being a disappointment to his parents, his boss was a relatively easy person to confront. Joe isn't as afraid of disappointing his new boss today, because Joe no longer has the fear that he is a disappointment himself.

Joe was stuck in his relationship with his boss because he was stuck in the *freeze* response. His fear of disappointment was signaling him to stop and evaluate the situation. But because he couldn't identify the real threat, he got stuck and couldn't decide if he needed to fight or flee. The freeze response is a natural response to fear, but it isn't healthy to stay in the freeze response. It is meant to be a temporary state of being.

If you are stuck in the freeze response, then you have some struggling to do. Like Joe, you may not know exactly what your struggle is, but you can be sure that there is something, or someone, with which you need to wrestle. Wrestling with your fears changes you. This is why God changed Jacob's name to Israel when he wrestled all night with the angel of God. The name Israel means, "He struggles with God." Getting stuck in life doesn't have to be a problem, as long as you are willing to wrestle with yourself and God. If you face your fears head-on, it will make you a new person, and more than likely you will no longer be stuck in a freeze response.

PART SEVEN

Happiness

70

Gratitude: The Key
to Happiness

Gratitude is a key element in happiness. This is not always easy to achieve, nor is it easy to understand exactly what this means. Some people are indiscriminately grateful in a naive manner because they believe that gratitude is simply positive thinking. They seem compelled to convince everyone (and perhaps themselves) that nothing bad can really happen to them because of the depth of their spirituality or their positive attitude. I don't believe this is what the Bible is instructing us to do.

The Bible instructs us to "give thanks in all circumstances." But it is important to make a distinction between thanking God *for* everything and thanking him *in* everything. God does not want us to live a life of denial, where we pretend to be grateful for everything that happens to us no matter how horrible. He's not instructing us to be grateful *for* all circumstances; he is telling us to look for something for which we can be grateful *in* all circumstances. This is genuine gratitude. Happiness does not come from the absence of suffering; it comes from finding comfort in it.

A few years ago, I invited Dr. Frederic Luskin, who served as director of the Stanford Forgiveness Project, to give a lecture to a group of psychologists. His group at Stanford conducted some of the largest research projects in the world on the effects of forgiveness, because they believed forgiveness to be a healing agent in the lives of victims of violent crimes. He helped many hurt, angry, and depressed individuals become more hopeful, optimistic, and self-confident. Dr. Luskin assisted many devastated people in their attempts to live happier lives.

As I listened to Dr. Luskin describe the horrible things that happened to the people he was trying to help, I found myself wondering if they could ever find healing for such atrocities. One woman had witnessed the murder of her child, another man had a member of his family violently taken from him never to be heard from again, and yet another woman had been raped. These people had suffered horrible circumstances and were in great pain.

I listened as Dr. Luskin described his work with one woman with incredible compassion and insight. He never tried to convince her that what had happened to her was anything other than horrific. He didn't suggest that the perpetrator of the crimes against her was anything other than wrong and culpable for his actions. But what Dr. Luskin did do was listen to the painful story of what happened to her, and sit with her pain for as long as she could bear to express it. And then, he quietly led her to the window, where she could feel the warmth of the sun on her face. It was a cold day, and the experience of the sun's rays was a comforting contrast to the coldness she felt throughout her life. With expert skill, Dr. Luskin helped this woman find a moment of gratitude in her life. Even if this brief moment of warmth in the sun was the only thing in her life for which she could be grateful, at least she had found it.

In that room of a few hundred people listening to Dr. Luskin, you could have heard a pin drop. We all seemed to get it at the same time. That moment of gratitude was the beginning point of this woman's healing. If she could find one thing for which she was grateful, then perhaps there could be more. Gratitude was the key to rebuilding her life. It was the beginning point of finding happiness in a life that appeared to have none.

Neither Dr. Luskin nor the Bible teach people to be grateful for the terrible things that happen to them. Sometimes bad things happen and good people have to suffer from them. But what they both do teach is that even in the midst of our suffering we can find something for which we can be grateful. It may be something as simple as the warmth of the sun or something as great as a relationship with the God of the universe, but finding gratitude is the foundation for our healing and the pathway back to happiness for those who have lost it.

71

Courage Is Not Fearlessness

What does it mean to have courage? The first synonym the dictionary associates with the word courage is *fearlessness*. But psychologically I don't think this is quite right. I have witnessed people act without fear in dangerous circumstances in ways I would not consider emotionally healthy, wise, or courageous. In fact, the feeling of fear can be very instructive at times, as it is often an emotion we would do well to heed rather than ignore. The absence of fear can be foolishness masquerading as courage.

I think courage is saying yes to your life in spite of negative circumstances.[1] It is not the absence of fear but faith in the presence of it. Courage is the choice to take action when you are afraid you can't. Not everyone can be fearless, but everyone has the capacity for courage. This is a good thing, because there is a powerful relationship between courage and happiness.

Brianna came to me for help because her marriage of fifteen years was in trouble. She had married the only man she had ever loved right out of high school, had two children with him, and now found herself in a life that she could not have predicted almost twenty years ago. She was very committed to her marriage vows, but he had become withdrawn and distant—so much so that she wasn't sure she even knew him anymore. He dismissed her pleas for getting help as something "they didn't need," and he was accepting more and more travel assignments from work to avoid things at home. Brianna was feeling just as lonely and afraid as she had during her unhappy childhood, and she didn't know what to do about it.

"I can't believe I am ending up like my parents," Brianna moaned.

"How so?" I asked.

"They didn't have much of a marital relationship, and now I don't have much of one, either," she said.

"You tried so hard to make things different for yourself."

"It didn't use to be this way," she went on. "We used to talk and do things together. But now he is either working or sitting alone in front of the TV at night. If I try to bring anything up, he just gets hurt and turns away."

"It's not easy talking about painful things, but life gets harder if you don't," I said.

"I know, I know," she replied. "It's just that he works so hard, and I haven't wanted to make things worse. I've tried to be supportive and helpful, but it just isn't working. I can't go on living this way."

Brianna grew up with an emotionally abusive mother and a passive father who couldn't protect her. She left home as soon as she was able and married her childhood sweetheart, a kind and thoughtful person who she knew would never hurt her like her mother had done. Unfortunately, she discovered over the years that she needed more from a husband than the absence of abusiveness. She also needed him to be emotionally present and connected to her. He was never rude or unkind like her mother, but his emotional unavailability was just as hurtful. Brianna was very unhappy in her marriage, and she was afraid that if she spoke up about it too firmly, her husband would leave her and then she would have nothing.

Brianna and I accepted that we could not change her husband; he wasn't in the room with us in our counseling sessions anyway. But that didn't have to limit her. She could take a look at her contributions to the problems in her marriage, and in her life, and try to face those things the best way she knew how. She grew up in a very unhappy childhood and now she was living in an unhappy marriage, but God had not abandoned her, and that meant she could ask him to give her the courage to do something about her unhappiness. Brianna could say yes to her life despite the negative circumstances.

Over the next several months, Brianna and I discovered that she made most of her decisions in life out of fear. She was afraid of her mother, so she learned to stand back and *not make waves* for fear of offending her. She married her husband because he felt safe and she was too afraid to do anything else. And she was contributing to many of her marital problems because she was afraid of what might happen if she tried to change things. She came to see that she was resenting him for not being different, but she was just as afraid of change too. Sure, she had told him many times that she was unhappy, but she was too afraid to actually do anything different herself to try to make a difference.

Over time, Brianna realized that her husband was not the source of her unhappiness—the real basis was her own fear. More precisely, the problem was her *response* to her fear. She was still acting like she did as a child, trying to *not make waves* to protect herself from her mother's abuse. But she didn't have to keep reacting this way. Now, when she was afraid in life, she could do something different. She could take some action to try to make things better.

Brianna is changing things in her life now. She identified a few goals for herself and started pursuing some accomplishments that she was too afraid to pursue before. She went back to college to obtain the degree she always wanted, she is developing some genuine friendships with a couple of women who she was afraid wouldn't accept her, and she insisted that her husband stop watching TV by himself in the evenings as a way to avoid their marriage. She changed all these elements in her life, not because she isn't afraid anymore, but because even though she is afraid, she is not going to let that fear stop her from asking for what she needs. This is the true definition of courage—saying yes to your life in spite of the negative circumstances. Brianna is becoming a true woman of courage, and not only is she a much happier person today because of it, her husband is as well.

The presence of fear is not really the problem in life. It is our lack of courage that is the real culprit. You need fear to help you identify danger. Brianna's fear helped her survive an abusive childhood by teaching her that not to speak up was the best strategy to help her avoid her abusive mother. But now that she is an adult, she needed a new strategy in response to her fears. This is where the courage to take a different action comes in. God expects us to feel fear at times, and thankfully he has given us the capacity for courage to deal with it when it comes.

72

Faith: The Power to Transcend Any Difficulty

Psychologists have studied the effects of religion in great detail, and the research indicates that authentic religion that is an intrinsic part of one's life has a positive influence on mental health in many ways.[2] Of course, religion is used in unhealthy ways by some people, but when psychologists look at religion very closely, they find that people who are intrinsically religious are generally happier than those who are not.[3] There is a positive relationship between heartfelt faith and happiness, which I also discussed in the portion of this book that covers anxiety.

Christina came to me for help because she was abused as a child, and as a result she struggled with low self-esteem, depression, and a deep fear of being hurt by others that made most of her relationships strained and difficult for her. She had been in therapy before, which was helpful, but she still was afraid of others to the point that she couldn't succeed in her job, and she had never had an intimate relationship with a man. Being vulnerable was just not something she could risk, given how hurt she had been in the past.

As a result of our many conversations together over time, Christina made significant improvements in her life. She became well respected at her job and courageously faced her fears of closeness with men in some important ways. Then, quite unexpectedly, Christina was diagnosed with cancer. It seemed so unfair that someone who had been forced to struggle with the effects of an abusive childhood should now be forced to struggle with cancer as well. But

Christina didn't spend much time thinking about it this way. Cancer was something that was happening to her; it didn't define her.

Christina had an intimate relationship with God, and she loved being a member of her church. She didn't view suffering in her life as punishment or bad luck; she saw it as an aspect of the world in which we live and something to be faced with faith that God would help her through it. Like others who view their religion as an intrinsic part of their lives, Christina believed her spiritual life was eternal and the challenges of her physical life were opportunities to develop her character and deepen her understanding of the world God made, not aggravations that alienated her from God or her happiness in this life.

Christina faced her battle with cancer with an optimism that some people couldn't understand, but everyone admired. She followed all her medical doctors' instructions carefully with the confident attitude that God would have a divine purpose in the outcome, no matter what that might be. I never observed her to be in denial about the seriousness of her condition. I often found her to be hopeful and consistently found her to be courageous in the face of physical death, which she feared on several occasions.

Over the next several months, Christina's faith in God gave her the resilience to face death with a courage that transformed her. She was offered promotions at work and asked to take a position of leadership at her church. Others sought out her wisdom and direction for problems in their own lives as a result of how she approached life, as well as the fear of death.

"It surprises me when people think dealing with cancer is such a big deal," Christina remarked to me in one session.

"Really?" I asked.

"I have had to face much worse things than cancer in life, but I guess cancer is something that they can see, so it is more disturbing to them."

"There are much worse things than death," I said.

"That's right," she said. "And once you have faced them, dealing with cancer is not as frightening as others might think."

Christina had cancer, but it didn't have her. Her faith in God gave her the ability to believe in a meaningful life even when her circumstances might suggest otherwise. Christina faced her suffering in life with a genuine faith that allowed her to be a happy person in the midst of unhappy circumstances. This was so impressive to others that they couldn't help being attracted to her. She even started dating a steady boyfriend, someone she could truly rely on, for the first time in her life.

Christina's cancer all but disappeared over the next several years as she lived a life of inspiration to everyone who knew her. She often gave her testimony at church, led a Bible study there, and was admired by everyone at work who had the pleasure of seeing her happy face daily. Her boss even moved her to the front office where she could greet people as they arrived, explaining that he wanted her to be the *face of the company* because of the happiness that she radiated.

Christina would have liked to live a long life on this earth, but eventually her cancer did return. As often happens with her form of cancer, it came back with a vengeance the second time, which resulted in Christina going to be with the Lord after only a few months of struggling with it. Right up until the week she passed, Christina's faith in God empowered her to live whatever time she had here on earth with as much happiness as anyone could have. It was an honor to witness her faith, which was so clearly the source of her contentment in life. If she were here, Christina would tell you that the key to life is to "rejoice in the Lord always." I will never forget the impact she made on me, because I don't know if I have ever witnessed a better example of how powerful the relationship is between genuine faith in God and true happiness.

73

The Myth of Materialism

In spite of the fact that most people believe money cannot bring happiness, most people still live as though it does. We work more than we should at the expense of our families and health, we spend more than we have, and we envy those who have more than we do. If money doesn't really bring happiness, then why are we attracted to the myth of materialism?

The truth is that having material things *does* bring some people happiness, at least temporarily. Personal happiness is an abstract feeling that comes and goes. Sometimes you feel it, and sometimes you don't. Dealing with the subjective nature of happiness is difficult, so one of the ways we deal with this is to attach happiness to things that are concrete. If you make your happiness contingent upon a concrete object that you can see and touch, then it makes it seem like your happiness is not so ephemeral. The main way people try to make happiness concrete is through materialism.

Materialism is the attempt to make happiness something you can control and depend on to be there when you need it. The good part of this strategy is that it works sometimes. The bad part is that it works only temporarily. This means that you will not be satisfied with a materialistic approach to achieving happiness for very long. Because materialism does work at least temporarily, you will likely try to do it again, only this time it will have to be more than the last time. Then you will discover that "whoever loves money never has enough."

A few years ago, I was invited to a party at the home of a very wealthy friend of mine. Everyone in attendance was of a similar socioeconomic status (except for me), so they felt comfortable discussing the details of their very privileged lives. I remember standing in a group of men making small talk when the conversation turned to the subject of jet aircrafts. One of the younger men in the group was trying to decide which airliner he should purchase for himself, as he needed one for his business. I was surprised at the detailed advice he received from the other men in the group. They all apparently owned their own personal jets and were able to offer him specific advice on the makes and models of the latest jet aircrafts. I got the sense that while they were all delighted with the choices they had made in this arena, they were all still quite aware of the *next step* they were planning to make to upgrade their aircrafts to bigger, faster jets that could go even farther than the ones they all had now.

You might think that these men were bragging about their material wealth or that this was a superficial attempt to impress each other as a way of establishing their worth in the group. But I don't think this was the main motivation for the conversation. They all seemed to know each other pretty well, and it appeared to me that they felt comfortable discussing their genuine concerns with a group of other men who could understand them. They weren't bragging about how much they had; they were all actually worried that what they had wasn't enough. If you have the kind of wealth to be able to afford owning a personal jet, when do you know that the one you have is enough? If you *could* have a better one, *shouldn't* you have a better one? Wouldn't you be happier then?

Most of us will never have to face this dilemma, but I think it illustrates a point. Even if money is no object, materialism can bring only fleeting happiness. I didn't believe these men to be unhappy, but I did think they were bored. They could keep purchasing things to make themselves happy, but because they had done this so often, the lasting effect of materialism had diminished. I witnessed for myself that evening that "whoever loves wealth is never satisfied with their income," because materialism works sometimes—but only temporarily.

74

Beauty Is Fleeting

Beautiful people tend to be more successful in life because we all want to reward them for their good looks.[4] Even though few people will admit they value physical beauty very highly, it is the most important variable in determining whether or not someone enjoys a first date.[5] Because beautiful people are intrinsically more desirable, we assume they must be happier as well. But you can't judge a book by its cover.

Bianca was fortunate. She was raised in a well-to-do family, graduated from an excellent private college, was very popular socially, and was extremely attractive. She was very aware of her good fortune in life and tried to be appreciative of it. She worked hard at her job and was kind to others, even when they were not as considerate of her in return.

Bianca learned to not complain about her disappointments in life, because she rarely received much sympathy when she did. If she tried to share her sadness with others, they would dismiss it as though she should have nothing to grumble about. After all, she was so blessed in so many ways, what could she really have to complain about anyway?

This led to a split between her personal feelings and the public persona that she displayed to others. Fearing she would be criticized for having any negative feelings, she tried to be as pleasant as possible. This seemed to be what others wanted.

"I feel guilty about being here," Bianca told me in our first session.

"You are not supposed to need therapy?" I said.

"Well, I suppose everyone can benefit from it, but I have so much to be thankful for." She paused and then continued with, "But I can't stop feeling so sad. It just doesn't make sense."

"I see. So you feel guilty about feeling sad."

"I guess that's right. I mean, there are so many people much worse off than me. I don't have the right to be whining about my problems with all that's going on in the world today."

"Well, it is going to make it difficult to talk about your problems if you see expressing sadness as *whining*," I replied.

"Well, that's the way I've always seen it. Maybe that's why I'm here," she said as she looked up at me.

Bianca was suffering from the *beautiful woman syndrome*. She was very aware that others were attracted to her, but this did not necessarily mean that they liked her. She enjoyed being desirable, but she also wanted to be *valued*, as well. She didn't go deeply into her thoughts and feelings around others, because they didn't seem to be interested. She learned that if she was superficially pleasant, then others liked being around her. Everyone liked how she looked, but she seldom knew if they really liked her.

Being around a beautiful woman helps us transcend the ordinary. Someone who looks special can make us feel special simply by being around them. But sometimes that same feeling of specialness can also have a painful effect on us. We can become envious of the specialness we see in her because it reminds us of the ways in which we are not that special. Then, just as quickly as we are attracted to a beautiful woman, we can resent her. Although she couldn't explain it, Bianca knew this happened, so she rarely felt safe enough to talk to others about how she really felt inside.

We give privileges to beautiful people because of the happiness we get out of witnessing their beauty. But if their beauty represents their only value to us, then we fail to see the person who is there. This is the price Bianca felt she paid in her relationships with others. It's true that Bianca's beauty contributed to her happiness in life, but she found the effect fleeting. Developing relationships she could trust that would bring enduring happiness was just as much work for her as it was for anyone else. Not only is physical beauty fleeting, but the happiness that it brings to everyone enjoying it is fleeting, as well.

75

Do You Anticipate Being Happy?

Anticipating happiness plays a role in how much of it you will have in your life. If you expect to be unhappy, then you will probably get what you're waiting for. If you expect to be happy, then you are more likely to end up with that. I'm not suggesting that you develop a naive attitude toward life; I'm suggesting that you take a look at your expectations.

A point I have made several times in this book so far is that the meaning people make out of their painful circumstances is more of a problem than the circumstances themselves. God has given us the amazing ability to overcome difficult obstacles based on the strength of our beliefs and expectations. But the opposite is also true. You can create obstacles for yourself simply based upon what you expect. If you believe that the suffering in your life means that you are doomed or unlucky, then you will be unhappy not only because of your circumstances but also because of your beliefs. Your attitude can work for you or against you, so it's important to be aware of your expectations.

Steven was raised by an angry father and a mother who was just as afraid of him as Steven was. He recalls numerous events in his childhood where slight infractions of household rules resulted in angry tirades by his father, who would swear and stomp around the house frightening both Steven and his mother. Confronting his father was out of the question. Steven learned how to live around him, feeling intimidated most of the time.

"I get this knot in my stomach whenever my boss stomps down the hall," Steven said.

"You're afraid he's angry with you?"

"Oh, I don't know," he mused. "I doubt that it really has much to do with me, but I can't help having this reaction. I can't stand it when people are loud. It just makes me so anxious."

"You had to learn to be quiet as a child. It wasn't safe to make too much noise," I said.

"You can say that again," Steven said with some uneasiness. "There was only one person in my house growing up who was entitled to make noise."

"What about when you were playing or making noise happily?"

"It didn't matter," Steven replied. "You never knew what was going to set him off. It was best to just keep quiet. Nothing was worth making him mad."

"So you learned to expect that just about any noise would lead to something bad," I said.

"That's right," he said emphatically. "It was better to expect the worst than actually have it happen."

Steven spent much of the time feeling anxious and afraid. He was afraid of disturbing others, and he didn't like it when they disturbed him. He had difficulty sleeping, worried about what others thought of him, and came across as self-conscious and uncertain. Steven believed that all disruptions led to someone getting angry, which made relationships very difficult for him. Steven was unhappy most of the time, in part because he never expected things to turn out happily for him. Steven expected to be unhappy, and as a result he often was.

After many months of working on this with me, things are changing for Steven. He still has a problem with anxiety, but this wasn't his biggest problem. Steven's problem with anxiety wasn't as big as his problem with expecting someone to get mad at him. Over time Steven saw that *believing* that all disruptions led to someone getting mad didn't necessarily mean that it *would* happen. Perhaps his boss could stomp down the hall because he was excited, or in a hurry, or maybe it didn't mean anything at all. Steven saw that *anticipating* unhappiness was creating more unhappiness than the actual events in his life. His childhood rule of expecting the worst wasn't helping him anymore.

As Steven began to release his expectation of unhappy endings for all disruptions in relationships, he noticed something happening for him. Instead of anticipating people would get angry, he could actually envisage them being happy at times. Now if he interrupts someone, he can imagine that they might be pleasantly surprised instead of irritated, and this is helping to release the knot in his stomach that was there for so many years. Perhaps some spontaneous noise can lead to happy encounters. Some interruptions in life are actually good news.

The Bible teaches us that "how beautiful on the mountains are the feet of those who bring good news." We all like positive people. Becoming aware of his beliefs and expectations helped Steven to see that anticipating unhappiness made him the bearer of bad news every time he expected someone to get mad. No one was attracted to that, including Steven. He is much happier now that he anticipates happiness in his interactions with others. Changing his beliefs and expectations is making him the bearer of good news these days, and everyone can see that he is a more beautiful person because of it.

76

It Takes Courage
to Be Imperfect

Happy people have an attitude of acceptance. Acceptance is the awareness of unsolvable problems that you choose to stop trying to change. It requires the ability to tolerate imperfections and the discomfort of failure. Happy people strive to accept circumstances, they tolerate their lack of control in life, and most importantly, they learn to accept themselves.

To be happy you must be able to accept your limitations. You must have the courage to be imperfect, which means you are motivated to grow while accepting who you are now at the same time. Living with this kind of courage is a happy balance between ambition and humility, and it is the path to being authentically happy.

Edward came for therapy because he was unhappy with his job. He had been an executive in nonprofit organizations for many years, but he was chronically unhappy with his place of employment. He had a history of leaving jobs after two to three years. Eventually he found something unacceptable about his job that made it impossible for him to stay there. He was never fired, but he always quit because he was unhappy.

"My work is very important to me," Edward explained. "I must work for an organization whose core values I agree with and one that allows me to utilize my talents and abilities. A man spends most of his life at work, so it doesn't make sense to me to feel any other way about it."

"You approach your work with a sense of moral obligation," I reflected.

"That's right," Edward said cheerfully. "I believe God placed me in this world for a purpose, and I must strive to fulfill that purpose. I can't accept anything less."

"Have you ever found a job that gave you that sense of purpose?"

"Not completely," he replied. "But that doesn't mean I should ever stop looking."

Edward was a hardworking and conscientious employee. He was good at his job and enjoyed working in the nonprofit world. But Edward was never happy. He believed that the root of his dissatisfaction was either the inconsistencies of each organization to live up to their stated values or their failure to provide him with an opportunity to utilize his abilities. He couldn't accept these shortcomings on the part of management, so he would eventually feel compelled to quit rather than stay and feel morally compromised.

At first Edward wasn't sure how I could help him in therapy, because he thought his unhappiness was rooted in an employment problem. But as our sessions went on, we discovered that his problem wasn't with how he felt about his employment; it was with how he felt about himself.

Edward's father was a very successful entrepreneur whom he admired but often disagreed with. He was proud of his father's accomplishments, but he was uncomfortable with how his father had achieved his goals. He argued with his father over the environmental and political ramifications of his business decisions and accused him of using the ends to justify the means. To Edward, his father seemed to value economic success over the social impact of his decisions. This seemed like moral relativity to Edward, and he vowed never to be like that himself.

As we explored the impact of Edward's upbringing upon his life today, we discovered many things. We discovered that his decision to work in the nonprofit arena was no accident. It was easy to understand why Edward emphasized moral integrity and social responsibility so highly in the organizations for which he worked, as a result of his relationship with his father. But as our therapy went on, we discovered something else. Edward's lack of acceptance for the shortcomings he observed in others was actually rooted in a lack of acceptance of his own limitations. It wasn't just the failures of others that made him unhappy; it was his own failures that disturbed him the most.

Edward was good at some things, but he couldn't accept being forced to work in areas that didn't utilize his talents and abilities. It made him feel like a failure, and he couldn't stand that. He complained that he was being underutilized, but it was really that he couldn't tolerate the feeling of inadequacy that came from working at tasks that weren't in his areas of strength. And Edward's intolerance for the moral inconsistencies of management turned out to be reflective of how difficult it was for Edward to accept his own discrepancies between what he believed he *should* do and what he actually *could* do. Observing their contradictions just made him feel worse about his own.

Edward's unhappiness at work had more to do with his unhappiness with himself than he knew. After several months of working on this, Edward didn't need to argue with his father, or anyone else, as much as he used to about the moral failures going on around him. He still is very committed to the nonprofit work that he does these days, but he is more accepting of his imperfect work environment. Learning to accept his own limitations and inconsistencies has helped him be more tolerant of everyone else's as well. Edward is discovering how the courage to accept his own limitations is helping him be happier with his work environment and be a much happier man in general, too.

The Bible tells us that the people who follow God have a very valuable spiritual gift inside of them. But even the most spiritually enlightened and mature among us "have this treasure in jars of clay."

We are all imperfect vessels, no matter how good our goals and ideals might be. Learning to accept ourselves as flawed containers of the great treasures that lie within us requires the courage to be imperfect. As Edward is learning, this is one of the keys to living a truly happy life.

77

Why the Humble Live Happier Lives

The Bible tells us that our knowledge of reality is only partial in this life. Your knowledge of others, and your ability to be known by them, is limited. This is a difficult thing for many people to accept. Most of us would like to believe that we can objectively know the truth with complete certainty. This is not to say there are no absolute truths. It is just to say that you can only know them with your limited human ability.

You are constantly learning in this life, ever growing in your knowledge. Everything you see is influenced by your history and perspective. This means you must be humble with what you know. As long as you are living in this human realm, you will be able to see things from only your own perspective. Being humble about what you think you know is an important aspect of happiness.

Henry and John were brothers who grew up in a middle-class family where they learned traditional family values and how to work hard to get ahead in life. They both married and started families in separate cities where they focused on their careers and home lives.

As the years passed, they tried to keep in touch, visiting each other about once a year. They didn't have any other siblings, so the relationship they had with each other was important, especially after their parents passed away. They didn't express how important they were to each other in words, but they both felt it in their hearts.

One year Henry was having some financial difficulties, so he called John to tell him that he wasn't going to be visiting him that year. Henry didn't want to explain why he wasn't coming because he was embarrassed to admit that he wasn't doing very well financially.

"Hello, John," Henry started off.

"Hey, Henry," John answered.

"How are things?" Henry asked.

"Fine," John replied. "And how about you?"

"Fine, just fine. Listen, about the trip up to see you this year. Some things have come up, and we are not going to be able to make it."

"Really?" John said, somewhat surprised. "Oh well, that's too bad. Is everyone okay?"

"Sure, we're all fine," Henry said awkwardly. "We just have too much going on, and I'm real busy at work so I just can't get away."

"Right," John said jokingly. "Like you ever let work get in the way of anything."

"Well, I may not make the kind of money you do, but my work is still important to me," Henry said defensively.

"Whatever," John said, still poking fun at Henry's excuse for not making the trip. "Well, when you start making the big bucks like me, then we'll schedule something."

"Look," Henry said, starting to get angry, "when I start making that kind of money, I'm sure I'll have better things to do anyway. Well, I've got to go. I just wanted to let you know."

"Yeah," John said. "Well, thanks for the call."

As they got off the phone, both men felt bad. Henry was embarrassed and angry at John, feeling mocked by him for not earning more money. John felt hurt because he always considered their family visits a sign of how important they were to each other. Now he felt Henry had more important things to do and was offering weak excuses to explain it away. Unfortunately neither man wanted to talk about how they really felt. It just wasn't something they did very often.

Several years passed, and the two brothers refused to speak to each other. Both felt offended by the other, and each considered it the other person's responsibility to make the first call to apologize. In spite of their wives urging them to talk to each other, many years passed with Henry and John living without any family connection at all. Each believed he was right in being angry with the other, so nothing changed.

Then something tragic happened. Henry developed cancer, and his doctors told him that he didn't have long to live. He was devastated. As he began to put his affairs in order, knowing that he was facing death, he couldn't keep from thinking about John. He hadn't spoken to his only brother in years, and he didn't want to die without having a final conversation with him. The reasons he had built up over the years to resent John no longer seemed to matter. He was going to die, and he wanted to make peace with his brother.

So Henry called John to repair their relationship. It turned out that neither of them were right about what had happened in that phone call many years ago. John didn't mean to mock Henry about the money he made; he was merely hurt and trying to cover it over with sarcasm. And Henry didn't mean to communicate to John that he wasn't important to him; he always looked up to him and was afraid he was disappointing him. Each of them had their own perspective on what had happened, but neither of them had the humility to consider they might not be right.

A lack of humility cost both John and Henry many years of happiness together. Insisting on being right turned out to be very wrong. The Bible tells us that "God opposes the proud but shows favor to the humble" (James 4:6). There are many reasons why this is true. One reason is that you can see things only from your own limited perspective. No matter how right you think you are, remember that in this life you will always "know in part" based upon your imperfect human ability. As John and Henry learned, this is one good reason why the humble live happier lives.

78

Why Contentment Is More Important Than Excitement

Lasting happiness comes from contentment more than excitement. The euphoria that comes when things are new is exciting. Falling in love, taking new adventures, and trying new things brings a certain kind of happiness to your life. But happiness that comes from the excitement of novelty doesn't last. Lasting happiness comes from learning "the secret of being content in any and every situation."

The danger of deriving your happiness from excitement is that excitement is addictive. When the rush of excitement wears off, then you must find something new to restore the lost exhilaration. If you must have excitement to be happy, then your happiness is dependent on your situation, so your circumstances are more in control of you than you are of your circumstances. This kind of dependency makes your happiness determined by something that doesn't last.

Shawn is a good-looking, energetic person who has many friends. He loves outdoor activities and is a really fun person to be around.

Although he has no difficulty making friends, he is not as successful at making marriages last. Shawn came to therapy because he was considering his third divorce. He was pretty sure that he wanted to go through with it, but he felt he should talk to a psychologist first.

"I have to tell you that I don't believe it is possible to stay happily married to the same person for a lifetime," Shawn said.

"Really?" I responded.

"That's right," he said. "I mean, people change so much over the course of a lifetime that you are just not the same person at fifty who took those vows when you were twenty. I think marriages should be for only seven years, at which time you can renew it or let it dissolve. It just makes more sense to do it that way."

"That's a very interesting notion. I'm guessing you have personal experience to support your theory."

"Correct," Shawn said confidently. "I don't believe the human male is capable of maintaining interest in the same woman for more than about seven years. It's in our genetic makeup to move on. Men just get bored. It's the way we are made."

Shawn's theory was not a new one to me. I am aware of some social anthropologists who make similar arguments to explain the widespread problem of affairs. But I operate with a different assumption about Shawn's explanation for his upcoming divorce. I don't believe that men are hardwired to lose interest in their partners; I believe they have a hard time feeling content.

As Shawn and I explored the details of his current situation, we developed a clearer picture of why he was unhappy in his marriage. At first Shawn's explanation was primarily a biological one: men grow bored with the same partner over time because they are biologically predisposed to do so. Over time we began to see that there were also some psychological explanations for his loss of interest in his wives.

Because there was so much conflict in Shawn's home growing up, he spent as much time as he could with his friends away from the house. He was a good athlete, so he found affirmation playing sports, socializing, and dating attractive girls. Because his home life was unhappy, he found happiness in extracurricular activities. The more things he could do to keep him away from his depressing home, the better.

By the time he was an adult, Shawn was an expert in several extreme sports, had a very active social life, and had experienced many sexual partners. He never experienced happiness at home, so he expected to find it only in exciting activities elsewhere. Shawn not only found his happiness in these exciting activities; he became dependent upon them. Just like an alcoholic, he was not just trying to find happiness; he was also trying to avoid the unhappiness that he had never learned to face.

After many months of honest conversations about this, Shawn began to expand his view of why he was going through his third divorce. He saw that his happiness in life was dependent upon novelty and excitement. It was only after taking the time to talk about the sad and difficult aspects of his life that he realized working through disappointments and hurts could produce a different kind of happiness—one that is content with who he is now without needing the excitement of novelty to distract him. Shawn discovered that he didn't have difficulty sustaining interest in a monogamous relationship; his difficulty was with resolving conflicts in relationships and coming to peace with the differences he encountered there. Like many men, he had never learned how to deal with his painful feelings well enough to experience contentment. As a result of his work with me, Shawn decided he didn't want a new wife; he wanted a deeper relationship with the one he had now.

Shawn still believes that men are hardwired to hunt and gather, so they are predisposed to be happier with the new and exciting parts of relationships. But he now believes that men *can* find lasting happiness in the contentment that comes from developing safety with the same person over time. Now he not only wants the happiness that comes from the exciting parts of his life, but he also longs for the happiness that comes from the security of being with someone he deeply knows will be his partner for life.

There is a happiness that transcends circumstances in life. The Bible tells us we can find this happiness if we learn "the secret of being content in any and every situation." By facing our pain rather than looking for excitement to cover it over, we are able to find a lasting form of happiness that comes from contentment.

79

Hope: The Expectation of Happiness

It is encouraging to believe that you will have a good life ahead of you. However, the two extremes of obsessing on an idealized future or a bleak one both produce unhappiness, because they are both driven by fear. In contrast, the ability to hope for a happy future is based upon a genuine love for life, which also helps you enjoy the present moment you have now.

The Bible tells us that some expectations are good for us. Hope is the expectation of happiness now and in the future. It is not a guarantee that your circumstances will be exactly as you want them, but a confidence that the love of God and your love of life will go forward with you. Hope is the capacity to love life, both now and in what is yet to come.

I am a consultant for an international ministry to people affected by disabilities. Joni and Friends was started in 1979 by Joni Eareckson Tada, who herself has been a quadriplegic since the age of seventeen. This is a worldwide organization devoted to raising awareness in Christian churches about the needs of those suffering from disabilities and equipping churches to reach out to meet the spiritual, emotional, and physical needs of those persons.

At one of the conferences held by Joni and Friends, I met a man named Nick Vujicic. Nick was one of the speakers at the conference, and he delivered a powerful message that few other people could have delivered. He is a great public speaker, but that wasn't the only reason he had such an impact on the audience. Nick gave a compelling sermon on the subject of hope. He was one of the happiest and most optimistic people I have seen in a long time. But what made his message even more impressive is the fact that Nick was born without any arms or legs.

Nick wheeled his way into the auditorium, seated in an electric wheelchair. He had just enough of a limb where one of his legs should have been to give him the ability to direct the wheelchair to the table at the front of the room. With practiced skill, he hopped up onto the table and positioned himself where he could see us, and where we all could clearly see him.

"I'm excited to be with you here on such a beautiful day," Nick began. "God has blessed us in so many ways, and I am grateful to be able to share some of the many ways in which he has so richly blessed me. We have so much to be thankful for, and I am honored to be able to talk with you about that today."

It was impossible to miss the contrast between what I was seeing and what I was hearing at that moment. Before me was a young man in his twenties with no limbs who was about to explain to me how good his life was. He was happy, energetic, and authentically hopeful about his future. Before the end of his message, he even mentioned his conviction that God had a special woman picked out for him as a wife someday. He had not met her at the time of that lecture, but he was completely hopeful that at some point in the future he certainly would.

Nick Vujicic loves life. The skillful manner in which he delivered his talk was so uplifting that by the end of his sermon I had forgotten that there was anything missing in his life at all. Nick's love for both God and life was contagious. And based upon this he had hope. If this man could have hope, then there was hope for us all.

Nick is a full-time public speaker and president of Life Without Limbs. He travels around the world encouraging others to find the happiness that he has found in life. His simple message that the love of Jesus Christ has empowered him to live a life of happiness and hope has impacted thousands of people. On the homepage of Nick's website he has the verse, "'For I know the plans I have for you,' declares the LORD, 'plans to prosper you and not to harm you, plans to give you hope and a future'" (Jer. 29:11). Nick has a life without limbs, not a disability. His hope is not based upon the fantasy that God will remove his greatest difficulties at some point, it is based upon his expectation that his love of God and life will be right there waiting for him in the future once he gets there. I am delighted to tell you that today Nick is married to a beautiful Christian woman and has two wonderful children. His love of God and life has certainly given him a hope and a future, and this has made Nick a very happy man.

80

Forgiveness: How to Free Yourself from Unhappiness

Resentment kills happiness. Yesterday's irritations can stay with you like scar tissue that seems impossible to get rid of. If you have been offended or demeaned in ways that you cannot forget, then you may struggle with resentment that impinges upon your happiness. Time alone does not necessarily heal resentment. The only cure for this kind of anger and ill will is forgiveness.

Forgiveness is a powerful tool for restoring happiness. Forgiveness is not excusing people, tolerating people, or even simply understanding them. As I explained in the section of the book that covered guilt, there are two levels of forgiveness. First, there is the decision not to return hurt for hurt. Second, there is reconciliation. This second level of forgiveness involves the hard work of coming to a mutual understanding of the pain that was caused, a heartfelt repentance for the injury, and a repair of the wound created in the relationship. Although this can take great effort, the benefit to your personal happiness is well worth it.

Julia came for therapy because she was unhappy in her marriage, and her marriage counselor thought she would benefit from some individual therapy. The frequent fights with her husband were disturbing to her, and even though she wanted to start a family, she felt she just wasn't ready. Sometimes she thought she had married the wrong person, and at other times she thought she was the problem. Her fights with her husband were so severe that she even hit him and threw things at him at times. She would yell at him so uncontrollably that her marriage counselor thought she had a borderline personality disorder, and her husband had come to resent her deeply for the way she treated him. This bothered her so much that she agreed to come for therapy for herself.

It didn't take long for us to discover the major reason Julia was having problems in her marriage. She had been molested for many years as a child, and she'd never fully dealt with it. Her husband knew about it, but he didn't know many of the details or what to say to her. And now that he was so angry with her, he had given up even wanting to discuss it. Julia was living with a deep wound that affected her relationships with all men, especially her husband. It is my experience that survivors of childhood molestation are often misdiagnosed with personality disorders, so I was glad that she was finally getting help.

"I get so angry with my husband," Julia confessed to me.

"Anger is a very effective way to keep him away from you when you don't feel safe," I said.

"I just don't know if this marriage is working out," Julia said with a worried look on her face. "I know he's angry and frustrated that we aren't intimate physically very often, but how am I supposed to want that when we fight so much?"

"Of course you aren't intimate physically very often. Your molestation as a child left you with some pretty confusing feelings about all that. It makes sense that you wouldn't feel safe having sex," I said.

"Mostly it feels *yucky* when we do it," Julia said in a strange, childlike voice.

"That sounds like something you've felt for a long time," I said, "because *yucky* is a word that children use when they are disgusted."

"Yeah," she replied. "If I really think about it, I guess it's always felt *yucky*."

Although Julia came for help with her marriage, we had a lot of other work to do, as well. We spent many hours working on the hurt, anger, and shame she felt as a result of the molestation. The man who molested her was deceased, so it wasn't possible to confront him with her feelings even if she had wanted to. So we worked through her pain in therapy. And, thankfully, Julia made a lot of progress.

As Julia understood herself better, her fights with her husband changed. She didn't feel as powerless anymore, so she could protect herself with her words instead of hitting, throwing, and yelling as she did in the past. She saw that her own past hurt caused her to hurt her husband in ways that she now regretted. She was able to explain to him the depth of her fears and the deeper reasons for her anger, and he was able to grasp it in a way that he never had before.

And then something unexpected happened. You might think that Julia forgiving the man who molested her would be the point of this story. But it isn't. In marriages like this, the partner who *wasn't* molested often has to suffer as a result of the childhood abuse that was perpetrated upon the violated spouse. The anger, rejection, and disgust directed at Julia's husband was very demeaning for him as a man, and over time had caused him to resent her. But by talking to her husband about the real reasons for her anger, and her regret over how she had treated him, she realized that her husband didn't resent her anymore for how she had acted. He wasn't just tolerating her as he had done in the past, or making excuses to his friends for the things she had done, but he was genuinely grasping what had gone on in a new light that allowed him to release the resentment he had about the hurtful things she did. She didn't know she needed it until it happened, but now she could see that he understood her and forgave her for all the times she had rejected and hurt him in the past. When Julia realized this, she loved him more than she ever had before.

Julia is much happier in her marriage today. She is even trying to get pregnant with her first child. She wasn't sure she was with the right man before, but feeling forgiven when she was at her worst changed all that. She understands what the Bible means when it says that the person "who has been forgiven little loves little," because when you feel the deepest level of forgiveness, you also feel the deepest level of love.

81

Why Happiness Is Not the Absence of Suffering

An important part of the life of Jesus was his suffering and death. He did not try to avoid it like most of us would; he embraced it as a necessary aspect of his existence. His physical vulnerability to pain was an essential part of his humanity and central to his message of love. According to Jesus, facing suffering with courage develops a greater capacity to love and live a meaningful and happy life.

Happiness does not have to be wiped out by suffering. This is a good thing, because suffering is unavoidable. Your happiness is not dependent upon *whether* or not you suffer; it is dependent upon *how* you suffer. Jesus made this point with his own life, as an example for ours.

Anna was raised in a strict and often punitive family in a small town where many of her relatives lived. She remembers most of her childhood being spent at extended family gatherings or church functions where she felt like she didn't fit in. Anna felt connected to her mother during her early years, but as she grew older, distance formed between them. She was an emotional child, so her creative and impulsive approach to life was disconcerting to her more traditional family and community. She was interested in art, music, and film, but her parents feared that these interests would lead to improper behavior, so they refused to let her pursue them. As she grew into her teenage years, the conflict between Anna and her parents intensified. She expressed feelings that would spring out of her spontaneously, and her parents would tell her that her feelings just weren't appropriate. Unfortunately, when your parents tell you that your most intimate feelings are bad, you develop the belief that *you* are bad, too. It seemed to Anna that everything about her was unacceptable to her parents, so she did what many young people do in her situation: she left home at eighteen and never went back.

By the time Anna was in her midthirties, she had suffered through several traumatic events, had gone through a number of failed relationships, and was discouraged about her chances of ever being happy in life. She came to therapy depressed and afraid there was something wrong with her. If her own parents didn't like who she was, then what hope was there of ever finding anyone who would?

"I know I'm all messed up," Anna said to me.

"How so?"

"Anyone from the screwed-up background that I came from would have problems," she complained. "That's obvious. But I can't go back in time and fix that. It's over. I will never get from my parents what I needed when I needed it. I've been damaged and no one can undo that."

"That's discouraging," I said.

"You're telling me," Anna said curtly. "I'm disqualified from ever being happy."

Anna's feelings about her painful childhood were not unusual. When someone is hurt at a young age, the damage feels permanent. The injury has been there so long that it is hard to imagine life without it. But from a psychological perspective, pain is not pathology. This means that suffering does not produce psychological problems, but how suffering is dealt with does.

As our therapy progressed, I discovered a problem in Anna's life that I often see. Her suffering in life was not as big a problem as the fact that she believed she was defective because of it. Anna had suffered great rejection and humiliation as a child. The emotions that sprang out of her felt like the essence of who she was, and when that was labeled as bad, then she felt like *she* was bad. This shame resulted in a series of bad choices based upon the self-perspective that she was *disqualified* from ever having a happy life.

After several months of exploring this with me, Anna is starting to feel different about her life. She is still in pain about her childhood, but she has found the courage to open up communication with her parents for the first time in many years. She doesn't expect *them* to change, but she wants to try to talk to them now that she feels *she* has. Anna is also suffering the consequences from all the bad choices she made over the years. But her perspective is different on that, as well. Now, instead of her suffering confirming that she is disqualified from happiness, she sees it as what happens when a sensitive woman tries to navigate through life surrounded by people who aren't emotionally responsive. It doesn't mean there is something wrong with her; it means there was something wrong with how she was treated. Being hurt no longer means she was damaged, and feeling pain doesn't mean that she is weak.

Anna has discovered something else. She found that her emotional sensitivity is actually an asset in life. What was once a liability is now a means for connecting on a deep and meaningful level with other sensitive and emotionally responsive people. Her sensitivity led to great suffering in her life, but it can lead to deep happiness, as well. Anna is still aware that she will get her feelings hurt in life, and probably often. But the joy she receives from deep emotional connections with others is a great source of happiness, too.

The life of Jesus tells us that there is a relationship between suffering and love. You must be vulnerable in order to love well, and this means you are going to get hurt. Jesus didn't have to become human—vulnerable to suffering and death. But he did this to help us see that this is the only way any of us can truly love. If you have suffered like Anna in your life, it doesn't mean you can't be happy. You can learn from the life of Jesus that it's not the absence of suffering that will make you happy but the presence of the courage to suffer well.

PART EIGHT

Love

82

The Christian Secret

In her bestselling book *The Secret*, Rhonda Byrne made the law of attraction very popular.[1] She helped concepts from quantum mechanics make their way into the common vernacular and popularized the notion that the universe is more connected than scientists thought in previous generations. Recognizing the interconnectedness of the universe is a comforting thing. We are not isolated beings striving to find meaning as disconnected individuals. We are all part of something greater in ways we are just beginning to understand.

The Bible also talks about the universe as connected and unified. There is a meaningful relationship between everything and a purpose for how the world was made. The story of the Bible is that we are certainly not all on our own. But the Bible is a bit more specific about the interconnectedness we experience. From the biblical perspective, it is not just an impersonal attraction that holds the universe together but a personal connection. According to the Bible, a personal God created the universe with a specific purpose and design. From this personal lens, we are able to see that the universe was designed to draw us toward a personal connection to each other and to God. And according to God's design, the way we do this is through love.

Andrew and Stephanie are an attractive and educated couple living in an upscale community. They enjoy attending cultural events, and they are well read and psychologically sophisticated. They are very spiritual people, but they do not consider themselves to be religious, as they don't believe that antiquated approaches to God are relevant in today's society. They have studied all the major religions and try to take what they find useful from each of them.

In many ways Andrew and Stephanie are very happy with the good life they have, so they came to marriage counseling out of their commitment to self-improvement. Because I believe this is an excellent motivation for seeking therapy, I was delighted to work with them.

"We don't really have any significant problems," Andrew announced in our first session.

"You are very fortunate," I said.

"We just want to work on our communication a bit," he said.

"I see. Are there any places where you find yourselves getting stuck?" I asked.

"Well, we did have one disagreement this week," Stephanie jumped in.

"That might be a good place for us to start. What happened?" I asked.

"It was actually pretty silly," Andrew said with some embarrassment.

"Often important issues show themselves in everyday events. Why don't you tell me about it?" I said.

"Okay," Stephanie said cautiously. "It was about Andrew's conversation with a friend of ours at a party the other night. She's a woman we both know, very attractive and friendly, and well, I just thought he was spending a lot of time with her and it made me uncomfortable. I tried to bring it up to him later, but it didn't go very well."

"I see," I said. "And what did you say?"

"Well," Stephanie said as she looked at Andrew out of the corner of her eye, "I tried to tell him that he hurt my feelings by giving her so much attention. I mean, right in front of all of our friends. It was so inappropriate."

"You see," Andrew said firmly, "that's what she does. Look, Stephanie," Andrew said, turning to face her, "don't put your feelings on me. It's not my responsibility if you have issues with insecurity around other attractive women. It's not like I was trying to *do* anything. How many times do I have to tell you—*I can't make you feel anything*. Your feelings are your responsibility, not mine."

This is a notion that I encounter often. And I wasn't surprised when Andrew turned to me after his confrontation of Stephanie, expecting me to be in full support of his perspective. Although I didn't challenge this idea in the first session, over time Andrew was going to find that I actually didn't agree with him. My experience in working with people in marriage counseling is that you *can* make someone else feel things, especially in marriage.

Intimate relationships are personal. That means when one person does something that has meaning for the other person, it is going to be felt personally. It might be an interesting philosophical idea that two people can live in an intimate relationship and be detached from any responsibility for the other's feelings, but that is not how it works in real life. You *can* make your lover feel hurt, and when you do, it should be the beginning of a conversation, not the end of it, which is what Andrew was trying to achieve with his declarations of psychological independence.

Over time I was able to help Andrew and Stephanie with their communication. I eventually got them to see that having a "response-ability" for each other's feelings was a good thing in marriage. We took the emphasis off of whether or not his or her behavior was *right*, and we put it on how they were making each other *feel*. Judging Andrew's behavior as inappropriate was not as helpful as letting him know that she was hurt. And responding to that hurt was something that Andrew *was* responsible for. Instead of asking themselves whether or not they were doing the *right* thing, they needed to ask themselves if they were doing the *loving* thing.

Some religions view God in impersonal terms, like a supernatural force empowering us to live better lives through influences like the law of attraction. But the Bible views God in very personal terms. He affects us personally, and we affect him and each other personally, as well. The way we manage this personal interconnectedness is through love. The Bible tells us that there are many virtues in life: "faith, hope and love. But the greatest of these is love." Discovering the secret that the law of attraction draws the universe together is a powerful, but incomplete, discovery. The Bible doesn't stop there. The Christian secret is that beyond the law of attraction is the power of connection. The greatest of all virtues is that you were designed to connect to God and others through love.

83

Why Love Is More Powerful Than Hate

The hallmark of the teachings of Jesus is love. His simple message of love for God and others has been translated into well over one hundred languages, with tens of millions of copies published each year. Jesus's instructions on love remain the most influential teaching of the past two thousand years.

Understanding the power of love is not always easy to do. Jesus's instruction "If someone slaps you on one cheek, turn to him the other also" appears to be a passive and submissive approach to conflict, which would not seem to be very effective at first. But if you look more closely, you will see that his instruction is not to turn and walk away, or cower in the face of conflict. Jesus specifically tells his followers to take a stand in the face of conflict, to not back down, and to continue to love others, even if they act in hateful ways toward you. The message here is that love is more powerful than violence or hatred, and those who live by its power will eventually triumph.

I had the opportunity to spend time—as a researcher, not an inmate—in the largest maximum security prison in the United States, located in Angola, Louisiana. Because the warden at the time, Burl Cain, is a Christian, he invited me to interview many of the inmates there in an effort to understand the effectiveness of his programs. The moral transformation in the lives of the men I met was absolutely astounding. I doubt that any other institution anywhere could provide better examples of how selfish criminals can be transformed into caring human beings, given the right circumstances.

One of the men I met there went by the name of Carolina. He was serving a life sentence for murder, and like most of the men there, Carolina will never leave the prison. He will die there as punishment for his crimes. He was notoriously violent, and according to our best psychological understanding of men like Carolina when he arrived at the prison, we don't believe there is any effective treatment for him, and he will probably be a danger to society for the rest of his life. But then, that was before Carolina met the love of God.

Even though Carolina only attended the meeting because he heard there might be some good food, God reached down and touched his heart in a Christian prison ministry meeting and changed his life. He didn't know God beforehand, and had never experienced love up until then, but the conversion experience Carolina had that evening was so profound that the lifetime of hatred in his heart was replaced by an overwhelming sense of God's love that he could not deny.

For the next several years, Carolina studied the Bible and sought out the Christian community in the prison that the warden actively encouraged. He knew he would never get out, but that didn't matter, because Carolina knew he was called to minister to the men there. More specifically, Carolina felt called to the men like him, the most violent men whom no one else would even dare speak to.

Convinced of his genuine rehabilitation, the warden sent Carolina to a neighboring prison as a kind of missionary to attempt to effect moral transformation in the lives of the inmates there. True to his calling, the first thing Carolina did was to walk right up to the most violent man in the prison and begin sharing the good news of how God can change a man's life. Not the least bit interested in hearing what Carolina had to say, the man responded in the most effective way he knew to end the conversation—he beat Carolina all the way down to the ground. As the guards were dragging the man to solitary confinement, Carolina struggled to his feet, spit out enough blood to speak, and embraced the man as he said, "It's okay, buddy, I forgive you."

When the man finally got out of solitary confinement, he was returned to Carolina's unit where everyone was waiting to see what would happen next. Quite the opposite of normal prison culture, Carolina did not seek revenge. Instead, for the next three months, he would quietly find out what the man needed in the way of food, cigarettes, or store supplies and purchase them out of his own money and put it on the man's bed. Confused and angry when he eventually found out who was doing this, the man confronted Carolina with, "Hey, you been puttin' that food on my bed?"

"Yup, and I'm getting sick and tired of it," Carolina replied.

"What?" the man reacted.

"That's right. I'm fed up with giving you what I want you to have. Now I want you to make out a list of what *you* want and not what I want you to have."

Which, of course, the man did. This exchange then went on for another three months until the man came to Carolina and said, "You're just not going to quit, are you?"

"Nope" was Carolina's reply.

"Well, I just can't take this anymore. Please don't give me anything else."

"I'm not giving you anything," Carolina said, "God is. He doesn't want you to live a life of destitution and despair. God wants me to care for you, so I'm obliged to do it."

And then the most violent man in the prison, the one who beat Carolina senseless, wept like a baby. He knew Carolina wasn't giving him things out of fear; the love he felt was strange and powerful in a way that he had never seen before. There was something happening between them that he could not understand, but he couldn't deny it either. The most powerful man in the prison was being overpowered by love.

Carolina went on to lead the man to Christ, and he grew to become one of the most faithful followers of God in the prison. To this day, he still talks about how Carolina reduced him to love. He just doesn't know any other way to put it.

Most of us will never have to *turn the other cheek* in the way that Carolina had to with this man. Nevertheless, the principle is the same for us as it is for Carolina. When confronted with hatred and violence, do not back down. Hatred is a powerful force, but the love of God is even more powerful. If you ever doubt it, just ask Carolina.

84

What Does It Mean to Love Your Neighbor?

Rio de Janeiro is one of the most beautiful cities in the world. Rio is an international vacation destination known for its picturesque beaches and breathtaking mountain views. But what is not as well known is that Rio is also home to some of the poorest and most desperate people in Brazil. The western edge of Rio, known as the *favela*, is so poor and crime ridden by drug lords that even the police refuse to travel down certain of its streets. The daily violence and hatred that exists in the *favela* is beyond what most people can imagine.

Geraldo Jordão Pereira was a publisher living in Rio who had been concerned about his community all of his life. Following in his father's footsteps, he built a successful publishing company that afforded him the ability to turn some of his attention to the social needs of the *favela*.

Through business acumen and the good fortune of publishing some of the bestselling books in the country, Geraldo created the first trust fund in the history of Brazil to support humanitarian efforts. By observing how community foundations operated in other countries like the United States, he established the Vera Pacheco Jordão Fund to inspire other businesses and entrepreneurs to support philanthropic work in his country for years to come.

Because Geraldo also published my books in Brazil, I had the opportunity to get to know him. I viewed him as a kind of Renaissance man, an entrepreneur who was also interested in art, literature, and social concerns. He was always dressed in a dapper fashion, complete with a smile on his face, and eager to discuss some current event of international interest. On one of my trips to Rio, I asked him about his work in the *favela*. I knew of the violence and poverty there and was curious about how his organization was dealing with it.

"I understand you are doing some work in the *favela*," I said.

"Yes," Geraldo replied. "It's going quite well."

"How did you get that started?" I asked.

"Well, because of my good fortune in the publishing industry, I realized that I needed to give something back. I have been very successful here in Brazil, and it has made me think. It just made sense to create a way to help others succeed in life as a result of the success I have experienced."

"So you created a foundation that will go on helping people even after you and I are gone," I said.

"That's right," Geraldo continued. "But not only that. We decided that we didn't want to just go around putting out fires in the *favela*. God knows there are plenty there. But what we wanted to do was to create a generation of firemen to do that work. We wanted to get to the root of the problem. So we established centers to train the women of the *favela* in marketable job skills. We didn't just want to give them better lives; we wanted to help them get better lives for themselves."

"That's brilliant. That must be very satisfying for you," I said.

"Yes. I love to go there and see their work," Geraldo said.

"You go into the *favela*?" I asked, surprised. "Isn't that dangerous?"

"Oh, not for me," Geraldo said calmly. "They know who I am."

Geraldo's comment struck me. I was aware that many people of his economic status in Rio not only refused to go into the *favela*, they had bulletproof glass installed in their cars just because it was nearby. But Geraldo wasn't afraid to go there because he genuinely loved the people he was helping, and he knew they respected him for that.

Geraldo didn't have to create the first community foundation in Brazil with the wealth he had acquired from his business success. He could have purchased artwork, built a bigger house, or created some monument to himself. But on a deep spiritual level, Geraldo somehow knew that the thing that would bring the most joy and satisfaction into his life would be to act in a loving way toward his neighbors. Geraldo discovered the truth that loving your neighbor as yourself is a very powerful way to live—more powerful than bulletproof glass.

Sadly, Geraldo Jordão Pereira passed away while I was writing this book. This world has lost a great man, but his impact upon us will live on. I like to think of him in heaven having a stimulating conversation with God about events of universal interest, dressed in a dapper robe, complete with his eternal smile on his face. At some point in the conversation, I can imagine God turning to him and saying, "Geraldo, it warms my heart that you understood what I meant when I asked you to *love your neighbor as yourself.* I love you, and I'm proud of you."

85

The Love of Money Is the Root of All Kinds of Evil

I sometimes hear people misquote the Bible by saying, "You know, the Bible says that money is the root of all evil." The Bible doesn't say that. It says "the *love* of money is a root of all kinds of evil" (italics added). This is an important distinction. Money is a tool that can sometimes be used for great good. It is something over which we are called to be good stewards. Money isn't evil. But the love of money can lead to all kinds of bad things.

The love of money is based on greed. It springs from a selfish fantasy that goodness in life can be contained within physical objects that you can obtain for yourself, and that once you have them you won't need anything else. Greed is an antidote to the pain of isolation. People who fall in love with money do so because they don't have the connection to God and others that they need to feel whole. Greed is basically an addiction to a concrete source of good feeling that is never really satisfying, because it is a substitute for love.

Bradley came for therapy because his mother told him to. He was a graduate student living in a nice apartment in a prestigious part of town. Bradley had everything he wanted, and he had grown up living that way. He came from a very affluent family because of the tremendous wealth that had been handed down from his grandfather. His parents made significant contributions to both his undergraduate and graduate schools, which was the main reason Bradley was able to get an education. His academic performance was consistently poor, but because of his parents' influence, the schools allowed him to stay. Bradley wasn't a bad person, but he was unmotivated and unable to find a direction in life. His mother was hoping therapy could help.

"I hope you stick it to them," Bradley said.

"To your parents?" I asked.

"Right," he said with a smile on his face. "I hope you send them a heck of a bill each month for making me come here."

"So you don't want to be here?"

"Oh, I don't know," Bradley said, backtracking a bit. "I don't have anything against psychology. It was one of my favorite subjects in school. It's just that my mother has all these ideas about who I'm supposed to be and all. I wish they would lighten up."

"So your parents make your life difficult," I said.

"Yes and no," Bradley replied. "They are putting pressure on me to finish this degree so I can develop a career in politics or something. I'm their legacy, you know, so I can't go and let them down. But on the other hand, I don't know of anyone who has it easier than me. I could buy and sell anyone at school. In that way, life's just not that hard for me at all."

Bradley was financially fortunate. He went on to describe his lifestyle of extravagance, which included casual liaisons with movie stars, using designer recreational drugs, living in homes around the world, and spontaneous events such as taking a girlfriend to Paris for the weekend just to go to dinner at his favorite restaurant there. Bradley had relationships, but they seemed more like an entourage than friends.

Yet, Bradley's life was a contradiction. Despite how exciting his life was, Bradley himself was bored. He didn't have to *try* to get ahead. Financially, Bradley had already arrived. Part of the satisfaction in obtaining things comes from the effort it takes to acquire them. Bradley was deprived of this.

Bradley lacked ambition. He didn't have to plan or work to get anything because everything had always been provided for him. He grew up in the care of nannies, went to boarding schools, and had a rather superficial and formal relationship with his parents, especially his father. He felt very well provided for by his parents, and even indebted to them for that, but he didn't feel loved. This left Bradley with an empty, lonely feeling inside that he covered over with his love for money and everything it could provide for him.

Greed is the perversion of ambition. God made each of us with a healthy drive to grow and be more than what we are today. This is healthy ambition that spurs us on to be all we can be while we are here on earth. Greed is the unhealthy notion that we can grab the goodness in life for ourselves without needing anyone, becoming a better person, or loving anyone else. Ambition is about growing toward goodness; greed is about stealing it for ourselves now.

I'm not sure how much I was able to help Bradley. I tried to help him come to grips with the roots of his lack of direction in life and help him deal with the lonely feelings of being unloved. But in many ways it was like trying to conduct therapy with an active alcoholic. Each time we touched upon painful feelings that might have benefited Bradley's growth if he'd explored them further, he would leave the session to reenter his world—which focused upon the benefits of money that would make those unpleasant feelings go away.

I want to make clear that the love of money is not found only among the rich. It is also found just as often among those who grow up under financial hardship. The love of money isn't about money; it's about the absence of love. Plenty of people from less privileged backgrounds grow up to fall in love with money as a result of feeling unloved. Unfortunately, they will have to learn Bradley's lesson: money will never love them back.

86

How to Heal Broken Hearts

I am very excited about the advancements in the science of marital counseling in the past few years. Researchers like Dr. John Gottman are identifying the signs of distressed marriages early on so we can help people repair their relationships before they end in divorce.[2]

And clinicians like Dr. Susan Johnson are developing techniques for conducting marital therapy that are substantially helping marital therapists heal broken hearts.[3]

Dr. Johnson's approach to marital therapy is called Emotionally Focused Therapy, because her goal is to assist couples in creating a secure emotional connection that will help them weather the challenges of married life. Couples who try to solve their problems intellectually can only go so far in resolving marital difficulties. It is only by getting to the emotional matters of the heart that the deepest problems can be solved.

Liam and Alexandra decided they needed marital counseling because of the distance they felt in their marriage. They didn't fight often, and when they did there was hardly any yelling or angry outbursts. Still, they had to walk on eggshells most of the time because of the tension between them. They were both very unhappy, and they knew they needed help.

Not all marriages express anger openly. Some people go inward with their anger and become depressed, unexpressive, or develop physical problems. But just because there isn't a volcano erupting doesn't mean there isn't a core of burning lava inside. Both Liam and Alexandra were hurt and angry, but they didn't know how to talk about it in any way that was helpful.

"I think we should talk about what happened when we bought the house," Alexandra said cautiously.

"Okay," I said. "It sounds like you have some unfinished business with that. Would that be all right with you, Liam?"

"I don't really see the point in going over that again," Liam said defensively. "We've been over that so many times, and I'd like to just move on. Why do you want to keep focusing on the past?"

"Talking about things in the past isn't necessarily helpful," I jumped in, "*unless* you have some present-day feelings about it that still need to be discussed. If that's the case, then we won't just be rehashing past events; we'll also be talking about what's going on between the two of you right now."

Liam and Alexandra were stuck because the only tool they were trying to use to get unstuck was their intellect. They talked about the facts of buying their house together, and they went over these facts many times. But the hurt and disagreement that resulted over the purchase of their home never got resolved. They were each under the impression that if they could just get the other to agree with their perspective, then the conflict between them would be resolved. But when it comes to marriage, this rarely works. In marriage you have two choices: you can be right or you can be happy.

Both Liam and Alexandra were raised in homes where conflict was not managed well. Liam never saw his parents fight, and Alexandra often witnessed her father bully her mother into submission. Neither saw an open expression of feelings leading to anything good. As a result, neither of them knew how to talk about their hurt feelings in their marriage. They tried to be fair and reasonable with each other, but because it is impossible for two people to always agree intellectually on everything, there were some issues that they just couldn't get resolved.

"How do you feel about buying the house?" I asked Alexandra.

"I feel lonely," she said softly.

"Lonely? Really? The biggest purchase of your life. The place where you are making a home together—and you feel lonely. How do you feel hearing her say that?" I asked, turning to Liam.

"How do I feel?" Liam said sharply. "I'll tell you how I feel. I feel lonely, too."

"Okay," I said quickly before he could go on. I could tell he was about to give me a list of reasons why he was justified in feeling as lonely as she was, and that wasn't going to help. She didn't need to hear his reasoning right now; she needed to know what was going on in his heart.

"I'd like to hear about that in just a minute," I said to Liam. "But what I'm asking you right now is, how do you feel when *Alexandra* feels lonely?"

"Oh," Liam said, somewhat caught off guard. "Well, it doesn't make me feel good. I mean, well, it makes me feel bad that she feels lonely. I don't want you to feel that way," he said, turning to Alexandra.

"And how does it make you feel to hear that?" I asked Alexandra.

"Not so lonely," she said, looking over at Liam.

The knowledge we use with our intellect helps us throughout our lives. Both Liam and Alexandra were successful people because they were both so knowledgeable and intelligent. But using your knowledge of a situation to justify yourself in a quarrel with your spouse is likely to make you appear defensive and uncaring. These types of painful disagreements are rarely resolved this way. Simply letting the one you love know that his or her pain matters to you can make all the difference. The circumstances surrounding your disagreement may well remain the same, but the disconnection between the two of you won't.

This distance between Liam and Alexandra was not magically resolved by one conversation. But learning the importance of focusing on the emotional connection between their hearts is getting them there. Agreement with what we know in our heads can only go so far in resolving distance that we feel in our hearts. The wisdom of the Bible is "knowledge puffs up while love builds up." When it comes to resolving marital conflicts, nothing could be more helpful.

87

Why God Created
Romantic Love

Love is a mystery. We use the word *love* to mean many things. We love our mothers, we love football, we love our country, and we fall in love. Some languages have many words for love to help make these distinctions. Perhaps the greatest confusion comes when we are talking about romantic love.

Romantic love has been observed by scientists in almost every culture in the world.[4] Whether it is called limerence, infatuation, or falling in love, the experience of romantic love is a powerful one. It can happen instantaneously, as with *love at first sight*, or it can develop in a relationship with someone you have known for a long time. Romantic love creates a feeling of *specialness* between lovers and constant thoughts of the other, as well as simultaneous hope, uncertainty, and mystery. It is often an all-consuming passion that sends hormones designed for excitement rushing through our veins. The experience is so wonderful that anyone who has fallen in love will tell you it's not about sex—it's about being in love.

Sadly, infatuation doesn't last. Our best estimates are that around two years into an intense romantic experience, things begin to change. The hormones of excitement drop off and are gradually replaced with hormones of contentment. The intrusive romantic thoughts that were once unavoidable are replaced by the concerns of everyday life. And if all goes well, infatuation will be replaced with attachment. The feeling of infatuation can be revived from time to time, but it doesn't typically remain at the same level of intensity that it did in the first couple of years. Romantic love is God's way of getting us into relationships, and the experience of secure attachment is his way of keeping us there.

I will never forget the day I was standing outside a large church in Los Angeles talking to a friend of mine when a beautiful blonde woman passed by. My friend and I were members of a men's group that met at the church on Saturdays, and because we were both single at the time, we often got together to discuss women and bemoan the fact that it was difficult to find the right woman even in a city the size of Los Angeles. But this blonde sighting was unusual. As she passed by, encircled by a covey of hopeful men, I had the impulse to speak to her. But I was speechless. I was overcome with my attraction to her, felt strangely self-conscious, and was only able to watch as one of the most attractive women I had laid eyes on for quite some time just strolled by.

Fearing I had just missed a rare opportunity, I went home and called one of the hapless men in her group of escorts and found out that her name was Barbara. Delighted with my Boy Scout preparedness, I eagerly went back to this same church and stood in the same spot in hopes of being offered a second opportunity to introduce myself. She didn't show. So I went back the next week, and the next, and the next. For three months I registered a perfect attendance at a church where I wasn't even a member in hopes of meeting a woman I had never spoken to and only seen once. I felt foolishly smitten, but bound on a quest that I could not abandon.

I guess people began to wonder why I was so interested in hanging out at the church, so someone offered me a job speaking to the singles class that met each Sunday. I knew it fit into my schedule, so I accepted. The morning came, and the classroom filled up with the typical two hundred or so young professionals. I was prepared to give one of my standard lectures on relationships. And who should walk in, march right down to the second row, and seat herself right in front of me? You guessed it, Barbara.

This was no time to become speechless. So I composed myself, prayed to God for the words to speak, and launched into a lecture that I honestly don't remember. Since I was the speaker, I was able to position myself by the door as everyone exited and seize my before-missed opportunity. This time I was ready.

As she approached to politely thank me for my presentation, I calmly said, "It's Barbara, isn't it?"

"Why, yes," she replied, somewhat puzzled.

"Oh, I think we have some friends in common," I said, trying to reassure both of us that I was not some kind of stalker.

Not about to let this opportunity pass again, I took the next few minutes to establish some areas of common interest between us and ask her if she would like to get together sometime to discuss them further. Still somewhat puzzled by my interest in her, she gave me her business card and invited me to call sometime.

I had never gone to such lengths before to meet a woman. I was somewhat ashamed of my brazen and even scheming approach to making her acquaintance. But I was feeling an instant attraction that pulled me into a direction that could not be denied. I am still a bit embarrassed by the story, but not the least bit sorry for having done what I did. You see, today Barbara is my wife.

Romantic love is a creative part of God's design for drawing us into relationships. It transcends our rational understanding and pulls on areas of our unconscious minds in ways that are too compelling to ignore. I know this is true not only because I am a psychologist, but because I am a man. Romantic love is a mystery you cannot solve, but one that has the power to change your life.

88

The Two Kinds of Sexual Love

Sexual arousal is a powerful aspect of a romantic relationship. This can happen in two ways. The first is erotic love. This is when a relationship has developed over time, and a close feeling of emotional and spiritual connection leads to the desire to be connected physically. Erotic love is sensual and completes the bond between two people who love each other. This is God's way of cementing a marriage together to make it last a lifetime. Erotic love is an important part of long-term intimacy.

The second form of sexual love is eroticized love. This is when someone feels sexual feelings and a desire for physical closeness with someone with whom they do *not* have a secure relationship. Eroticized feelings are an attempt to make up for what is missing emotionally and spiritually with a physical connection. These sexual feelings try to cover over the lack of connection between people with the euphoria of sexual arousal. These feelings can be quite intense, and because they are an attempt to cover over deeper feelings, they can become addicting.

In the book of 2 Samuel in the Bible, we learn of King David and his relationships with his many children from several different wives. In chapter 13, David's son Amnon is said to fall in love with Tamar, David's beautiful daughter from a different wife. This was a complicated situation, so Amnon's attraction to Tamar grew into an obsession that was so intense that "he made himself ill" (2 Sam. 13:2). He knew it wasn't right for him to lust after his half sister, but the taboo seemed to make his attraction to her even stronger. This is how eroticized feelings start. There is a disconnection that is painful, or the other person is unavailable in some way, so eroticized feelings of physical desire serve to cover over the painful feelings that cannot be resolved. Amnon had no idea if he truly loved Tamar; all he knew was that he wanted her with a passion that was consuming him. The whole situation was making him literally sick.

As is often the case with eroticized feelings, Amnon became manipulative in order to get what he wanted. He developed a plan with his uncle, Jonadab, who was "a very shrewd man" (2 Sam. 13:3), to trick his father and Tamar into giving him an opportunity to act on his eroticized lust. He told David that he was sick and that he would like for his sister Tamar to come to his house to prepare some food for him. Not thinking much of it, David asked Tamar to do exactly that. When she went to Amnon's house, he told everyone else to leave. He then grabbed her and said, "Come to bed with me, my sister" (2 Sam. 13:11). Tamar protested with, "Don't do this wicked thing. What about me? Where could I get rid of my disgrace? And what about you? You would be like one of the wicked fools in Israel" (2 Sam. 13:12–13). Tamar was appealing to their relationship, but it fell on deaf ears because Amnon was not motivated by concern for their relationship. He was consumed with his eroticized love.

Because eroticized feelings cover over painful feelings, Amnon couldn't get in touch with any concern for Tamar, fear of his father, or even his own good judgment. Eroticized feelings are an antidote to feelings of insecurity, so Amnon was numb to his sense of conscience and guilt. He couldn't tell what was right or wrong anymore, so he raped her.

Then something interesting happened. The very next verse says, "Then Amnon hated her with intense hatred. In fact, he hated her more than he had loved her" (2 Sam. 13:15). Once the eroticized feelings are satisfied, the medicated effect against the underlying pain goes away. Stripped of the numbness of eroticized feelings, Amnon was left with the pain of what was really going on. He didn't have a genuine relationship with Tamar; she even offered to become his wife at this point, but he refused her. And now he had created even more brokenness between them, as well as between himself and his father. As often happens with eroticized love, Amnon flipped from loving Tamar to hating her almost instantly. You see, Amnon's eroticized feelings for Tamar had nothing to do with loving her; they were a sexual fantasy that served to cover over his lack of relationship with someone he viewed only as an object of his desire, not a woman he truly loved.

The story doesn't end well for Amnon. David was furious with him, and Tamar's brother Absalom eventually killed Amnon for revenge. Eroticized feelings don't lead to better relationships, because they are not based upon good feelings and good connections. Eroticized feelings are an attempt to cover over painful feelings of insecurity, and as Amnon learned, it is better to face the underlying pain than to cover it over with sexual actions that will only make things worse.

Erotic love is a wonderful expression of sexual love. It facilitates bonding between life partners because it adds a physical connection between two people who truly love each other. But eroticized love can be a dangerous distortion of sexual love. If the painful feelings that it covers over are not identified and worked through, the result is not very loving at all.

89

Earning Approval
Isn't Being Loved

The approval of others is earned by your behavior. If you act in ways that are respectful of others, then they in turn will approve of you. But there is a difference between feeling approval and feeling loved. You have a need to feel loved for who you are, in addition to feeling approval for what you do. Earning the approval of others is a good thing, but it becomes a problem if you feel you have to earn their love, too.

Anita is an attractive, conscientious, and successful working mother. She is happily married with two delightful children whom she loves very much. Anita is also very proud of the fact that she is well respected at the law firm where she has a thriving practice as an attorney. It isn't easy, but she seems able to make it work both at the office and at home.

On the surface, Anita appears to have it all. She is very organized and efficient. She *has* to be, since she literally has two full-time jobs—one at the office and one at home. Even though it is difficult at times, Anita and her husband came to the conclusion that it was best for the family if Anita was finding fulfillment through her career as well as through being a mom. Anita wanted both a career and a home life, and they could rely on their extended family members to help out now that the kids were in school.

But even though Anita would tell you that she has every reason in the world to be happy, sometimes she isn't. Some mornings she will wake up sad and not know why. And sometimes when she is driving home, she will get thoughts of driving right past the house, right out of town, and off into the sunset. She doesn't have any idea of where she wants to go; she just feels like getting away from everything.

Because she was disturbed by these feelings and thoughts, Anita came to therapy. She was grateful for her wonderful life, so she was upset about this contradiction within herself and she wanted me to help her make it stop.

"I was listening to a song on the radio the other day, and I got another one of my thoughts," Anita confessed to me.

"Tell me about that," I said.

"It was by that new female artist, you know, the one who is doing that national tour," she said as her face brightened up.

"I think I know the one," I said.

"Well, as soon as I thought about her traveling across the country, I got the image of taking off, too. I know I'd never do it, but it just felt so nice to think about getting on a plane and going on a permanent vacation," she said.

"That sounds relieving," I said.

"That's right," Anita said with a smile. "It sounds like a relief."

"That would be nice," I said.

"Well, actually it wouldn't," Anita said as her face changed to a frown. "I mean, how selfish is that? I have a family who loves me and a career that most women would kill for, and here I am planning to abandon it all. What kind of person would even have these thoughts?"

Anita was confused about her reaction to her life. She loved everything about it, except for how she felt from time to time. Anita worked hard at everything she did, but hard work alone wasn't going to help her with this problem. In fact, her hard work was actually part of the problem itself.

Anita grew up the only child of parents who divorced when she was very young. She doesn't remember her father, but she has many memories of how hard her mother worked to make a good life for her. Anita is grateful for the love and support her mother gave her growing up, and even though it was difficult much of the time, she wouldn't trade her relationship with her mother for any other family she knew.

But Anita not only felt admiration and love for her mother, she also felt an obligation to *be good* for her. She knew her mother was worn out by being a single mom, so Anita tried to never cause her any problems or be a burden to her in any way.

Anita kept her room clean, always did her homework ahead of time, and never got into trouble like some of her friends did at school. Anita believed that in order to be a good daughter, she needed to avoid doing anything bad.

Anita's mother was very proud of her. Anita beamed each time her mother described her to others as such a *perfect* daughter. She knew her mother loved her, but without realizing it Anita became more concerned with whether or not she *approved* of her. Anita's focus wasn't on whether or not she was *pleasing* her mother; she was most concerned about whether or not she did anything to *displease* her. Her mother already had enough on her plate, and Anita was going to make sure she didn't do anything to add more.

It is important to feel approval from your parents. This means doing things to please them, as well as avoiding things that might displease them, too. But that is not all you need from your parents. You also need to feel loved for who you are, even when your behavior falls short. Because of the circumstances of her childhood, this was missing for Anita. She knew she could earn her mother's approval, but she mistakenly thought she needed to earn her love, as well. These are two different things. There is a time for working for approval, and there is a time for being loved on faith. Anita had a good grasp of how to accomplish this first area in her life, but she needed to work on the second one.

The escape fantasies that were plaguing Anita were caused by working too hard. She not only worked for the approval of everyone, but she also worked to earn their love. This was exhausting, so she developed fantasies of relief. Anita discovered that you can work to earn the approval of others, but love must be freely given. So Anita and I began working on the underdeveloped area in her life of feeling loved for who she was. Working hard belonged to the area of approval, so she couldn't just work harder at feeling loved; she needed to do something completely different.

Now Anita not only asks herself what she *should* do; she also asks herself what she would *like* to do, as well. This allows the people around her to know her more intimately and love her simply for who she is. Anita is working on ways to feel love in her life independent of her behavior. Trying to earn love out of an obligation to be good wasn't working; opening herself up to experience love based on her faith that God and others love her no matter what she does seems to help. These days, Anita isn't having as many disturbing thoughts as she used to have. She is still a hardworking woman who has the respect of her community, her law firm, and her family. But she is adding some new ways to feel good about her life by being loved simply for who she is. Anita found out the hard way that just as the Bible says, "If I give all I possess to the poor and give over my body to hardship that I may boast, but do not have love, I gain nothing."

You need to feel both approval and love to feel good about your life. You will earn the approval of others with the goodness of your behavior, but you cannot earn their love. Love is something that is freely given. You can't make others love you, but you can give them the opportunity to give you their love as a gift by letting them know who you really are.

90

How Brotherly Love Can Change Your Life

Many churches have discovered the importance of getting people together in small groups for prayer and support. In this more intimate setting, people are able to open up to each other and share their concerns in ways that make them feel connected to each other and to God. Sometimes the groups are organized according to gender, so the women have a chance to meet together while the men can do the same. The group dynamic changes when you are only meeting with members of your own sex.

Several years ago, I helped organize small groups for the men of a large church. The women of the church had annual retreats and had been meeting in small groups for many years, but nothing had been done for the men. So I met with a group of other men to plan a men's ministry for the church. The men of the church were just as much in need of the intimate prayer and support that the women were receiving; it's just that men are not very good about asking for what they need spiritually.

The time I spent in that small group of men planning the men's ministry turned out to be one of the most meaningful events of my adult life. In our planning to organize small groups for the church, we became one. Twenty years later, some of those men are still my closest friends. We laughed, cried, shared our stories, and prayed for each other in ways that we would never have done if women had been present. The conversation changes when both men and women are together. It is not better or worse; it's just different.

I remember one Saturday morning sitting in a circle with the other six men of our small group. They were all leaders in the community and the church, so I was honored to be among them. We were going around the circle "checking in" with each other. This was the time when each man could say whatever he wanted to the group. We were there to support each other in our lives with only one rule—whatever was shared in the group stayed in the group. Vincent was the next to share with the group. He was a well-known community leader and a man who had a good reputation throughout the church.

"I'd like you guys to pray for me," Vincent started off.

"Okay," several members mumbled. This was a typical request, and we didn't think much of it.

"Well, you guys know me, and most of you know my wife, too. We've been happily married for years now, and I want things to stay that way," Vincent said, looking down at his feet.

Then he lifted up his head and said, "Well, there's this place out in the valley that I've been driving out to lately, and I'd like you guys to pray for me that I'd stop doing that. I know my wife wouldn't want me going out there anymore, and I figured you guys could help me stop doing it."

At first I was shocked. I wasn't sure if he was talking about a strip club or perhaps something worse. But what we all knew was he was asking us for help with something that he certainly wasn't talking about with anyone else. I was sitting in a room *at a church* with other church leaders and listening to the honest confession of a man asking other men for support with the greatest struggle of his life. Just then I felt honored to be among men who could be that genuine with each other. We weren't priests listening through the dark screen of a confessional; we were a small group of men trying to support each other to live better lives.

Afterward I asked Vincent how he came up with the courage to share such an intimate struggle with the group.

"I knew if I confessed it to you guys, I probably wouldn't go back," he said.

My respect for Vincent went up that day. I didn't know the details of his sexual struggles, and I didn't really need to know. I knew he was honest. The kind of honesty that Vincent and the other members of our small group had with each other created a bond between us that was strong and healing. As we learned how to be better men with each other, we all observed something interesting happening outside of the group. We became better men to the women in our lives, too.

The Bible reminds us, "Behold, how good and how pleasant it is for brothers to dwell together in unity." My experience in that small group of men confirmed that. There are many forms of love, and brotherly love is one of the important ones. Men need to love men in order to love women better. This means that men need to experience other men as friends rather than competitors. Our honesty bound us together in the way God intended brothers to live, and we were all better men because of it.

91

How God's Love Heals

Most forms of love are conditional. Romantic love can be fickle. The love of a friend can change depending upon the behavior of the friend. The love of a family member can be colored by hurtful events over the course of a lifetime. But the Bible talks about the love of God as being unconditional. God loves you no matter who you are or what you have ever done.

Human love is different. You cannot act in whatever way you like and still get people to feel close to you. Human love requires you to take responsibility for yourself and accept that human relationships have conditions. The reality is that at times you will not live up to the expectations of others, and those you care about will go on failing you, too. It is difficult to love someone who repeatedly hurts and disappoints you. Fortunately, God's love can help.

Peter was a difficult person to love. He was arrogant, aggressive, and very argumentative. Peter had few friends, but that didn't seem to bother him much. His wife was somewhat passive, so she didn't confront him, which led Peter to believe that he was justified in his pushy behavior. He wasn't happy about it, but Peter came for therapy because of the stress he was experiencing after some serious financial losses. He wanted to make sure that the stress wasn't going to cause even more problems for him.

"I can't believe those idiots didn't see this coming," Peter complained to me.

"It's frustrating when the people you rely on don't come through," I said.

"It was their job!" he yelled. "I mean, if people just did their jobs, then I wouldn't be in this jam."

"I know," I said.

"I was on top of my part of the deal. It's just that I can't get over how stupid I was for getting involved with such numbskulls," Peter snapped as his face turned red.

Peter spent a lot of time complaining about how everyone else was not as smart or effective as he was. He believed his stress resulted from their incompetence. But his efforts to get everyone else to change weren't reducing his distress. He was entrenched in a pattern of blame and negativity that only resulted in making him more miserable. Peter was an unhappy man, and he was spreading his unhappiness onto everyone else he knew. Peter thought everyone other than himself was inadequate.

It wasn't hard to see that Peter was the one struggling with feelings of inadequacy. His father had been hard on him growing up, and his mother never protected him from the harsh criticisms he received. Peter grew up feeling inadequate, and that led to an adult life of feeling unhappy with everyone else.

Working with Peter became more difficult when he turned his disappointment toward me, as well. He often felt as though I didn't understand him or that I was off the mark in my comments. He wasn't entirely sure what I should be doing for him, but he was pretty sure it was something better than what I was doing for him now. This doesn't happen very often, but I was trying to help someone that I didn't particularly like.

I didn't like feeling this way about one of my patients, so I prayed to God for help. This is something that we do at the counseling center where I work. We discuss our difficult cases, examine the transferences[5] involved, and ask God to guide us as we navigate through the pain of those we are seeking to help. I don't completely understand how prayer works, but my experience is that it does.

Sometime after that, during one of our difficult sessions, a thought occurred to me. I was just like Peter. When I feel exposed or inadequate, I try to defend myself with rationalizations. I was taught to be a critical thinker in graduate school, so defending myself with critical thinking was an automatic defense mechanism for me. But approaching philosophical ideas with critical thinking is not the same thing as using criticism as a defense mechanism. One of the reasons I didn't like Peter was that I didn't like this same defense mechanism in myself.

Remembering that I can be defensive and critical of others helped me to care for Peter. God doesn't need me to be any different than I am to love me, and I believe God feels the same way about Peter. I think Peter's therapy became a place where God was trying to communicate his unconditional love to Peter through me. I'm not sure that I personally loved Peter more, but I felt an unconditional love of him that I believe came from God. Sometimes therapy becomes holy ground where God makes himself known in more obvious ways than at other times. I believe my therapy with Peter was one of those times.

I wish I could say that Peter became a completely different person as a result of his therapy, but that didn't happen. He did become less critical of his wife, launched a more positive direction in his career, and became a less miserable person in our sessions. At one point near the end of our treatment, Peter referred to me as his *best friend*. I was surprised and privileged to hear it. Peter didn't feel close to anyone, so I was honored to think that he could feel close to me. I don't believe that would have happened without the help of God's love.

My relationship with God is the one place in my life where I don't have to defend myself. I can feel exposed and inadequate and not feel ashamed. My relationship with God makes me feel completely seen for who I am, inadequacies and all, and still loved. The unconditional love of God is foundational in my life, and it empowers me to love others even when my own love fails.

The story of the Bible is that God created the world so that we could love him and he could love us. The New Testament tells us that he sent his Son into the world to prove it. Romans 5:8 says, "God demonstrates his own love for us in this: While we were still sinners, Christ died for us." God loves us even when we are at our worst. Different from other forms of love, God's love is unconditional. We don't have to be any different from who we are to experience God's love. It is a powerful experience to receive God's love, and a healing experience to give it away.

Notes

Part One Hurt and Suffering

1. C. S. Lewis, *The Problem of Pain* (New York: Macmillan, 1962), 24.

2. C. S. Lewis, *A Grief Observed* (New York: Bantam Books, 1983/1976), 31.

3. Lewis, *A Grief Observed*, 4.

4. Robert Stolorow, *Trauma and Human Existence: Autobiographical, Psychoanalytic, and Philosophical Reflections* (New York: Analytic Press, 2007).

5. You may want to read more about this in my book *Who's to Blame? How to Escape the Victim Trap and Gain Personal Power in Your Life*, by Carmen Berry and Mark W. Baker (Colorado Springs: Pinon, 1996).

6. Proverbs 1:33.

7. Hebrews 12:11.

8. I must give credit to Sandra Wilson and Ronald Eggert, who have written a book by the same title, published by Discovery House in 2001.

9. See my chapter on the unconscious in *Jesus, the Greatest Therapist Who Ever Lived* (San Francisco: HarperOne, 2007), 189–211.

10. James 3:1.

11. Alcoholics Anonymous (AA) is the largest self-help organization in the world dedicated to helping people overcome addictions, particularly alcoholism. Celebrate Recovery (CR) is a Christian organization similar to AA in its effectiveness in helping people recover from addictions but openly acknowledges Jesus Christ as our Higher Power.

12. Dag Hammarskjöld, *Markings* (New York: Ballantine Books, 1985).

13. Paul Althaus, *The Theology of Martin Luther* (Philadelphia: Fortress, 1966), 32.

Part Two Guilt and Shame

1. Luke 10:38–42.
2. James 2:26.
3. Jim Collins, *Good to Great: Why Some Companies Make the Leap and Others Don't* (New York: HarperCollins, 2001).
4. Genesis 2:25.
5. I discuss this more extensively in the chapter "Understanding People: Are They Good or Bad?" in *Jesus, the Greatest Therapist Who Ever Lived*.

Part Three Anger

1. I am grateful to my friend and colleague Dr. Sharon Hart May for the distinction between anger of hope and anger of despair. I highly recommend her book, *How to Argue So Your Spouse Will Listen: Six Principles for Turning Arguments into Conversations* (Nashville: Thomas Nelson, 2007).
2. This is one of the terms used by Dr. Susan Johnson in her approach to marital counseling called Emotionally Focused Therapy. My work with couples has been significantly influenced by her. You might want to look at her book *Hold Me Tight: Seven Conversations for a Lifetime of Love* (New York: Little, Brown, 2008).
3. Joseph M. Jones, *Affects as Process: An Inquiry into the Centrality of Affect in Psychological Life* (Hillsdale, NJ: Analytic Press, 1995).
4. Paul Ekman, *Emotions Revealed: Recognizing Faces and Feelings to Improve Communication and Emotional Life* (New York: Owl Books, 2003).
5. This is one of the helpful terms that comes from the research of Dr. John Gottman. You can find other helpful ideas in John Gottman and Nan Silver, *The Seven Principles for Making Marriage Work* (New York: Three Rivers, 1999).

Part Four Anxiety

1. Hans Selye, *Stress without Distress* (New York: Signet, 1991).

Part Five Sorrow

1. Job 7:4.

Part Six Fear

1. When I asked a federal judge in Chicago if crime pays, he said, "Sure, some career criminals can evade the law for a lifetime, but studies show that their lives are riddled with disease and paranoia. They typically die younger than normal and often are miserable."

Part Seven Happiness

1. Paul Tillich, *The Courage to Be* (New Haven: Yale University Press, 1952).

2. Raymond Paloutzian and Crystal Park, *The Handbook of the Psychology of Religion and Spirituality* (New York: Guilford, 2013), 464.

3. Scientists have distinguished between people who are intrinsically religious and those who are extrinsically religious and nonreligious. P. Scott Richards and Allen Bergin, *A Spiritual Strategy for Counseling and Psychotherapy* (Washington, DC: American Psychological Association, 1997), 83.

4. Elaine Hatfield and Susan Sprecher, *Mirror, Mirror: The Importance of Looks in Everyday Life* (Albany, NY: State University of New York Press, 1986).

5. Mark Snyder, E. D. Tanke, and Ellen Berscheid, "Social Perception and Interpersonal Behavior: On the Self-Fulfilling Nature of Social Stereotypes," *Journal of Personality and Social Psychology* 35 (1977): 656–66.

Part Eight Love

1. Rhonda Byrne, *The Secret* (New York: Atria Books, 2006).

2. Gottman and Silver, *Seven Principles for Making Marriage Work*.

3. Susan Johnson, *The Practice of Emotionally Focused Marital Therapy: Creating Connection* (New York: Brunner/Mazel, 1996).

4. Helen Fisher, *Anatomy of Love: A Natural History of Mating, Marriage, and Why We Stray* (New York: Fawcett Columbine, 1992), 50.

5. *Transference* is a technical term for the relationship between the therapist and the patient in psychotherapy that focuses upon the unconscious aspects of the relationship that are out of conscious awareness.

Acknowledgments

This book is the product of many years of effort and the contributions of many lives. I am grateful to Dr. Robert Stolorow and Dr. Howard Bacal, who taught me how to listen to emotion in the lives of others as well as within myself. I am thankful for my colleagues and friends at La Vie Christian Counseling Center who have partnered with me to do the healing work of psychotherapy for over two decades. I want to thank Dwight Case, Don Morgan, Eugene Lowe, and J. D. Hinton for supporting me emotionally and allowing me to lean on their spiritual wisdom for many years. And I am especially thankful for Jim Hart of Hartline Literary Agency, who helped bring this book to life in the United States.

I could not have written this book were it not for the vulnerability of my patients and their willingness to share with me their deepest feelings in their pursuit of finding emotional health. And my greatest gratitude always goes to God for giving me the opportunity to do this work and blessing me with my wife, Barbara, and three children, Brendan, Aidan, and Brianna, who so patiently sacrificed their time with me so I could give some of it to all of you.

About the Author

Dr. Mark Baker has been practicing as a clinical psychologist for over twenty-five years. He holds graduate degrees in theology and psychology, and he has postgraduate certification in psychoanalytic psychotherapy. He is also the author of *Jesus, the Greatest Therapist Who Ever Lived*, in which he took a psychological perspective on the teachings of Jesus. Dr. Baker lives with his family in Southern California.